VOLUME 5

Crisis in Papua

September–December 1942

MICHAEL CLARINGBOULD
PETER INGMAN

AVONMORE BOOKS

South Pacific Air War
Volume 5: Crisis in Papua
September–December 1942

Michael John Claringbould
Peter Ingman

ISBN: 978-0-6489262-9-0

First published 2022 by Avonmore Books

Avonmore Books
PO Box 217
Kent Town
South Australia 5071
Australia

Phone: (61 8) 8431 9780
avonmorebooks.com.au

A catalogue record for this book is available from the National Library of Australia

Cover design & layout by Diane Bricknell

Cover artwork captions:

Front: Para-fragmentation bombs spill from A-20A War Bond Special near Sanananda Point in November 1942. Note the Perspex in the nose has been painted over as part of the strafer modification.

Rear: A pair of H6K4 Mavis flying boats join up and commence their descent towards Rabaul at dusk after separate long-range searches for Allied shipping.

CONTENTS

Peter Ingman (left) and Michael Claringbould in front of B-25J 44-31508 at Parafield Airport, South Australia, in October 2020. The aircraft has been painted to represent B-25C N5-131 Pulk of No. 18 (Netherlands East Indies) Squadron named after Dutch pilot Fred "Pulk" Pelder.

Michael Claringbould – Author & Illustrator

Michael spent his formative years in Papua New Guinea in the 1960s, during which he became fascinated by the many WWII aircraft wrecks which still lie around the country. Michael has served widely overseas as an Australian diplomat, including in South East Asia and throughout the South Pacific where he had the fortune to return to Papua New Guinea for three years commencing in 2003.

Michael has authored and illustrated various books on Pacific War aviation. His history of the Tainan Naval Air Group in New Guinea, *Eagles of the Southern Sky*, received worldwide acclaim as the first English-language history of a Japanese fighter unit, and was translated into Japanese. An executive member of Pacific Air War History Associates, Michael holds a pilot license and PG4 paraglider rating. He continues to develop his skills as a digital 3D aviation artist, using 3DS MAX, Vray and Photoshop to attain markings accuracy.

Peter Ingman – Author

A keen aviation historian, Peter's key interest is in the early stages of the Pacific War. Two of his books, *Zero Hour in Broome* and *Carrier Attack Darwin 1942* (both with Dr Tom Lewis) have received many favourable reviews in Australian media. A former business executive, Peter has travelled widely throughout northern Australia and the South Pacific conducting research for his books. He is the Chairman of the South Australian Aviation Museum History Group. This is his tenth book.

Other Books by the Authors
Michael Claringbould and Peter Ingman

South Pacific Air War Volume 1: The Fall of Rabaul December 1941–March 1942 (2017).

South Pacific Air War Volume 2: The Struggle for Moresby March–April 1942 (2018).

South Pacific Air War Volume 3: Coral Sea & Aftermath May-June 1942 (2019).

South Pacific Air War Volume 4: Buna & Milne Bay June-September 1942 (2020).

Michael Claringbould

Black Sunday (2000).

Eagles of the Southern Sky (2012, with Luca Ruffato).

F4U Corsair versus Zero the Solomons 1943-44 (Osprey, 2022).

Nemoto's Travels The illustrated saga of a Japanese floatplane pilot in the first year of the Pacific War (2021).

Operation I-Go Yamamoto's Last Offensive – New Guinea and the Solomons April 1943 (2020).

P-39 / P-400 Airacobra versus A6M2/3 Zero-sen New Guinea 1942 (Osprey, 2018).

P-47D Thunderbolt versus Ki-43 Hayabusa New Guinea 1943/44 (Osprey, 2020).

Pacific Adversaries Volume One Japanese Army Air Force vs The Allies New Guinea 1942-1944 (2019).

Pacific Adversaries Volume Two Imperial Japanese Navy vs The Allies New Guinea & the Solomons 1942-1944 (2020).

Pacific Adversaries Volume Three Imperial Japanese Navy vs The Allies New Guinea & the Solomons 1942-1944 (2020).

Pacific Adversaries Volume Four Imperial Japanese Navy vs The Allies - The Solomons 1943-1944 (2021).

Pacific Profiles Volume One Japanese Army Fighters New Guinea & the Solomons 1942-1944 (2020).

Pacific Profiles Volume Two Japanese Army Bomber & Other Units, New Guinea and the Solomons 1942-44 (2020).

Pacific Profiles Volume Three Allied Medium Bombers, A20 Series, South West Pacific 1942-44 (2020).

Pacific Profiles Volume Four Allied Fighters: Vought F4U Corsair Series Solomons Theatre 1943-1944 (2021).

Pacific Profiles Volume Five Japanese Navy Zero Fighters (land-based) New Guinea and the Solomons 1942-1944 (2021).

Pacific Profiles Volume Six Allied Fighters: Bell P-39 & P-400 Airacobra South & Southwest Pacific 1942-1944 (2022).

Pacific Profiles Volume Seven Allied Transports: Douglas C-47 series South & Southwest Pacific 1942-1945 (2022).

Peter Ingman

Zero Hour in Broome (2010, with Dr Tom Lewis).

Carrier Attack Darwin 1942 (2013, with Dr Tom Lewis).

Mark Vc Spitfire versus A6M2 Zero-sen Darwin 1942 (Osprey, 2019).

P-40E Warhawk versus A6M2 Zero-sen: East Indies and Darwin 1942 (Osprey, 2020).

The Royal Australian Air Force in South Australia during WWII (2021).

INTRODUCTION

This fifth volume of the *South Pacific Air War* series chronicles the air war in New Guinea from 9 September until 31 December 1942. It can be read alone or as a continuation of the first four volumes which span the first nine months of the Pacific War.

As explained in *Volume 4*, after the American invasion of Guadalcanal on 7 August, the Solomons became a separate and distinct theatre from the Allied perspective. Then, from early September the Fifth Air Force was formed to control and coordinate USAAF and RAAF units in New Guinea, and it is the activities of these units (plus some operating from northern Queensland) that form the basis of this volume.

Note that the New Guinea/Solomons boundary was often blurred around southern Bougainville, with Fifth Air Force units often venturing into the northern Solomons. Likewise Allied air units from Guadalcanal sometimes ventured into New Guinea air space. However, from the Japanese standpoint there was no geographical delineation between these areas, all of which formed their single "South Seas" theatre. Indeed, regular reference is made to events in the Solomons in this volume. Not only was Japanese airpower extensively engaged there, but the knife-edge nature of critical campaigns meant that the Fifth Air Force was at times directed to attack targets such as Rabaul and the Shortlands area to relieve pressure on Guadalcanal.

The subtitle *Crisis in Papua* is apt because against this background the Japanese advance over the Owen Stanley Ranges posed an immediate threat to Port Moresby and its invaluable airbases. The Fifth Air Force was quickly directed to the new roles of close support and aerial supply of ground forces, while also trying to interdict Japanese convoys.

The strategic picture evolved remarkably quickly during subsequent months, ending with the Battle of Buna-Gona in November and December. During this period Allied aerial attrition reached an all-time high, reflecting rapidly increasing activity which eclipsed that seen in previous months.

The Japanese too were forced to adapt their air power in the face of horrific losses in the Solomons, caused by their decision to staunchly defend Guadalcanal. In November the entire IJN air force was tactically restructured, while at the same time key JAAF units were redeployed from Southeast Asia to reinforce New Guinea. These initial JAAF units would experience their first combat in this strange new theatre before the year ended.

Never before has this campaign been chronicled in such detail, with Allied accounts matched against Japanese records for a truly factual account of the conflict.

Michael John Claringbould & Peter Ingman
Australia
October 2021

Glossary and Abbreviations

(Japanese terms in italics)

BG	Bombardment Group (USAAF)
BS	Bombardment Squadron (USAAF)
Buntai	Equivalent to a *chutai* but usually accompanied by administrative or established command status.
Buntaicho	Leader of a *buntai*
Chutai	Japanese aircraft formation normally comprised of nine aircraft.
Chutaicho	Flight leader of a *chutai*.
CO	Commanding Officer
Dokuritsu Chutai	Independent Squadron (JAAF)
Flyer1c	Aviator First Class (IJN)
FG	Fighter Group (USAAF)
FS	Fighter Squadron (USAAF)
FCPO	Flying Chief Petty Officer (IJN)
FPO1c	Flying Petty Officer First Class (IJN)
FPO2c	Flying Petty Officer Second Class (IJN)
FPO3c	Flying Petty Officer Third Class (IJN)
Hayabusa	Peregrine Falcon (JAAF name for Ki-43 fighter)
Hiko Sentai	Air Regiment (JAAF)
Hikocho	Administrative commander of a *Kokutai,* senior to the *Hikotaicho* (operational commander).
Hikotaicho	commander of a *kokutai*
HMAS	His Majesty's Australian Ship
IJA	Imperial Japanese Army
IJN	Imperial Japanese Navy
JAAF	Japanese Army Air Force
Katakana	Phonetic characters used in written Japanese, usually used for geographic place names.
Kokutai	An IJN air group, consisting of between three and six *chutai*.
Ku	Abbreviation of *kokutai*
Lieutenant (jg)	Lieutenant (junior grade)
PRS	Photo Reconnaissance Squadron (USAAF)
RAAF	Royal Australian Air Force
Sentai	An abbreviation of Japanese *hiko sentai* defining a JAAF flying regiment.
Shotai	A tactical formation typically of three aircraft (although sometimes two or four aircraft).
Shotaicho	Flight leader of a *shotai*
Sokei	A colloquial Japanese abbreviation of *shiki-souhatu-keibaku* often used to refer to the Ki-48 light bomber.
SNLF	Special Naval Landing Force (IJN)
SoPAC	South Pacific Area
SWPA	South West Pacific Area

TCS	Troop Carrier Squadron	USN	United States Navy
US	United States	USS	United States Ship
USAAF	United States Army Air Force		

Explanatory Notes

Place names are, where possible, consistent with 1942 usage, and with local spelling conventions, for example Nadi rather than Nandi.

Measurements are also consistent with 1942 usage: generally, miles and miles per hour are used; Altitude is given in feet, even though Japanese aviators used metres.

Japanese individuals have their surnames first, followed by first name, as per Japanese usage.

Allied code names are used for most Japanese aircraft because these names are widely recognised by readers.

Addendum to *Volume 3*:

p.138: The name of Flyer1c Shimizu Matsuhiro is written incorrectly as Flyer1c Matsuhiro Shimizu.

p.223: The date given for the loss of B-26 40-1402 is 7 May 1942 but should be 10 May 1942.

Addendum to *Volume 4*:

- The loss of the submarine *S-39* off Rossel Island in mid-August 1942 was not included in *Volume 4*. The circumstance of this loss is described in Chapter 1 of this volume.

- While the chronology of this volume commences on 9 September 1942, some more detailed information on P-39 and A-20 ground attack missions in the Kokoda area during 1 – 8 September can be found at the beginning of Chapter 2.

- As an observation to *Volume 5* there are numerous discrepancies between official sources, such as individual squadron records and intelligence summaries. These are particularly apparent pertaining to numbers of Allied aircraft completing attack missions during this period. This is complicated by the presence of aircraft that might have acted as escorts or reserves and for some reason did not actually participate in the attack, in addition to those that aborted for technical reasons. For example, page 150 of *Volume 4* states that 13 A-20s participated in the first A-20 mission in the Pacific against Lae on 31 August. Allied air summary logs suggest that the actual number that took part in the attack was either ten or as few as six. If 13 A-20s did participate in the mission it would mean that all three flights, each of six A-20As and drawn from the 8th and 89th Bombardment Squadrons, had arrived at Port Moresby by 31 August (as opposed to the second and third flights arriving on 2 and 8 September as stated in *Volume 4*).

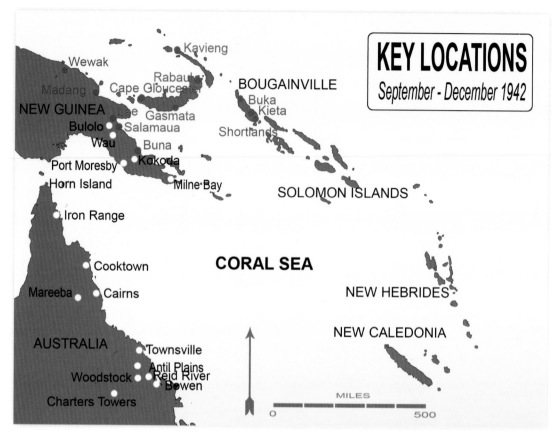

Key locations of the wider South Pacific region as featured in this volume. Key Allied bases and airfields are in white with black text while Japanese locations are in red. While increasing numbers of Allied squadrons moved forward to Port Moresby during this period, many were still based in northern Queensland at locations including Townsville, Reid River, Charters Towers, Mareeba and the newly built Iron Range. Note that Madang, Wewak and Cape Gloucester were under Japanese control but were not occupied until December 1942.

Right: A map showing key New Guinea locations featured in this volume. Note that the overall area was divided into two territories, the Australian colony of Papua and Mandated New Guinea which was a former German colony administered by Australia after WWI. The distinction ceased to have any meaning after the outbreak of the Pacific War, although in the context of this title references to "Papua" usually mean the general area bounded by Port Moresby, Buna and Milne Bay. Japanese centres are in red, and the Kokoda inset map shows the approximate extent of their advance as of 9 September.

NEW GUINEA THEATRE
September 1942

KOKODA CAMPAIGN
September 1942

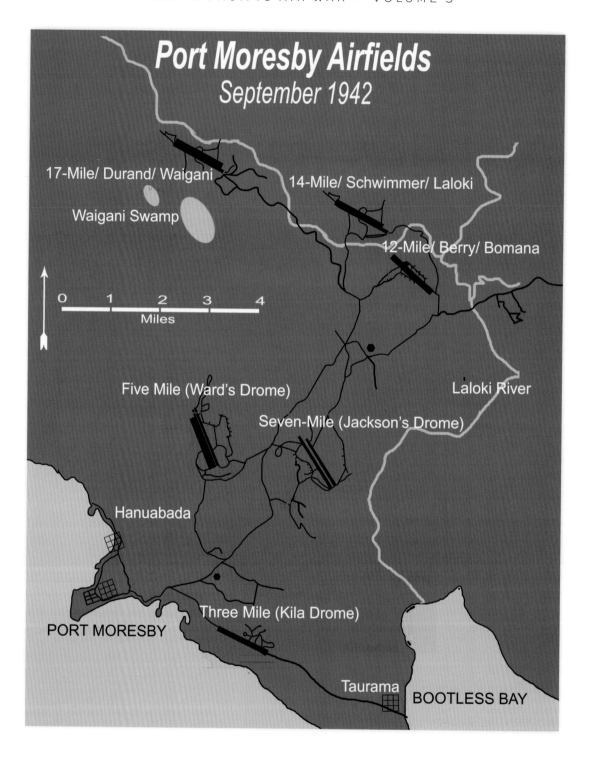

Port Moresby Airfields
September 1942

17-Mile/ Durand/ Waigani

14-Mile/ Schwimmer/ Laloki

Waigani Swamp

12-Mile/ Berry/ Bomana

0 1 2 3 4
Miles

Five Mile (Ward's Drome)

Laloki River

Seven-Mile (Jackson's Drome)

Hanuabada

Three Mile (Kila Drome)

PORT MORESBY

Taurama BOOTLESS BAY

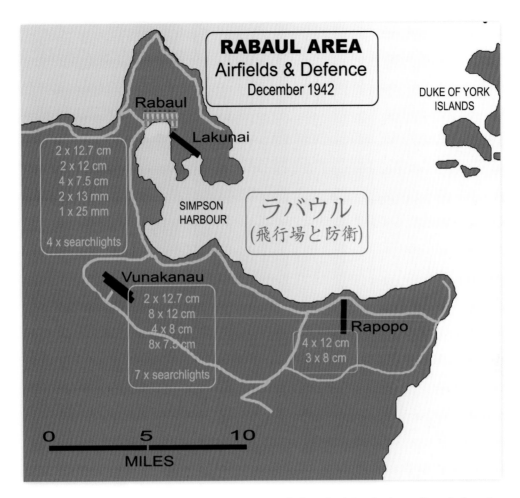

RABAUL AREA
Airfields & Defence
December 1942

Rabaul

Lakunai

DUKE OF YORK
ISLANDS

2 x 12.7 cm
2 x 12 cm
4 x 7.5 cm
2 x 13 mm
1 x 25 mm

4 x searchlights

SIMPSON
HARBOUR

ラバウル
(飛行場と防衛)

Vunakanau

2 x 12.7 cm
8 x 12 cm
4 x 8 cm
8 x 7.5 cm

7 x searchlights

Rapopo

4 x 12 cm
3 x 8 cm

0   5   10
MILES

Rabaul was home to two airfields which had originally been built by the Australians. Lakunai was mostly used as a fighter strip and was famously situated alongside an active volcano, Tavurvur. Vunakanau had been greatly expanded by the Japanese and was the main IJN bomber base in the South Pacific. Construction of a runway at Rapopo was begun by the JAAF in December 1942 but would not be ready for use until January 1943. This map lists the anti-aircraft guns at these locations in December 1942.

Left: By September 1942 Port Moresby was a very busy aviation centre and was home to the six airfields seen in this map. In addition, another airfield had been built at 30-Mile (Rorona). The original pre-war civil 'drome was at Three-Mile (Kila) but was unsuitable for use by larger aircraft. Seven-Mile was the best facility and had been built by the RAAF in 1941. The other airfields had all been built in 1942 after an influx of engineering and construction units had arrived in Port Moresby and were in varying stages of development. Most of the airfields were eventually known by three names: their distance from Port Moresby central post office in miles, a geographic name and a name commemorating pilots and soldiers who had lost their lives in the area. Seven-Mile was known as Jackson's, after the CO of the RAAF's No. 75 Squadron, John Jackson, who was shot down and killed on 28 April. Today, the location still bears his name as Port Moresby's Jacksons International Airport. Berry, Durand and Schwimmer were all USAAF P-39 pilots killed between April and August. Wards was named after an Australian army officer who helped build it but was killed in fighting on the Kokoda Track in August.

A No. 6 Squadron Hudson drops four 250-pound bombs over northern Papua. It was common for Allied aircraft to drop unexpended bombs on Japanese positions while returning to Port Moresby after armed reconnaissance missions.

CHAPTER 1

ALLIED OVERVIEW

By the start of the second week of September 1942, the attention of Allied commanders in New Guinea was firmly focused on the unfolding campaign high in the Owen Stanley Range that runs down the spine of Papua. As detailed in *Volume 4* of this series, Japanese forces had landed in the Buna area on the northern coast of Papua in late July where they had established a supply base and airfield. Follow-up convoys brought several contingents of IJA troops, which pushed inland and had captured Kokoda on the northern side of the ranges by the end of July.

From Kokoda a track, passable only by foot, ran for some 60 miles over the mountains to Owers' Corner on the southern foothills of the Owen Stanleys. Owers' Corner was only about 25 miles by road to the outer airfields of Port Moresby. With plans for a sea invasion of Port Moresby having been frustrated following the Battle of the Coral Sea in May, the Japanese sent several thousand IJA troops across the track where they were met by Australian troops. The unfolding series of battles became known at the time as the Kokoda Track Campaign or now more simply the Kokoda Campaign.

However, sending such a large body of troops over the mountains was logistically demanding, given that the track rises to a height of over 7,000 feet and undergoes severe undulations such that it took fit men several days to cross. Further, military operations in such an environment were governed by the availability of supplies and ammunition, all of which had to be carried by foot. Both sides employed small armies of native "carriers", but the carriers also had to carry their own food. This meant that the further into the mountains they ventured, the effective load per carrier lessened dramatically.

Matched with these gruelling physical conditions was an environment prevalent with malaria, leeches and dysentery. Not surprisingly, the combat effectiveness of troops in such an environment dropped quickly. The Japanese were fully aware of these challenges, and at this initial stage their advance along the trail was more of a reconnaissance in force to establish a route for a future attempt to capture Port Moresby. However, at the time the Allied commanders were unaware of this and incorrectly viewed the tenacious Japanese advance along the track as a direct threat to Port Moresby and its invaluable air bases.

The first troops encountered by the Japanese were Australian militia troops of the 30th Brigade which had garrisoned Port Moresby since the start of 1942. Briefly, the airstrip at Kokoda, which was the only one along the track, had been used to reinforce and resupply these troops before its capture by the Japanese at the end of July. In mid-August Australian reinforcements were sent up the trail, in the form of the 21st Brigade which had landed in Port Moresby just a few days earlier. These men were well-trained Australian Imperial Force soldiers and had seen combat in the Middle East the previous year.

However, the welcome arrival of the 21st Brigade greatly complicated the supply situation, as the number of troops deep in the mountains would more than double. This was somewhat alleviated by the airdropping of supplies on a dry lake bed high in the mountains named Myola. Nonetheless, during a number of pitched battles during August the Australians were forced to retreat back along the track, as it was almost impossible to secure the jungle-clad flanks of defensive positions in the steep mountainous conditions.

By the start of September, the Australian retreat meant the abandonment of Myola, and during 6-9 September the 21st Brigade fought from positions at Efogi, a short distance to the south. The Australians were again forced to withdraw and illustrating the difficulties of the terrain one of the brigade's three battalions lost contact with the main force altogether, its remnants only emerging from the jungle more than a fortnight later.

Hence from the Allied point of view by the start of the second week of September the situation was dire indeed with the defending Australian forces now just a few ridges north of the roadhead at Owers' Corner. While the nuances of the land campaign are outside the scope of this volume, General Douglas MacArthur's South West Pacific Area (SWPA) headquarters in Brisbane held grave concerns about the fighting efficiency of the Australians at this time. Lieutenant General Sydney Rowell, who had only taken over command of New Guinea Force in mid-August, was effectively replaced after only a month in the job.

Major General George Kenney, USAAF, had arrived in Australia in late July and had taken over as MacArthur's air commander. After visiting New Guinea, Kenney records in his memoirs that he believed:

> Rowell was planning a withdrawal to his [Port Moresby] perimeter defense line, which would put most of our airdromes in the hands of the Japs.

Kenney subsequently reported to MacArthur that he believed Rowell had become defeatist, and reports of further Australian withdrawals in the second week of September only seemed to confirm this view. Thus, Kenney's view of the situation paralleled MacArthur's, and the two soon established a good working relationship. Indeed, from this point onwards MacArthur's headquarters arguably became "air minded", with air power forming a key pillar of offensive moves in the theatre. There is some irony in this, as MacArthur's use of his own air force during the defence of the Philippines was a disaster, and by September 1942 his headquarters had a negative reputation for micro-managing air operations in the SWPA.

Kenney's arrival restructured several fundamentals of Allied air power in the SWPA. First, the joint Australian-American Allied Air Forces command was dissolved. Kenney received permission to bring all American air units in the theatre under his own air force command. The Fifth Air Force designation was chosen as it was not in use elsewhere and reflected on the original V Interceptor Command and V Bomber Command of the US Far East Air Force which had defended the Philippines in 1941. The Fifth Air Force was officially constituted on 3 September 1942. Kenney's force, at least on paper, consisted of three fighter groups and five bombardment groups, along with two transport and one photographic reconnaissance squadron(s).

An 8th FG P-400 Airacobra being refuelled at 30-Mile 'drome in late 1942, with the nose of a 49th FG P-40E discernible behind it. Between May and September 1942 six squadrons of Airacobras formed the bulk of Allied fighter strength in New Guinea and sustained heavy losses.

B-25C 41-12938 Ole Cappy seen at 14-Mile with its crew. This was one of the original 405th BS Mitchells which flew from California to Queensland via Hawaii in August 1942.

The commander of the 89th BS, Major Ernest Nenneman, at the controls of his assigned A-20A 40-169 Eight Ball during an exercise off Port Moresby in late 1942. The successful local modification of the A-20As with 0.50-inch calibre machine guns in the nose in September gave an important boost to Fifth Air Force low level attack capability.

Since April the brunt of the defence of Port Moresby had been undertaken by the 8th and 35th Fighter Groups, both equipped with P-39D/F Airacobras. Losses had been heavy, with 82 Airacobras lost in combat and to accidents – more than any other Allied type in the theatre. By early September two squadrons (the 41st and 80th FS) were based at Port Moresby. Four other squadrons (the 35th, 36th, 39th and 40th FS) were resting in Townsville, but within the next two months these would be rotated northwards to New Guinea.

Since early 1942 the 49th Fighter Group, equipped with P-40E Warhawks, had been based in the Northern Territory and had defended Darwin against regular raids from Japanese units based in islands to the north. Despite starting the campaign with a cadre of largely untrained and inexperienced pilots, the group was superbly led by Lieutenant Colonel Paul B Wurtsmith. Kenney was so impressed with Wurtsmith that he would soon be appointed to lead the newly organised 5th Fighter Command.

Meanwhile the 49th FG would soon move from Darwin to New Guinea, so that Wurtsmith would soon have three fighter groups (nine squadrons) under his command in the theatre – a more than four-fold increase over the pairs of squadrons which had defended Port Moresby since April. Kenney had qualitative plans for his fighter force too. Aware that the P-39s and P-40s were poor performers at high altitude and lacked the range to escort bombers to distant targets such as Rabaul, prior to leaving the US Kenney had requested a batch of new Lockheed P-38 Lightning twin-engine fighters. Kenney was familiar with the type after commanding the Fourth Air Force based in San Francisco where he had witnessed the speed, high altitude performance and long range of the P-38s. However, the new type was technologically far advanced from the existing P-39s and P-40s, and various teething problems meant the Lightning fighter would not make its combat debut in New Guinea until late November 1942.

To date the bulk of offensive air operations in the SWPA had been in the hands of the 3rd, 19th and 22nd Bombardment Groups, all of which had seen much service. The 19th BG operated B-17E Flying Fortress heavy bombers, while the 3rd BG flew a mix of A-20A Havocs and B-25C Mitchells and the 22nd BG flew B-26 Marauders.

Illustrating the fact that replacement aircraft arriving from the US had been barely enough to replace combat losses, another heavy bomber unit, the 43rd BG, had also been in Australia since early 1942 but had not received its own aircraft. Instead, all newly arriving B-17s were being sent to the 19th BG. Only in recent weeks was it possible to start allocating the 43rd BG some B-17Fs. By integrating with experienced crews from the 19th BG, one squadron from the 43rd BG, the 63rd BS, had begun flying combat operations in August. The 403rd BS was the next unit of the 43rd BG slated for operational status and received four new B-17Fs in early September.

At this time the 19th BG had seen more continuous combat than any other air unit in the SWPA, with some personnel having served since the Philippine and Java campaigns in the first weeks of the Pacific War. Kenney formed the view that some of these long serving crews had become exhausted and demoralised, going so far as referring to the group as a "broken-down outfit". Not surprisingly, in October the longest serving crews were sent home, while others were transferred to the 43rd BG. The following month the entire 19th BG returned to the US. By that time another heavy bomber unit, the B-24 equipped 90th Bombardment Group, had begun to arrive in Australia.

Mirroring the situation of the 43rd BG was that of the 38th BG, ground components of which had also arrived in Australia in early 1942. It was not until late August that the 71st and 405th Bombardment Squadrons, equipped with B-25C/Ds, arrived at Breddan Field near Charters Towers in Queensland. Some 37 Mitchells had departed Hamilton Field in California on 7 August. The flight was not without incident, as after having been blown off course by strong winds off the eastern Australian coast on 14 August two of the bombers crashed near Casino in New South Wales. Fortunately, most of the crewmen baled out safely.

At this time, the 38th BG had two other squadrons administratively attached to it, but which were serving in the South Pacific Area. As explained in the table below, it was not until April 1943 that two additional B-25 squadrons reached Australia, meaning that until then the 38th BG would operate effectively at half-strength in the SWPA.

Meanwhile, as detailed in the earlier volumes of this series, incessant Japanese air attacks on Port Moresby had forced the American bombers to be based in Queensland. They would fly shuttles up to Port Moresby and back to fly their combat missions, but this large amount of transit flying greatly reduced the combat efficiency of the force.

However, the Japanese attacks on Port Moresby had recently slackened given their focus on the Solomons, and Kenney was determined to move his bombers to permanent bases closer to the frontlines. Already the 89th Bombardment Squadron, from the 3rd BG, had completed its move with its A-20As to Port Moresby – the very first USAAF multi-engine bomber unit to be permanently based there. While the other three squadrons of the 3rd BG would not make the same move until January 1943, the two newly arrived squadrons of the 38th BG would move to Port Moresby by late October 1942.

Another factor in this move north was the construction of an airfield at Iron Range. Situated on the east coast of the remote Cape York, this airfield was roughly midway between Cairns and Port Moresby. Engineers had arrived at the site in June, and ships were able to bring in supplies via a jetty at nearby Portland Roads. Despite thick rainforest the first airstrip was ready within two months. An American B-18 was the first aircraft to land there on 18 August, and two B-26 squadrons from the 19th BG had relocated to the new base by the end of September. These were joined the following month by three B-17 squadrons from the 43rd BG.

Conditions at Iron Range were very primitive and tropical ailments of all kinds were common. However, the construction of this base went unnoticed by Japanese reconnaissance and was a significant achievement at this time, bearing some similarities to the successful construction of the Milne Bay base during the same timeframe (see *Volume 4*).

On 3 September Kenney appointed Brigadier General Kenneth Walker to head Fifth Bomber Command. Walker had arrived in the SWPA a few weeks before Kenney and had flown several combat missions over New Guinea to experience frontline conditions first-hand. Walker was an advocate of conventional high altitude bombing tactics, which had delivered disappointing results in the theatre so far.

In contrast to Walker, Kenney was a believer in low-level attack tactics, the development of which would have a decisive impact on Fifth Air Force doctrine in coming months. Prior to leaving the US, Kenney had requested 3,000 parachute fragmentation bombs that were being held in the war reserve:

No one else wanted them, so they were ordered shipped to Australia on the next boat.

Developed in the 1920s, "parafrags" were small 23-pound bombs fitted with highly sensitive fuses and parachutes. Designed to be dropped in large quantities, these weapons would slowly float to earth before detonating and breaking up into 1,600 small pieces. Even at 100 yards distance the fragments would punch a hole through the aluminium skin of an aircraft. As direct hits were not needed to inflict damage, such weapons were ideal for attacking parked aircraft dispersed over a wide area.

On 5 August, Kenney had visited the 3rd Bombardment Group at Charters Towers which had been struggling to get a squadron of A-20As into operational service. The fighter-like A-20As were ideally suited to Kenney's low-level attack tactics but lacked the range to engage targets on the other side of the Owen Stanley mountains from Port Moresby. They were fitted with a pack of strafing machine guns in the nose, but these were only of the relatively light 0.30-inch calibre.

At Charters Towers Kenney was intrigued to find an officer making an unauthorised installation of the considerably heavier 0.50-inch calibre machine guns in the nose of an A-20. The officer was Paul Irving Gunn, widely known as "Pappy" Gunn because he was over 40 years of age. Gunn had been a naval machinist before training as a fighter pilot in the 1920s, and at the start of the Pacific

Seen in dark USAAF uniform, Brigadier General Kenneth Walker socialises with RAAF officers in Townsville in late August 1942, shortly after arriving in Australia from the United States. Walker would soon be appointed to lead Fifth Bomber Command in the newly raised Fifth Air Force. Immediately to his right are (left to right) Group Captain Arthur Cobby and Air Commodore Frank Bladin. Cobby, who was the highest scoring ace of the Australian Flying Corps in WWI, had just taken over as commander of the North Eastern Area which was the RAAF command covering Northern Queensland and New Guinea. Bladin was commander of the North Western Area where he had been responsible for the defence of Darwin. The 49th Fighter Group had been at Bladin's disposal for most of 1942 but was now slated to move to New Guinea.

Destined to play a key part in the subsequent air campaign was No. 30 Squadron equipped with powerfully armed Beaufighters. A19-4 is seen at Charters Towers shortly before deploying to Port Moresby with a red inner roundel and yellow surround still visible. This aircraft was hit by anti-aircraft fire over Lae on 18 November and made a wheels-up landing at Wards 'drome. Sent to an aircraft depot for repairs, it did not return to service until 1944.

War he was an airline pilot in the Philippines. When MacArthur's Air Corps took over the airline, Gunn was commissioned as a captain and subsequently flew a Beech Model 18 full of refugee pilots to Australia. Following several busy months of operations, including flying B-25s in combat, by August Gunn was employed as an engineering and maintenance officer with the 3rd BG.

Gunn proved to be a talented engineer with a typically American "can-do" attitude. In due course he was destined to become one of the legendary characters in the Fifth Air Force, but his first challenge came directly from Kenney. The general asked for 16 A-20As equipped with 0.50-inch calibre machine guns, bomb bay fuel tanks and bomb racks to hold 40 parafrags. He wanted them ready within two weeks. Working day and night Gunn narrowly missed the deadline, but a squadron of the newly fitted out A-20As was ready for operations in early September (as noted above, the 89th BS had moved forward to Port Moresby at this time).

Kenney also recognised the need for air transport in the mountainous New Guinea terrain, but the Fifth Air Force could boast just two transport units, the 21st and 22nd Troop Carrier Squadrons. These operated a motley collection of Douglas and Lockheed transports, over half of which were former Dutch aircraft which had escaped from Java in early 1942. The 22nd TCS was based at Essendon in Melbourne but would move to Townsville in October, while the 21st TCS was based at Archerfield in Brisbane. Kenney had requested additional troop carrier squadrons from the US, and two were scheduled to arrive in October.

Also serving with the Fifth Air Force was the 8th Photographic Reconnaissance Squadron which had been operating its small fleet of unarmed F-4 Lightnings from Townsville since May. On 9 September the unit moved forward to a new permanent base at Port Moresby. Allied commanders often framed their plans around photographs of enemy positions provided by this unit.

It should be noted that Kenny also made considerable improvements to his logistics and maintenance organisations. Townsville was chosen as the site for a large new air depot, to some extent replacing a large facility which had been built at Tocumwal, some 1,000 miles to the south. Within weeks eleven 200-foot-long hangars were under construction with most of the work completed by the end of 1942.

The following table summarises the USAAF units that Kenney had at his disposal on 9 September 1942. Note that during August his staff reported that of 430 combat aircraft that were on strength, only 151 were operational:

75 fighters	P-39s, P-40s
33 medium bombers	B-25s, B-26s
43 heavy bombers	B-17s

This situation would improve in coming months, both through deliveries of replacements and better maintenance. However, after the Guadalcanal landings Kenney faced the possibility that aircraft intended for delivery to the SWPA could be diverted to the neighbouring South Pacific theatre in times of emergency. Much to Kenney's frustration, this happened on several occasions, the first of which was in late August when 30 P-39s were re-routed from Australia to New Caledonia.

5th Air Force, USAAF, North Queensland and Papua, 9 September 1942

8th FG:

     35th & 36th FS, P-400s & P-39D/Fs Airacobras, Townsville, Queensland

     80th FS, P-400s & P-39D/Fs Airacobras, Port Moresby, Papua

35th FG:

     39th & 40th FS, P-400s & P-39D/Fs Airacobras, Townsville, Queensland

     41st FS P-400s & P-39D/Fs Airacobras, Port Moresby, Papua

49th FG (moving from Northern Territory)

     7th FS, P-40E Warhawks, arrive Port Moresby 19 September

     8th FS, P-40E Warhawks, arrive Port Moresby 25 September

     9th FS, P-40E Warhawks, arrive Port Moresby 10 October

3rd BG:

     8th BS, A-20A Havocs, Charters Towers, Queensland

     89th BS, A-20A Havocs, Port Moresby, Papua

     13th & 90th BS, B-25C Mitchells, Charters Towers, Queensland

19th BG:

     28th, 30th & 93rd BS, B-17E Flying Fortresses, Mareeba, Queensland

     435th BS, B-17E Flying Fortresses, Townsville, Queensland

22nd BG:

     2nd & 408th BS, B-26 Marauders, Reid River, Queensland

     19th BS, B-26 Marauders, Woodstock, Queensland (to Iron Range, Queensland, 15 September)

     33rd BS, B-26 Marauders, Woodstock, Queensland (to Iron Range, Queensland, 29 September)

38th BG

     71st & 405th BS, B-25C Mitchells, Breddan Field, Queensland

     Note: ground components of the 38th BG had arrived in Australia in early 1942, while the 69th & 70th Bombardment Squadrons, both equipped with B-26s, were sent to New Caledonia and Fiji. These squadrons subsequently remained in the South Pacific Area while still administratively attached to the 38th BG. Only in February 1943 were they finally transferred to the 42nd BG. It was not until April 1943 that two newly raised replacement squadrons, the 822nd and 823rd Bombardment Squadrons, arrived in Australia to bring the 38th BG back to its full strength of four squadrons.

> **5th Air Force, USAAF, North Queensland and Papua, 9 September 1942 (continued)**
>
> 43rd BG:
>
> > 63rd BS, B-17F Flying Fortresses, Mareeba, Queensland
> >
> > 64th BS, B-17F Flying Fortresses, Fenton, Northern Territory (to Iron Range, Queensland, 12 October)
> >
> > 65th BS, B-17F Flying Fortresses, Torrens Creek, Queensland (to Iron Range, Queensland, 13 October)
> >
> > 403rd BS, B-17F Flying Fortresses, Torrens Creek, Queensland (to Iron Range, Queensland, 17 October)
> >
> > Note: only one of these squadrons, the 63rd BS, had yet flown combat missions. The others were not yet ready for operations.
>
> Independent Squadron:
>
> > 8th PRS F-4 Lightnings, Port Moresby, Papua (arrived 9 September)

The formation of the Fifth Air Force also resulted in parallel changes to the RAAF organisational structure, which took primary responsibility for the defence of continental Australia. All operational units based in Australia came under a new organisation called RAAF Command, which became responsible for maritime patrol around Australia's coast as well as the campaign being conducted from Darwin and the north-west.

This left several squadrons based in Papua which were formed into a new command called No. 9 Operational Group. This unit became operational on 1 September and was under Fifth Air Force control. It was commanded by Group Captain William "Bull" Garing, a 32-year-old career air force officer who had flown Sunderland flying boats in Europe before returning to Australia in 1941.

On 9 September the fighter defence of Milne Bay was still being provided by Nos. 75 and 76 Squadrons equipped with P-40Es. Both of these units had seen much action during the Milne Bay operations from 25 August until 7 September. However, they would soon be withdrawn to the Darwin area to replace the 49th FG.

Also involved in the Milne Bay operations was No. 6 Squadron flying Lockheed Hudsons in the maritime reconnaissance role. This squadron was based at Horn Island but maintained a forward detachment at Milne Bay.

As outlined in *Volume 4,* No. 100 Squadron's Beaufort torpedo bombers had made their combat debut in New Guinea in June, prior to being withdrawn to Victoria for anti-submarine patrol duties. In early September a detachment of six Beauforts had been sent north to Milne Bay and these made an unsuccessful torpedo attack on Japanese ships on 7 September. Meanwhile the remainder of the squadron had relocated to Bohle River airstrip, Townsville, by 24 September.

It should be noted that during July and August six 22nd BG B-26s conducted torpedo training

By September 1942 the wider Port Moresby area was a mass of airfields and military camps criss-crossed by interconnecting roads busy with traffic. Here American vehicles travel between newly constructed aircraft revetments at Wards 'drome. Note that they are driving on the left-hand side as a concession to operating on Australian territory.

at the RAAF torpedo training facility at Nowra, some 75 miles south of Sydney. Almost none of the USAAF crews then in Australia had torpedo experience given that it was a weapon mostly employed by the USN in American usage. The training was not popular and with the Marauders urgently needed for conventional bombing duties it had been cancelled by the end of August. For this reason, No. 100 Squadron's torpedo attack capability remained a unique niche function in the SWPA theatre.

However, the supply of aerial torpedoes was far from assured. Since the start of the Pacific War, there had been no direct supply of American aerial torpedoes to either the USAAF or the RAAF in the SWPA. Instead, control of local torpedo stocks was vested in the USN, and only a slim stock was available for the RAAF. The Beauforts were able to carry the American Type XIII torpedo, albeit with some minor modifications. However, the Type XIIIs were heavier and bulkier than the British torpedoes for which the Beaufort had been designed. This meant that the Beaufort's flying performance was degraded due to the additional weight and drag of the American munition.

Instead, the RAAF preferred the British Mk. XII torpedo, of which the RAAF received 50 transferred via the RAN in 1942. Of this number, 15 were allocated to Nowra for training, leaving just 35 for operational use.[1] Given that the needs of a single torpedo bomber squadron were estimated at 75 torpedoes per six months, the stock of 35 torpedoes would barely last No. 100 Squadron until the end of 1942. Indeed, by January 1943 the Australian Air Board was recommending the acquisition of many hundreds of torpedoes, both through local

---

1   Torpedoes used for training had the warheads removed and were recovered and reused. The wastage rate was estimated at 5% of the number of torpedoes dropped.

manufacture and from the US.[II] However, in the immediate term the supply of aerial torpedoes in the SWPA remained poor and plagued by uncertainty, and this scarcity helps explain why No. 100 Squadron remained the sole torpedo attack unit in New Guinea at this time.

When the Beauforts made their flight north in September they each made a stop at Nowra and collected a torpedo. These first torpedoes to arrive in New Guinea were drawn from among the small stock of American Type XIIIs. During October No. 2 Mobile Torpedo Unit was sent to Papua to support No. 100 Squadron.

Another RAAF type to recently make its combat debut in New Guinea was the Bristol Beaufighter, two of which had flown alongside the Beauforts in the 7 September attack. The Beaufighter was a fast twin-engine fighter powerfully armed with four 20mm cannons and was ideally suited to Kenney's preferred low-level attack tactics.

No. 30 Squadron had received its first British-built Beaufighter Mark 1Cs in June 1942 and began a hurried training program at RAAF Richmond outside of Sydney. In early September three aircraft were forward deployed to Milne Bay where they participated in the 7 September mission, although one of the aircraft was written off in a ground accident. By this time the squadron had moved north to a temporary base at Bohle River airstrip, Townsville, with 23 Beaufighters.

In early September an advance echelon of No. 30 Squadron's ground personnel moved by flying boat from Townsville to Wards 'drome (Five-Mile), Port Moresby. Most of the squadron soon followed by sea, with the movement completed by 14 September.

Also destined for New Guinea service was No. 22 Squadron, which in April had received 22 Douglas DB-7B light bombers originally ordered by the Dutch Navy for use in Java. Similar to the A-20A flown by the USAAF, these were called Boston Mark IIIs in RAAF service. From Richmond the squadron had spent some months training and flying anti-submarine patrols off the New South Wales coast. By early September it had begun to move north to Papua with an advance party sent to Wards 'drome.

Although a few Bostons arrived at Wards in late September, most of the squadron remained at Townsville for several weeks. During this time, the Bostons were flown south to Amberley where they were fitted with four nose-mounted 0.50-inch calibre machine guns, mirroring the modifications to the USAAF A-20As. Bostons were also sent to Charters Towers to ensure they could deploy small fragmentation bombs and American parafrags. Because of these tasks the squadron would not be properly settled at Wards until early November.

Another RAAF unit at Port Moresby was No. 1 Rescue and Communications Flight, which was operating an Anson, a DH-89 and a Tiger Moth in the light transport capacity. These maintained communications with isolated outposts using small airstrips or makeshift landing grounds. On 1 October the unit was expanded to squadron strength and soon received at least two DH-84s, three additional Avro Ansons and three additional Tiger Moths. By the end

---

II   Australian manufactured torpedoes were not available until 1944 by which time such munitions were freely available from outside sources. The newly established RAN Torpedo Factory was instead used for repairs and maintenance.

of 1942 the unit had carried about 15,000 pounds of supplies and rescued dozens of people, including downed aircrews and sick and wounded troops.

Other RAAF squadrons were based in North Queensland but would regularly operate into or nearby the New Guinea theatre. Most notable were the Catalina flying boats of Nos. 11 and 20 Squadrons which had seen much service since the first days of the Pacific War. Based at Bowen south of Townsville, these flying boats flew anti-submarine patrols as well as long range night bombing missions against Japanese bases. By October they were increasingly using Cairns as an operating base, as it was some 300 miles further north than Bowen. In mid-November both squadrons were permanently based at Cairns.

Since February No. 33 Squadron had been operating three Short Empire flying boats in a transport capacity from Townsville, with regular shuttle flights to Port Moresby. However, on 21 August these flying boats and their crews were taken over by the newly formed No. 41 Squadron. The new unit was also allocated four ex-Dutch Navy Dornier flying boats, but these would require extensive and lengthy overhauls and would not in fact be ready for service until mid-1943.

No. 33 Squadron had also been operating a handful of DH-84 Dragon biplanes since March, and these had been regularly used for flights to New Guinea. Now in response to the growing need for air transport No. 33 Squadron converted to wholly land-based operations. However, the availability of transport aircraft was scarce indeed, and among those allocated to the squadron was a Lockheed Vega and a Ford Trimotor (both of which at this time were non-operational), alongside the Dragons and some Tiger Moths. The Trimotor was undergoing conversion to an air ambulance, and as will be seen in November was among aircraft used by No. 33 Squadron to directly support Australian troops fighting on the Kokoda Track.

Another RAAF unit that would soon be in the area was No. 7 Squadron. This had been a Hudson training unit in Victoria and by September it had re-equipped with Beauforts and was undergoing torpedo training at Nowra. The squadron was then sent to Ross River airfield in Townsville where an advance party arrived on 25 October, and operational flying commenced on 7 November. Subsequently the Beauforts often visited Milne Bay, Horn Island and Port Moresby while flying convoy protection patrols.

Since the early months of 1942, the wider Port Moresby area had resembled a large construction site. By September it boasted six airfields each of which was being upgraded with ever increasing numbers of protective revetments built among newly graded dispersal areas. Such facilities made aircraft reasonably safe from air attack, although there was always a danger of aircraft being caught in the open as had happened on 17 August when several valuable transports were destroyed or damaged at Seven-Mile.

Port Moresby had faced relentless air assault for months and it was not yet apparent how much this would slacken due to the Japanese campaign in the Solomons. Also, as noted earlier, by the second week of September the IJA advance over the Owen Stanleys was becoming perilously close to Port Moresby. Allied commanders needed confidence that both the air and ground

---

RAAF, North Queensland and Papua, 9 September 1942

(Papua based units under the command of No. 9 Operational Group)

Nos. 75 and 76 Squadrons, P-40Es, Milne Bay (soon to move to Darwin area)

No. 6 Squadron, Hudsons, Horn Island (forward detachment at Milne Bay)

No. 1 Rescue and Communications Flight, Anson, DH-89, DH-82, Port Moresby (to expand to squadron strength from 1 October; became No. 1 Rescue and Communications Squadron on 30 November)

No. 100 Squadron, Beauforts, moving from Laverton, Victoria, to Bohle River, Queensland (move completed by 24 September; forward detachment at Milne Bay)

No. 30 Squadron, Beaufighters, Bohle River, Queensland (moving to Port Moresby by 14 September)

No. 22 Squadron, Bostons, Townsville (moving to Port Moresby by November)

Nos. 11 and 20 Squadrons, Catalinas, Bowen, Queensland

No. 41 Squadron, Empire FBs, Townsville, Queensland

No. 33 Squadron, DH-82s, DH-84s, Townsville, Queensland

---

threats to Port Moresby were in abeyance before full use could be made of the excellent new airfield facilities. Nevertheless, there was a growing amount of USAAF and RAAF airpower that would soon be available for permanent basing in New Guinea, and these moves would unfold over the final months of 1942 and early 1943.

Since the beginning of the Kokoda Campaign in late July, Allied airpower was increasingly called upon in direct support of land units. However, with the campaign fought under a jungle canopy and with few distinctive features in the mountains, such direct support was rarely effective. Another key target for air attacks was the Buna beachhead area where new supplies were landed, usually under the cover of darkness.

Buna was in relatively easy range of Port Moresby, even for P-39s. For that reason, the Japanese had been forced to abandon their use of a small airstrip there which had briefly been used by Zeros and Vals. As a result, most of the Allied air operations over the Buna-Kokoda area were now flown without aerial opposition, although the possibility remained if Zeros operated from forward bases at Lae, Buna or Gasmata.

The other main target for Allied bombers was Japanese ships. These needed to regularly run into Buna and Lae on resupply missions from Rabaul and had become skilled at unloading under the cover of darkness. During daylight they made use of low cloud cover where possible, and often entire voyages took place without detection by Allied reconnaissance, which was plentiful. Ships were premium targets and often entire squadrons of bombers were placed on standby in anticipation of a sighting in clear weather.

From a strategic point of view the obvious target was the Japanese base at Rabaul, and MacArthur's air force was increasingly asked to attack it as a means of lending assistance to the South Pacific Area. This was done via the B-17 heavy bombers of the 19th and 43rd Bombardment

Groups, but Zero fighters enjoyed some success in shooting these down during August by employing frontal attacks. The Fifth Air Force would respond in the forthcoming period by almost exclusively raiding Rabaul under the cover of darkness.

Routine reconnaissance flights were made on a daily basis by long-ranging B-17s, often from the 435th BS at Townsville which regularly overflew Rabaul and other Japanese bases. These flights were supplemented by RAAF Hudsons flying sea search missions eastwards from Milne Bay.

B-25C 41-12906 Eager Eagle was one of the original 38th BG Mitchells which arrived in Australia in August and is seen at 14-Mile. The 38th BG flew its first combat mission on 15 September.

Two No. 6 Kokutai Model 32 Zeros patrol overhead a flotilla of IJN destroyers. Convoy protection became an increasingly important theme for Rabaul's fighter force in the final months of 1942.

CHAPTER 2

JAPANESE OVERVIEW

For the six months leading up to September 1942 the bulk of Japanese air operations in New Guinea had rested on the shoulders of two hard-worked units: No. 4 *Ku*, flying Betty bombers, and the famed Tainan *Ku* with Model 21 Zeros (as well as small numbers of C5M Babs reconnaissance aircraft). However, during August both units had suffered serious losses over Guadalcanal. As noted in *Volume 4* by the end of August an anonymous Japanese diarist at Buna had simply noted:

> The Tainan *Kokutai* has been annihilated.

In fact, the Tainan *Ku* received some reinforcements and continued operations, although it was qualitatively a shadow of the elite unit it had been in mid-1942. Although it still retained a core cadre of experienced pilots, numbers had been substantially reduced and those remaining were badly fatigued. Furthermore, most incoming replacements lacked experience.

The situation of No. 4 *Ku*, however, was vastly more serious. Up until late September it had seen seven months of combat from Rabaul during which it had lost two *hikotaicho* in succession, six *buntaicho*, exactly 40 aircraft and the equivalent of 30 crews (in excess of 200 personnel). On 25 September most of the unit's survivors flew back to Japan in six Bettys to regroup. A handful of crews remained at Rabaul where operations were limited to flying a few sector patrols in October.

In the lead-up to the Buna landing in July and the subsequent Milne Bay operations, a mixed Zero fighter and Val dive-bomber unit had arrived in Rabaul, No. 2 *Ku*. Then the American invasion of Guadalcanal in early August had seen an influx of reinforcements flown into Rabaul, including a fighter unit, No. 6 *Ku*, and elements of three Betty bomber units, the Kisarazu, Misawa and Chitose *Ku*. These were further reinforced in September by detachments from two units in the Netherlands East Indies: No. 3 *Ku* (Zeros) and the Takao *Ku* (Bettys); and one unit from Malaya: the Kanoya *Ku* (Bettys and Zeros).

On paper it would seem that the strength of Japanese airpower at Rabaul had been greatly expanded during August-September. However, this is a *non sequitur* as the losses over Guadalcanal were massive. Confirmed Betty losses exclusively in the Solomons during September 1942 were:

Chitose *Ku*	3
Kisarazu *Ku*	8
Misawa *Ku*	7
Takao *Ku*	6
Total	24

The loss of 24 Bettys within just one month compares to the loss of 31 Bettys to all causes in the South Pacific between 20 February and 7 August, as detailed in previous volumes of this series. Quite simply, the IJN was bleeding aircraft and crews at an unsustainable rate over the Solomons. Indeed, this loss total of 24 Bettys in one month represents 30% of the 79 operational Bettys available at the end of September. At that time there were 77 operational Zeros available (a table below gives a detailed breakdown of these numbers).

In the first months of the Pacific War the impressive range of the Betty had enabled it to strike Allied targets usually with the benefit of surprise. Flying at medium to high altitude and usually with a Zero escort, the Bettys were often able to release their bombload before the defenders had a chance to react.

However, the situation in the Solomons was very different. Rather than striking unprepared targets, the Bettys were attacking Henderson Field on Guadalcanal and ships in the same vicinity regularly during the same few hours of each day. Given the range from Rabaul, there was little opportunity to vary these predictable mission profiles, which greatly enabled the Americans to defend against these attacks. In addition, the Americans benefitted from coastwatchers on Bougainville which were often able to give a detailed warning of these incoming attacks.

The Betty's sluggish take-off performance, especially when fully loaded with bombs and fuel, meant operations were confined, at least at this stage, to Rabaul and more distant Kavieng. The use of these bases against targets such as Port Moresby and Guadalcanal limited the bombers to a standard load of just 12 x 60-kilogram bombs, which often rendered limited destructive effect. More powerful was the Betty's ship-killing potential when lugging torpedoes, but such weapons meant low-level attacks where the lightly built Bettys suffered from the growing potency of light and medium calibre shipborne anti-aircraft defences.

Given that the Betty's biggest Achilles' heel was lack of armour and self-sealing fuel tanks, such anti-aircraft defences were understandably much feared by the "land attack" bomber crews, especially as they had no parachutes. On the plus side, Mitsubishi's big twin ditched cleanly, stayed afloat, and carried a large inflatable dinghy for the crew. This saved several fortunate Betty crews rescued after surviving long durations in South Pacific seas. Ironically this also resulted in a boon to the Allies when many Betty crew members were captured in August and September 1942, gifting the Allies a trove of intelligence which meant they were well-versed on the bomber's performance and shortcomings.

To combat the high attrition of their Betty force the Japanese increased their use of night attacks. However, these missions more often ran into bad weather, especially over the Owen Stanleys, and the reduced bombing accuracy meant the results were usually little more than of nuisance value.

The main Betty base was Vunakanau. Positioned on a plateau near Rabaul, Japanese aircrews often called it affectionately by its unofficial name "*Yamano hikojo*" translating as the mountain airfield. Off-duty ground crew tended nearby gardens where fertile soil proffered fresh produce in abundance. As "bomber central" Vunakanau was still an expanding base, and by September it had yet to receive a concrete runway. Its dirt runway was well-drained, however, and the

A Betty is guided into a revetment at Vunakanau after a mission. The type was the workhorse of IJN offensive operations in the South Pacific, but after the start of the Guadalcanal campaign Betty attrition became a serious problem.

A Mavis flying boat crew disembark into a launch in Rabaul harbour after a flight. Note they are man-handling a 7.7mm machine gun ashore for servicing. In early September a dozen Toko Ku Mavises had arrived in Rabaul.

airfield was rarely out of commission for more than 24 hours as a result. Its useable runway length was around 1,300 metres and it had fifteen earthen revetments, which afforded excellent protection from air raids. More were under construction.

Each Betty *kokutai* was losing two to three Bettys per month due to accidents, mainly bad landings or tyre blowouts. The Japanese model for repair and maintenance of airframes was different to that of the Allies which operated dedicated repair units. Instead, each *kokutai* had its own internal engineering units, usually one repair *buntai* per two *buntai* of Bettys. Each repair *buntai*, comprising around 250 technicians, had a dedicated heavy repair section made up of sub-sections for engines, metal work, instruments and miscellaneous systems.

Although Vunakanau had no hangars, major repairs were conducted in the southern area of the field where large Casuarina trees offered good shade. Spare parts were plentiful and so was fuel. Larger parts were often cannibalised from other aircraft as required. Thus, in some cases three decommissioned bombers could be rendered into a single airworthy airframe. Mitsubishi issued a suite of specialist took kits which accompanied each aircraft to the field. Similar to their Allied counterparts, technicians were often assigned to specific aircraft in which they took considerable pride. Furthermore, these engineer-specific crew often flew as tail gunners in their dedicated Bettys, providing further incentive to ensure airworthiness.

The Guadalcanal campaign had cost many experienced fighter pilots, and an inventive way was briefly explored to bolster the ranks. Several incoming bomber pilots were hand-picked as fighter material and given opportunity to show their potential. Few made the cut. Once such example was FPO1c Nishimura Toshio who arrived at Rabaul in late September as a replacement Betty pilot. He was given ten hours flying time in Zeros, complaining he had never flown one before, before being reassigned back to bombers.

When it came to replacement aircraft, the Japanese had a considerable advantage over the Allies. Whereas US aircraft had to be delivered from North America, halfway across the world, a Betty could be flown from the Japanese factory to Rabaul in just two days. The preferred route was to fly from Kisarazu or Yokosuka to Saipan for an overnight stop. They would then fly to Rabaul the following day. Both sectors were about the same distance of around 1,250 miles, a flying time of about seven and a half hours. Betty deliveries were flown in groups as small as two aircraft, up to full *chutai* size but never singly. Very few aircraft were lost on these delivery flights, as the standard of oceanic navigation was very good.

From Lakunai, the Tainan *Ku* operated a "Land Reconnaissance" unit, made up of around 20 pilots and observers, and led by the detachment operations officer Lieutenant Hayashi Hideo. The detachment operated six C5M2 Babs single-engine reconnaissance aircraft. Shortly after arriving in New Guinea, the Tainan *Ku* had agreed to trial the new Nakajima J1N1-C twin in the reconnaissance role. Designed as a long-range escort fighter, the first three to become operational were initially deployed in early July 1942 (see *Volume 4*). After one was lost to Airacobras on 2 August the two remaining twins continued to be widely deployed. However, a second was lost to Wildcats over Guadalcanal on 14 September and the sole surviving J1N1-C would eventually return to Japan before the end of the year (although not before flying a sole bombing mission in the Solomons on 3 December).

Following the American invasion of Guadalcanal in early August, the Japanese lost the airfield they had been building upon which so much of their regional strategy depended. All of a sudden, they were fighting an air campaign at extreme range, given the 600-mile distance between Rabaul and Guadalcanal. Under such conditions a good portion of their airpower couldn't even contribute to the fight, namely the shorter-legged Model 32 Zeros as operated by the likes of Nos. 2 and 6 *Ku*. The land-based Val dive-bombers of No. 2 *Ku* faced the same problem, even when their armament was reduced from a single 250-kilogram bomb to two underwing 60-kilogram bombs.

The answer was to get airfields on Bougainville operational. In January, the Japanese had captured the small airstrip at Buka on the northern tip of this island which had been occasionally used by RAAF aircraft. In recent weeks Allied reconnaissance and a nearby coastwatcher, Jack Read, had noted increased construction activity at this location as hundreds of native labourers had been conscripted for the task. The first Zeros arrived at Buka in late September.

As noted in *Volume 4* of this series, in July the Japanese had commenced and then abandoned work on an airfield at Kieta due to poor drainage. More promising was a location at Buin on the southern tip of Bougainville. This location was roughly midway between Rabaul and Guadalcanal. In addition, it was adjacent to the Shortlands which was being used as an anchorage and also for floatplane and flying boat operations.

Airfield construction at Buin commenced in late August, and Rabaul instructed that it should be ready to handle a full *chutai* of nine dive-bombers by 20 September 1942. However, this deadline proved overly optimistic in the face of heavy rains and Allied bombing attacks, and the first aircraft would not arrive until October.

All South Seas locations were allocated a three-letter code beginning with the letter "R", for which Buin was "RXP". Whilst the Japanese continued to refer to the airfield in *katakana* as "Buin", the Americans referred to it as "Kahili" or "Kahilli", in a reference to the nearest village pronounced "Kilee" by its inhabitants. The location was a strategic cross-roads with both the Fifth and the 13th Air Force regularly ranging over the area.

The IJN air commanders at Rabaul had made extensive use of floatplanes and flying boats since the very start of the South Pacific campaign. Indeed, the Yokohama *Ku* had been a lynchpin of these operations ever since December 1941. Alongside its far-ranging Kawanishi H6K4 Mavis flying boats, the unit had added a fighter wing, flying Nakajima A6M2-N Rufes. However, the Rufes and several Mavises were destroyed at their moorings during early morning air strikes on Tulagi on 7 August. In subsequent days, many Yokohama *Ku* personnel perished on the ground fighting US Marines. Only a small portion of the Yokohama *Ku* remained at Rabaul operating a handful of surviving Mavises.

As an interim measure a detachment of Toko *Ku* Mavises was sent to Rabaul from Palau in the Central Pacific. The first batch of six Mavises arrived in Rabaul harbour on 28 August after a delivery flight of around eight hours. The flying boats had been loaded with extra engineers and equipment. Some of them carried a total of 13 crew instead of the usual patrol compliment of between nine to ten men.

In total around a dozen Toko *Ku* Mavises had arrived at Rabaul by the end of the first week of September, although unusually one had vanished on the flight from Palau. By 2 September the first of these had forward deployed to the Shortlands where they began crucial surveillance flights of search sectors P, Q and R (see map on page 36), with flight times often reaching 11 hours or more.

The sector searches took the Mavises directly overhead or abeam of Guadalcanal where they often crossed paths with American aircraft. These included 13th Air Force Flying Fortresses,

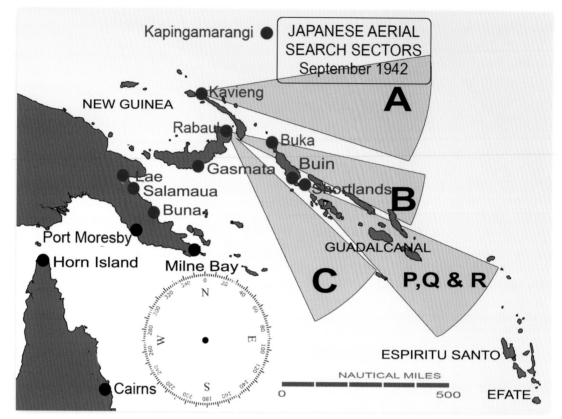

Japanese search sectors in the South Pacific in September 1942, usually flown by Betty bombers or Mavis flying boats. Several Mavises were lost due to aerial clashes with 13th Air Force Fortresses while flying the P, Q and R sector over the Solomons.

some of which were based at Espiritu Santo and were on their own way to Bougainville. These clashes between unlikely enemies proved costly for the Toko *Ku*, resulting in heavy losses. The first Mavis loss was on 5 September when one was shot down by a Fortress. By 21 September four more had been lost in these encounters, meaning that the Toko *Ku* detachment had lost half of its strength during just three weeks of operations in the South Seas.

The Yokohama *Ku* also lost two flying boats to aerial clashes with Fortresses on 31 August and 1 September. Accordingly, the tired and washed-out aircrews of the Yokohama *Ku* were ordered back to Japan on 23 September, with the unit's handful of remaining Mavises transferred to the Toko *Ku*. In view of the recent flying boat losses, it was decided to call forward three additional No. 14 *Ku* Mavises, which would fly down via Truk in early October. Alongside their surveillance role the Mavises also flew regular transport missions and occasionally were called on for search and rescue of downed aircrews.

The maze of Japanese command and administrative structures is exemplified by the circumstances of the floatplanes of the "R Area Air Force". On 14 July the 11th Seaplane Tender Division was created, consisting of the seaplane tenders *Chitose and Kamikawa Maru*, under the overall command of the Second Fleet. The tail code format used by the floatplanes of these ships was determined at fleet level, and the Second Fleet used red codes.

On 28 August these floatplanes with their red tail code surrounded by white piping became known as the R Area Air Force. This unit was commanded by Rear Admiral Jojima Takatsugu and was shore-based in the Shortland Islands. The *Kamikawa Maru* contingent was first to arrive at the beginning of September where it offloaded eleven Rufes and two Petes to take part to the Guadalcanal air battle. *Chitose*'s floatplanes arrived the following month and both units focused on the Solomons theatre.

From the Allied viewpoint the South Pacific campaign at this juncture was neatly divided between two theatres and two commands, New Guinea (SWPA) and the Solomons (SoPAC). However, the Japanese made no such distinction. For them, from the vantage of Rabaul or Tokyo, it was all the same "South Seas" theatre.

It was Vice Admiral Mikawa Gun'ichi's Eighth Fleet command based at Rabaul which was forced to respond to the competing demands of the situations in both Papua and Guadalcanal. It was the latter theatre, with its rapidly increasing amount of airpower based at Henderson Field, that was the cause for most concern. In New Guinea significant worries were caused by "long-range bombers" (Flying Fortresses) regularly finding and attacking IJN vessels; and the "furious bombings" of the wider Buna area which threatened the supply of the IJA force in Papua.

Accordingly, the "Base Force", meaning Rabaul air power, reprioritised its aerial commitments in mid-September as follows:

- Annihilation of enemy air power on Guadalcanal
- Regular patrols of waters southeast of Guadalcanal and New Guinea
- Air cover for shipping throughout all areas

These priorities *de facto* moved the focus towards the Solomons theatre and meant that Allied airpower in the New Guinea would be less challenged than in recent months.

Meanwhile, Tokyo continued to authorise more reinforcements to the theatre. The increase in both size and diversity of inventory

IJN 12cm heavy anti-aircraft guns overlooking Rabaul harbour. By late 1942 Rabaul and its airfields were well defended by anti-aircraft guns and searchlights.

had the potential to complicate the command structure at Rabaul. In mid-September 1942 Vice Admiral Tsukahara Nishizo was commanding the 11th Air Fleet which had three separate "attack force" operational headquarters based at Rabaul. Keen to avoid confusion, Tsukahara decided to clarify the chains of command. Accordingly, he rearranged his aerial units into two strike forces, the 5th and 6th Attack Forces, sub-structured into "Forces", which divided operational commands between fighter and bomber forces as outlined in the table below.

Fifth Attack Force

Force	Commander	Units	Main Base
1st Force	*Hikocho* Tainan *Ku*, Captain Saito Masahita	Tainan *Ku*, No. 3 *Ku*, Kanoya *Ku* fighter wing	Lakunai
2nd Force	*Hikocho* No. 4 *Ku* Captain Moritama Yoshimitsu	No. 4 *Ku* (ordered to depart on 23 September)	Vunakanau
3rd Force	*Hikocho* No. 2 *Ku* Commander Yamamoto Sakae	No. 2 *Ku*	Lakunai
4th Force	*Hikocho* Toko *Ku* Commander Ito Sukemitsu	Toko *Ku* (reassigned inventory from the Yokohama *Ku*)	Malaguna (Rabaul) Shortlands
6th Force	*Hikocho* No. 6 *Ku* Commander Morita Chisato	No. 6 *Ku*	Lakunai
1st Special Duty Detachment	Captain of seaplane tender *Akitsushima*	Seaplane tender *Akitsushima*	Assigned to 11th Air Fleet
2nd Special Duty Detachment	Captain of *Mogamigawa Maru*	*Mogamigawa Maru*	Assigned to 11th Air Fleet

Sixth Attack Force

Force	Commander	Units	Main Base
Ko (甲) Force	*Hikocho* Kisarazu *Ku*, Captain Konishi Yasuo	Kisarazu *Ku*	Vunakanau (redeployed from Kavieng)
Otsu (乙) Force	*Hikocho* Misawa *Ku*, Captain Sugawara Masao	Misawa *Ku*	Vunakanau
Hei (丙) Force	*Hikocho* Takao *Ku*	Takao *Ku*	Vunakanau

In similar comparison to Kenney's worn-out 19th BG, the Bettys and crews from the tired and depleted remnants of No. 4 *Ku* were ordered back to Japan on 23 September. They would return home in stages, as would also the return to Taroa of the *chutai* of Chitose *Ku* Bettys which had forward deployed to Rabaul at the end of August 1942. Ten Chitose *Ku* Zeros which had arrived at Rabaul on 2 September would remain *in situ*, however, and were reassigned to the Tainan *Ku* along with their pilots.

The gap left by the departing No. 4 *Ku* Bettys would be filled by the Takao *Ku*, diverted from its Kendari base in the Netherlands East Indies, in parallel to the incoming No. 3 *Ku* fighter detachment from the same area. Formed in April 1938, the Takao *Ku* had first served in the China theatre. By late 1942 it was an experienced and substantive unit, boasting six *chutai* of Bettys. The first Takao *Ku* echelon of Bettys arrived at Vunakanau on 22 September, from where they flew their first mission in the South Seas two days later; these were five separate sector searches which would also serve as area familiarisation flights. Soon Takao *Ku* Bettys would start appearing regularly over both New Guinea and Guadalcanal.

Note that the Bettys of the Kanoya *Ku* were omitted from the structure above. This was because it was a "borrowed" unit and on 1 October its fighter and bomber wings would be separated, with the bomber wing redesignated as No. 751 *Ku*. The bombers would move to Kavieng where they would fall under a separate command structure as will be described in subsequent chapters. Also omitted were the floatplanes of the R Area Air Force which retained their autonomous command.

Two ships are noted as part of the Fifth Attack Force. One of these was the modern seaplane tender *Akitsushima* which had been in the South Seas since mid-year and had regularly circulated between Rabaul, Buka and the Shortlands. It primarily serviced Mavis flying boats, but also undertook search and rescue missions and supply runs. Equipped with a useful anti-aircraft armament of four 5-inch dual purpose guns and ten 25mm medium calibre guns, it had sustained "trifling damage" from an air raid while at Buka on 1 September, likely incurred from the RAAF Catalina night attack on that date. During the next three months the *Akitsushima* sustained 11 more air attacks but without further damage.

The second vessel allocated to the Fifth Attack Force was the aircraft transport *Mogamigawa Maru* which was used to deliver Zeros and other aviation supplies to the theatre from Japan.

A tally of relevant unit operational records indicates Rabaul-based aircraft offensive strength at the end of September 1942:

Bomber Units	Serviceable Aircraft / inventory	Available aircrew
Kisarazu *Ku*	15 G4M1 / 21	23 crews
Misawa *Ku*	12 G4M1 / 15	23 crews
Takao *Ku*	19 G4M1 / 20	20 crews
Kanoya *Ku*	16 G4M1 / 23	18 crews
TOTAL	**62 / 79**	**84 crews**

Fighter Units	Serviceable Zeros	Available pilots
Tainan *Ku*	Model 21 x 8	39
No. 6 *Ku*	Model 21 x 12	15
	Model 32 x 13	15
No. 3 *Ku*	Model 21 x 20	27
No. 2 *Ku*	Model 32 x 16	14
Kanoya *Ku*	Model 21 x 8	9
TOTAL	**77 Zeros**	**119 pilots**

This modest inventory of 139 serviceable aircraft (excluding about a dozen flying boats and the floatplanes of R Area Force), was expected to handle both New Guinea and the Solomons. The bottom line for the Japanese commanders at Rabaul was that it could attain neither sufficient aircraft replacements nor reinforcements, a problem shared to some extent with their Allied counterparts. The declining quality of aircrew morale and experience was also worrying.

No surprisingly, as will be seen, IJN air activity in New Guinea in September was considerably reduced from previous months as the main focus of higher command was the recovery of Guadalcanal. However, two big developments lay just around the corner. The first was a substantive IJN restructure of air units destined for the start of November. The second was the imminent arrival of the Japanese Army Air Force (JAAF) in New Guinea, initially in the form of a single reconnaissance unit. However, this modest beginning presaged a flood of JAAF units which would soon be rushed to the theatre.

The Achilles Heel for MacArthur in the SWPA was a lack of naval power. His sole surface unit capable of offensive action was Task Force 44, which comprised Australian and American cruisers and destroyers. TF44 had been temporarily transferred to the SoPAC command at the start of the Guadalcanal campaign. Due to losses in that theatre, including of the heavy cruiser HMAS *Canberra*, when TF44 was returned to the SWPA in early September it was somewhat weaker than when it departed, consisting only of the heavy cruiser HMAS *Australia*, the light cruisers USS *Phoenix* and HMAS *Hobart*, and several USN destroyers. Virtually all of MacArthur's other warships, mainly destroyers and corvettes, were wholly employed escorting convoys. This included regular runs from Townsville to Port Moresby and Milne Bay.

Up until 6 September IJN ships, including cruisers and destroyers, had been entering Milne Bay almost with impunity. However, the return of TF44 to the SWPA enabled a counter to be put on any future such movements. On 7 September TF44 departed Brisbane, and three days later began patrolling the Coral Sea to the south of Port Moresby, from where it could respond to any enemy naval movements approaching Milne Bay. The force largely remained in this position for the rest of the year. The Louisiades, a lengthy string of reef-strewn islands off the eastern tip of Papua, formed a natural boundary for naval operations. IJN warships operated freely to the north of them while TF44 patrolled to the south.

Japanese naval operations in the New Guinea area were the responsibility of Vice Admiral Mikawa Gun'ichi's Eighth Fleet based at Rabaul. This was a fleet well-balanced for New Guinea operations that included cruisers, destroyers, transports and smaller craft. It had proven capable of landing the forces at Buna and Milne Bay, and subsequently reinforcing and resupplying the IJA force in Papua via the Buna beachhead.

In addition to the Eighth Fleet, a great bulk of the IJN's best combat ships were currently operating in the Truk-Rabaul area with a focus on the Solomons. This included aircraft carriers, battleships and heavy cruisers that theoretically could have been diverted for operations in New Guinea at short notice. For this reason, a developing theme in New Guinea became localised Japanese naval superiority versus Allied air strength.

The waters between north Queensland and Papua were shallow and generally unsuitable for submarine operations. However, the Eighth Fleet had deployed two small coastal submarines

Engineers attend the engine on a E8N2 Dave floatplane on the shoreline of Malaguna Bay near Rabaul. A Pete is seen in the background. By September most of the floatplanes in the theatre were concentrated with the R Area Force in the Shortlands.

to this area, the *RO-33* and *RO-34*. The former vessel had been sunk off Port Moresby by an Australian destroyer on 29 August. The *RO-34* did return briefly to Papuan waters in late September but was mostly employed in the Solomons.

Since April eleven USN S-class submarines had been operating from Brisbane. Designated as Task Force 42.1, these were short range boats dating from the 1920s, but which rendered useful service in the waters around New Guinea, sinking several Japanese vessels. Illustrating the dangers of operating near the Louisiades, on the night of 13-14 August the *S-39* had grounded on rocks off Rossel Island. Over the next two days heavy seas pounded the submarine and it took on a 60-degree list. The crew abandoned the boat and was rescued by the corvette HMAS *Katoomba* on 16 August. The wreck of the *S-39* remained on the rocks where it continued to break up.

After the US landing at Guadalcanal many of TF42.1's submarines were redirected to the Solomons, but in September a few spent some time in New Guinea waters waiting to intercept any further Japanese ships that approached Milne Bay. However, these elderly S-class submarines were becoming increasingly difficult to maintain, and by November all had been directed back to the US for refits. They were replaced by more modern long-range submarines, the operations of which fall outside the scope of this volume.

On 12 September No. 76 Squadron Kittyhawks prepare to strafe suspected hiding locations of the Japanese marines marooned on Goodenough Island.

CHAPTER 3

CRISIS IN PAPUA I: 9 – 16 SEPTEMBER 1942

As noted in Chapter 1, the first week of September brought bad news for the Allies on the Kokoda front. The hard-pressed Australian 30th Brigade had been forced into a series of fighting withdrawals which had brought the IJA troops onto the southern slopes of the Owen Stanleys. The dry lake bed at Myola, where large quantities of rations and supplies had been air-dropped, had been abandoned and captured by the Japanese. Reinforced by the newly arrived 21st Brigade, the Australians had made another stand at Efogi, a short distance south of Myola, during 6-9 September.

While the Japanese had around 4,000 troops between Kokoda and Efogi, the nature of fighting on a narrow and jungle-clad mountain trail meant that only around 1,500 IJA troops were on the frontline, mainly from the 144th Infantry Regiment. Facing them were a similar number of Australian troops. An advantage the Japanese possessed was the availability of a small but crucial number of artillery pieces which had been painstakingly disassembled and hauled across the mountains.

While the Australians lacked artillery, they did have the availability of air support from nearby Port Moresby. Between 1 and 8 September, P-39s flew 109 ground attack sorties over the area, including against Kokoda, Myola and Efogi. The P-39s (recorded mostly as "P-400s" in Allied records) strafed with 20mm cannons and machine guns, and on most occasions also dropped a single 100- or 300-pound bomb. Illustrating the difficulty of these missions, the War Diary of the 21st Brigade reported nine "P-400s" bombing and strafing Efogi at 1100 on 7 September. However, the last "stick" of bombs was dropped over Menari, which was the next village south of Efogi and well behind the Australian lines. Fortunately, there were no casualties.

It will be recalled that a squadron of A-20As was being hastily equipped with 0.50-inch calibre machine guns and bomb racks to tote small 20-pound fragmentation bombs (called "parafrags" when equipped with parachutes). The first of these specialised low-level attackers arrived at Port Moresby in late August and flew their first mission against Lae on the last day of that month. They comprised three flights, each of six machines, drawn from the 8th and 89th Bombardment Squadrons.

Between 2 and 9 September, the A-20s flew 43 sorties against targets along the Kokoda Track.[I] A typical raid occurred at Efogi at 0815 on 7 September. Each of eight bombers dropped 8 x 100-pound bombs, and in total some 6,000 0.50-inch and 1,200 0.30-inch machine gun rounds were expended. The War Diary of the 21st Brigade recorded:

> 8 A-20s dive-bombed and strafed Efogi. Excellent job.

This was a successful attack, and Japanese records show 11 men were killed and another 20

I   In addition, seven sorties were flown against the Salamaua area on 3 September, when three 13th BS B-25s also struck nearby Mubo.

were wounded. However, such successes were the exception rather than the norm due to the difficulty of identifying targets under the jungle canopy.

During the fighting at Efogi the Australians lost 87 killed, as against 56 Japanese killed from the 144th Infantry Regiment. The battle was a disaster for the Australians, who were forced to make a disorderly withdrawal after a successful Japanese flanking manoeuvre. As a result of this retreat the brigadier commanding the Australian force was relieved of his command.

A worse development for the Australians was that the relatively fresh 2/27th Battalion had been separated from the remainder of the 21st Brigade due to the arduous terrain. It would not re-join the main force for another two weeks. However, the Japanese did not pursue the retreating Australians closely, giving them a few days to regroup in a defensive position at Ioribaiwa.

Meanwhile the Fifth Air Force was also hitting Buna airfield during this period. On 5 September, a maximum strength effort was made by the newly arrived A-20As when 17 of the bombers attacked the airfield – it would be the largest formation of A-20As to assemble for an offensive mission for some time. The bombers dropped 47 x 100-pound and 185 x 20-pound bombs, with crews recording fires starting near the runway and two enemy aircraft destroyed. The bombers were escorted by seven P-39s which expended 4,000 rounds of machine gun ammunition and reported silencing an anti-aircraft position.

A trio of 89th BS A-20As head out on another combat mission after departing Kila 'drome. In early September the squadron was often attacking targets on the Kokoda Track and at Buna.

As detailed in *Volume 4*, construction of an airfield at Buna had commenced with much urgency in late July. On completion of the first grassy runway, along with a modest suite of square earth revetments, the Japanese commenced levelling a second runway which was never used. Despite the location suffering from drainage problems after heavy rains, nine No. 2 *Ku* Model 32 Zeros had arrived at Buna on 22 August. These were joined briefly by some D3A1 Val dive-bombers from the same unit before the location was largely abandoned on 28 August in the face of heavy Allied air attacks.

On the afternoon of 8 September, the last flyable Zeros left Buna for good. These were No. 2 *Ku*'s last airworthy Model 32s, which withdrew to Lae. The abandoned and wrecked aircraft left behind on the edge of the field were repeatedly strafed and bombed by the Allies, in the mistaken belief they were active aircraft.

By this time some 18 A-20As had arrived in New Guinea, mostly allocated to the 8th BS. However, as noted in *Volume 4*, this squadron was recalled to Australia due to perceived morale problems following the disastrous loss of five A-24 dive-bombers over Buna on 29 July. Instead, the 8th BS crews handed over their machines to the 89th BS, although a number of 8th BS crews remained flying with the 89th BS for some weeks.

The 10 September was quiet, with no Allied attack missions flown. The following day six 89th BS A-20As struck Buna in a mission recalled by crew chief Sergeant Hugh Ellerbee as the squadron's first.[II] Ellerbee described the mission:

> We established our camp area on a hill overlooking Kila Kila runway. From here we flew our first strike at the Japs. This mission was one we didn't like to talk about. Somebody had goofed up on the distance there and back. We lost some planes by running out of gasoline ditching in the water. The others barely got to the landing strip. One had to be towed from the end of the runway back to its revetment. The pilots were out of gasoline and with all the excitement of the first mission, got back to Kila about dark. Naturally all of the personnel had gathered to welcome them back. One pilot hadn't safetied his guns. On his approach to the strip he accidentally hit the trigger and a 50 cal in the nose shot a burst causing quite a stampede of personnel …

The morning also saw half a dozen 408th BS B-26s drop 72 x 300-pound bombs over Buna airfield. They were followed in the late afternoon by the 89th BS, when 15 A-20As were flown mainly as strafers, dropping 25 x 100-pound bombs and expending 6,000 x 50-inch and 1,200 x 0.30-inch calibre machine gun rounds. One the way back Lieutenant Charles Brown flying *Little Ruby* experienced engine trouble and to avoid flying back over the mountains he diverted to Milne Bay. However, he didn't make it and he and his gunner were forced to bale out 60 miles short of their destination. Both were hospitalised.

The remainder of the force did indeed experience fuel shortages on their return flight as described by Ellerbee. Lieutenant Turner Messick flying *The Comet* was forced to ditch not far from Port Moresby. Messick and his gunner were rescued.

II   The 89th BS had already flown missions including a 5 September strike against Buna. The 11 September mission may have been the first for certain crews.

Also on 11 September a lone A-20A flew an armed reconnaissance over the Myola-Efogi section of the Kokoda Track, dropping 8 x 100-pound bombs and expending 5,000 rounds of machine gun ammunition. Such missions were repeated by the 89th BS on 14, 15 and 16 September.

The sizeable raid against Buna airfield on 11 September was repeated early the following day, this time by a force of five 408th BS B-26s and nine 89th BS A-20As accompanied by eleven 41st FS P-39s. Through light rain and poor visibility, Captain Don Hall led the A-20As from *Cactus Don* as they strafed from just 70 feet and loosed 320 x parafrags. The B-26s, meanwhile, dropped 58 x 300-pound bombs from 5,000 feet. The pilots reported large fires having been started and some 17 aircraft destroyed on the ground. However, these were mostly existing Model 32 Zero wrecks of the Tainan and No. 2 *Ku* as described above, as the location was no longer in routine use by Japanese aircraft even though anti-aircraft guns still defended the area.

The ordeal was not over for Buna airfield as seven 28th BS B-17Es also attacked on 12 September. Through rain squalls the pilots descended to below 3,000 feet to drop 84 x 300-pound bombs and to strafe the area, firing 5,000 rounds of 0.50-inch calibre ammunition. However, this low-level approach made the large bombers easy targets for medium-calibre anti-aircraft guns. Two bombers were made unserviceable after receiving hits, while Captain Crawford described seeing hits on a third aircraft after it made its bomb run, B-17E 41-2663, flown by Lieutenant Gilbert Erb:

> The huge machine was hit on the nose by a shell, right before my eyes. I saw the flames spurt out, the Fortress reel like a drunken man and then plunge down on a crazy path towards the water. Just as the plane was about to strike the water, it levelled out and made a neat water landing.

The bomber ditched about twenty miles southeast of Buna only some 50 yards offshore. The water impact broke off the tail section, then about a minute after the ditching a large explosion sent a water spout a good hundred feet in the air. In fact, four men had already parachuted from the stricken bomber before Erb regained a semblance of control and was able to ditch. Of the five still inside the fuselage, three drowned but Erb and his injured bombardier got out and made it safely ashore. After meeting up with two of the parachutists, Erb was able to lead the party of four to safety at Milne Bay weeks later, although by then exhausted and in poor condition. The two other parachutists were captured and killed by the Japanese.

Meanwhile, further south the first 22nd BG B-26s had begun using their new base at Iron Range on Cape York in Far North Queensland. This was less than two hours flying time from Port Moresby. Seven 19th BS Marauders were led by Lieutenant Walter Krell from Iron Range to Port Moresby on the afternoon of 12 September in preparation for a raid on Lae the next day. Krell was ordered to use the relatively new field at 14-Mile (Laloki) which had just been laid overall with steel Marsden matting to take the heavy bombers. However the crews were frustrated to find no arrangements for messing or accommodation had been made leaving them to scrounge beds and food from ground personnel.

The next morning Krell led his seven B-26s while another formation of seven B-26s (from the 2nd and 408th BS) departed from Seven-Mile. The latter formation reached the target first and dropped 70 x 300-pound bombs over Lae airfield from 7,700 feet. Krell's bombers followed

Buna was last used by Japanese aircraft on 8 September, after which various abandoned aircraft were regularly attacked during Allied raids in the mistaken belief that they were operational. This Tainan Ku Model 32 Zero, V-187, was one such abandoned aircraft. It was captured by the Allies at Buna on 27 December 1942.

fourteen minutes later, and 129 x 100-pound bombs were dropped over the runway and dispersal area. Another two-dozen bombs failed to release and were jettisoned over Salamaua. Japanese anti-aircraft fire was active and two aircraft were hit by single bullets, while the American pilots reported leaving two bombers burning on the ground.

After refuelling at Port Moresby, it was towards evening by the time Krell led his formation back to Iron Range. He was still unfamiliar with the newly created strip and landed *Kansas Comet* (40-1433) short of the runway in a zone where the trees had been cleared but other obstructions remained such as tree stumps and ant hills. Landing at high speed, the Marauder struck one such obstruction and burst a tyre. After careening down one side of the runway out of control the bomber struck a truck parked nearby. The fuselage was torn open and fuel from ruptured tanks was set alight. Krell and four crewmen survived, although with bad bruising, cuts and burns. Sadly, Krell's Australian co-pilot, Pilot Officer Graham Robertson, was killed as was the truck driver.

Volume 4 of this series describes how one element of the Japanese Milne Bay attack force never arrived at its destination. This was 353 men of the 5th Sasebo SNLF which was being transported to a point north of Milne Bay via barges from Buna. However, following a stop on Goodenough Island, the barges had been thoroughly strafed and disabled by RAAF Kittyhawks on 25 August. With their only radio destroyed, the Japanese marines (known as the Tsukioka Unit, after their CO Commander Tsukioka Torashige) were effectively marooned. Only on 9 September did their plight become known when messengers reached Buna using a native canoe.

Goodenough Island is part of the D'Entrecasteux group of islands which are separated from the eastern tip of Papua by a narrow straight and which lie north of Milne Bay. Spanning a distance of around 100 miles, the three largest islands in the group are Goodenough, Fergusson and Normanby, all of which are mountainous. Indeed, the highest peak on Goodenough Island stands out an imposing 8,000 feet.

On 8 and 9 September a Tainan *Ku* C5M Babs from Rabaul had been searching this vicinity for suspected Allied airbases following the recent discovery of Milne Bay. On 10 September the Babs, crewed by pilot FPO2c Kudo Shigetoshi and radio operator Lieutenant (jg) Ki'izuka Shigenori, flew over the island and made contact with the waving stranded troops. Kudo dropped a package containing 50 packets of cigarettes and a message saying two destroyers would arrive the following day.

Later that day the destroyers *Yayoi* and *Isokaze* departed Rabaul to undertake the rescue. The *Yayoi* was one of the vessels that had bravely entered Milne Bay to evacuate troops just a week beforehand, so the mission to Goodenough Island would have appeared relatively easier.

The D'Entrecasteux Islands and the surrounding waters of the Solomon Sea were the subject of daily reconnaissance cover by the detachment of No. 6 Squadron Hudsons operating from Milne Bay. However, on 11 September it was a B-17E that first spotted the two destroyers near the Trobriand Islands, which was a small group located a short distance to the north of the D'Entrecasteux Islands.

That afternoon a force of five 28th BS B-17Es which had departed Port Moresby spotted the destroyers on the open sea in broad daylight. As the destroyers took evasive action, the Fortresses descended to low altitude to make their attacks. Captain Crawford, flying 41-2645 *Miss Carriage*, recalled:

> The Japs in both warships were blazing away with everything they had. It was like all hell was let loose. They knew they were caught with their pants down.

The *Yayoi* was essentially a WWI-type destroyer dating back to the mid-1920s, while the *Isokaze* was modern, having been launched in 1939. The *Isokaze* was well armed, with three twin 5-inch dual purpose guns. Probably for this reason the weight of attack fell on the older ship, although the *Isokaze* still reported minor damage from a near miss.

The destroyers were pattern-bombed by the Fortresses, flying at just 1,500 feet, with a total of 28 x 500-pound bombs. One of these, dropped by the B-17E flown by Lieutenant James Ellis, scored a direct hit on the stern of the *Yayoi*, leaving it dead in the water as its crew abandoned ship.

The Fortresses were flying so low their gunners strafed the enemy ships as the bombs were unloaded. *Miss Carriage* had just been hit by shrapnel when was it knocked upwards, throwing both pilots against the ceiling as the cockpit seemed surrounded by smoke and flames. As the pilots regained control, it was realised that bullets from the ball gunner had mistakenly exploded the last bomb dropped from the plane. Fortunately, the battered aircraft made it back to base.

Around 45 minutes later four No. 6 Squadron Hudsons arrived on the scene, with one pilot noting:

> Got a pleasant surprise to see five Fortresses below the cloud.

The Hudson pilots spotted the *Yayoi* down by the stern but stubbornly afloat. Diving from 4,000 to 1,500 feet, the Hudsons loosed 19 x 250-pound bombs, and likely scored several near misses. These contributed to leaks which led to uncontrollable flooding, and the outdated destroyer sank after the Allied aircraft had departed with the loss of 68 crewmen.

That evening the *Isokaze* returned to look for survivors but found only an oily residue on the surface. The main group of some 87 survivors, including *Yayoi*'s captain, were able to reach Normanby Island, which was around 20 miles away.

The sinking of the *Yayoi* was something of a landmark: it was the first IJN warship to be sunk in New Guinea waters by land-based aircraft.[III] It was also a feather in the cap for the soon to be departing 19th BG, which had made many unsuccessful attacks against Japanese warships in the theatre during the previous six months. The low altitude attack was the exact opposite of the bombing doctrine that the 19th BG had first employed: attacks from extreme altitude.

From coastwatchers and native sources the Allies were aware of the marooned Japanese forces on both Goodenough and Normanby Islands, and kept a close watch on the area. RAAF Kittyhawks from Milne Bay made strafing attacks on Goodenough on 12 and 13 September, and planning was underway to land Australian troops on the islands to conduct a mopping-up operation.

At this time Japanese air activity in Papua was limited to single flights by a Tainan *Ku* C5M Babs, which checked the northern Papuan coast on 12 and 14 September for signs of Allied forces. Nothing was seen, and these flights resulted from erroneous reports by the naval commander of Buna airbase that there had been an Allied landing nearby. The source of this information is discussed in Chapter 3. At this time the naval garrison at Buna airfield was made up of 400 troops from the 5th Yokosuka SNLF and the 5th Sasebo SNLF, together with the 14th and 15th Establishment Units which consisted mainly of labourers. Among the anti-aircraft weapons held by the garrison were two 8cm guns, one 25mm gun and three 13mm machine guns. It should be noted that similar units from the airbase at Lae[IV] were being transferred to the Solomons, reducing the capacity for air operations at that location.

Meanwhile the *Isokaze* had abandoned its rescue mission and returned to Rabaul. In subsequent days Allied air reconnaissance was keenly watching for further IJN movements in the area. The Hudsons from Milne Bay encountered very poor weather on 12 and 13 September, as noted by pilot Sergeant John Clark:

> Visibility was bad and we flew through rain most of the time. It is more the rule than the exception for rain and low clouds to be around this area.

Further north a B-17 on one of the routine reconnaissance flights had better luck, locating and strafing a "sub-chaser or minelayer" 50 miles south of Kavieng on 12 September. In response nine 30th BS B-17s flew up to Port Moresby from Mareeba. The following day three of the

---

III   The light carrier *Shoho* had been sunk be carrier-based aircraft in May, while some warships had been sunk by submarines, most notably the heavy cruiser *Kako* in August.

IV   Since August Japanese air operations at Lae had been much reduced due to the withdrawal of all Tainan *Ku* fighters due to the Guadalcanal operations. No. 2 *Ku* and occasionally Nos. 3 and 6 *Ku* Zeros still used the base, however.

bombers experienced mechanical failures leaving six to search for the ship. This formation found what they reported as "a cruiser towing a destroyer" south of New Britain, and the cruiser was targeted with 48 x 500-bombs.

The ships were in fact the light cruiser *Tenryu* and the destroyer *Hamakaze* which had left Rabaul the previous day to search for *Yayoi* survivors. Finding nothing and realising that a rescue of any survivors from the D'Entrecasteux Islands would need friendly air cover, the captain of the cruiser was returning to Rabaul when the B-17Es attacked. None of the bombs hit and no damage was incurred.

On the same day as this attack another search plane located a Japanese convoy south of Rabaul, almost certainly one connected to the reinforcement and resupply of Guadalcanal. Accordingly at 0330 on 14 September seven 63rd BS B-17Fs took off from Mareeba. It was the first independent mission for the fledgling 43rd BG, but it got off to a disastrous start.

The B-17F flown by Captain Herschell Henson, 41-24391 *Hoomalimali*, suffered an engine failure soon after take-off. The plane dived into a small valley, and fully loaded with bombs and fuel it was destroyed in a terrific explosion. The shockwave damaged homes in the Mareeba township some three and a half miles away. The next morning the badly dismembered bodies of the ten crew were recovered over a wide area strewn with wreckage. Meanwhile the other six Fortresses searched the approaches to Milne Bay for the Japanese convoy but hampered by bad weather nothing was seen and they returned to Mareeba.

Meanwhile the USN was running its own critical resupply convoys to Guadalcanal, and a request was sent to General MacArthur to bomb Rabaul on 15 and 16 September. This task was a throwback to the maximum strength B-17 raid that had been made on Rabaul on 7 August to coincide with the American invasion of Guadalcanal. While 16 Fortresses had been assembled for that raid, less than half of that number could now be marshalled for each of a string of missions that would unfold over the two days.

On the morning of 15 September five 28th BS B-17Es departed Port Moresby. Underlying the importance of the mission the lead bomber was co-piloted by Brigadier General Kenneth Walker of Fifth Bomber Command, albeit flying primarily as an observer. Only four of the bombers made it to the target area around midday and dropped 16 x 500-pound bombs over the harbour. However, nothing was observed due to cloud. There was an attempted interception by six No. 6 *Ku* Zeros flying a CAP, while another 14 Zeros from both the Tainan and No. 6 *Ku* were scrambled. The Zeros and two Fortresses exchanged fire but due to the cloud the bombers escaped without damage.

Later that afternoon at 1730 four 30th BS B-17E/Fs departed Seven-Mile for a night raid over Vunakanau. At 2200 and taking advantage of no moon the bombers approached the target at just 6,500 feet, releasing 20 x 500-pound bombs over the northern end of the runway. Despite the dark conditions the low flying Fortresses exposed themselves to accurate anti-aircraft fire.

Lieutenant Ray Holsey's *Frank Buck* 41-2659 was hit and two engines were knocked out, with another giving trouble. When still 65 miles short of Port Moresby and running low on fuel

The 49th FG began moving to New Guinea from the Darwin area in September, with the 7th FS arriving first. This 49th FG P-40E is seen at Rorona (30-Mile) outside of Port Moresby.

Holsey was able to make a safe emergency landing on a beach near Hood Point. Remarkably, this plane was flown out two weeks later after mechanics had repaired the engines and a 3,000-foot runway of steel matting was laid out by hundreds of native labourers.

Not so fortunate was Captain Robert Williams and his crew in B-17F 41-24427. They never returned from the mission and remain MIA. No trace of the bomber has ever been found.

The 16 September saw two further B-17 Rabaul raids attempted. During the first, five 28th BS B-17s found the target area covered by cloud. Four returned to base with their bombs while the fifth aircraft bombed and strafed Gasmata, an alternate target. That evening six 30th BS B-17s dropped 36 x 500-pound bombs on Vunakanau and on a ship alongside a wharf in the harbour. Explosions and fires were observed at the airfield.

In connection with these raids three RAAF Catalinas raided Buka aerodrome on Bougainville during the night of 15/16 September. These were lengthy missions of almost 19 hours duration, with an assortment of 20-, 25-, 250- and 500-pound bombs dropped. Small fires were observed as a result. A fourth Catalina failed to locate the target in bad weather and jettisoned its bombs over the sea.

A day after the 43rd BG flew its first independent mission, on 15 September the 38th BG undertook its first combat mission. As noted in Chapter 1, the 71st and 405th Bombardment Squadrons were new arrivals in the theatre, having only recently flown their B-25Cs across the Pacific. Some 35 Mitchells had arrived in Brisbane by mid-August where the crews celebrated their feat with a huge party at Lennon's Hotel. Lennon's had opened in mid-1941 and claimed to be the most modern hotel in Australia, boasting 140 rooms and 16 fully equipped apartments, as well as a flat roof suitable for sunbaking and parties. It had a long association with American forces in Australia during the war, and many senior officers had permanent accommodation at the hotel including MacArthur and Kenney.

When the 38th BG B-25s arrived at Charters Towers a short time later the de-icing equipment was removed from the leading edges of the wings and vertical stabilisers in line with the expected low-level role for the unit. Initial plans were for the 38th BG to move to Rorona (30-Mile), which was north-west of Port Moresby. On 7 September 1942, Captain John Thompson, the acting commanding officer of the 71st BS, called for volunteers for an advanced detail to go there. However, the plans were changed the next day, likely because of the Australian defeat at Efogi and Kenney's concerns the Japanese troops would break through: Rorona was the closest Port Moresby airfield to the Kokoda Track.

Instead, both squadrons deployed to Horn Island, where 13 B-25s had arrived by 9 September. On the evening of 14 September, the squadrons were alerted for their first combat mission to the Buna area, scheduled to depart early the next morning. Crews were roused at 0400 for a hasty meal of cold mutton and lukewarm tea before a dozen B-25s took-off led by Lieutenant Colonel Theodore Castle.

The bombers stopped off at Port Moresby for refuelling and briefing. Castle ordered the 405th BS to attack targets in the Buna area, while the 71st BS struck at supply barges hidden along the shore at nearby Sanananda Point. Both squadrons dropped a total of 60 x 300-pound bombs from 3,000 feet, flying just under a low cloud base. Moderate anti-aircraft fire was encountered, but the mission was successfully completed without losses and the B-25s returned direct to Horn Island that afternoon.

Interestingly the escort for this mission was provided by P-40Es of the 7th FS. This was the first squadron of the 49th FG to arrive in Port Moresby from the Darwin area. It was their first mission in New Guinea, although the entire group would not be properly settled until its ground crews arrived by ship in October. While *en route* to Port Moresby P-40E 41-24874, flown by Second Lieutenant Robert Hazard, had been lost during a ferry flight between Cairns and Horn Island on 11 September. After his engine failed at low altitude Hazard crashed into the ocean off the east coast of Cape York. A search found no trace of him or his aircraft.

The next day, 16 September, saw nine A-20As depart for a follow-up attack on the barges spotted near Buna. However, the formation ran into bad weather and returned to Port Moresby where *The Comet II* 40-3148 crash-landed at Kila 'drome and was wrecked. An escort of 16 Airacobras did penetrate the weather, however, and these strafed the barges. In addition, a single 435th BS B-17E hit the same target with 7 x 300-pound bombs.

16 September also saw six B-26s from the 2nd and 408th Bombardment Squadrons searching for a reported Japanese cruiser off Lae. After searching for three hours in bad weather without making any sightings the aircraft returned to base.

Meanwhile two US Army divisions had arrived in Australia in recent months and MacArthur was keen to deploy American troops to New Guinea as soon as possible. The 126th and 128th Infantry Regiments of the 32nd Division were being prepared for the move. At a conference in

On the night of 15/16 September 30th BS B-17E 41-2659 Frank Buck was landed on a beach 65 miles southeast of Port Moresby after being damaged by anti-aircraft fire over Rabaul and running low on fuel. Remarkably it was flown out two weeks later after a runway of steel matting was laid out on the beach. Frank Buck was a fictitious adventurer from a 1930s radio series who caught animals for zoos.

Brisbane on 13 September Kenney pleaded with MacArthur to let him fly one of the regiments to New Guinea. MacArthur was dubious, asking how many men he would lose flying the route. Kenney famously replied:

> ... we haven't lost a pound of freight on that route and the airplanes don't know the difference between 180 pounds of freight and 180 pounds of infantryman.

MacArthur allocated one company of the 126th Infantry Regiment to Kenney as a trial. On the morning of 15 September, 230 men together with their weapons and packs boarded Douglas and Lockheed transports at Amberley outside of Brisbane. All of the men were safely carried to Port Moresby that day. While MacArthur moved the rest of the 126th Regiment by sea, he was open to air movement of the 128th Infantry Regiment. This was done with the cooperation of the Australian Government who allocated a dozen civil airliners for the operation. These were joined by other aircraft such as bombers which had just completed overhaul in Australia prior to returning to combat duty. The operation commenced on 18 September and was completed on 24 September, two days before the remainder of the 126th Regiment arrived in Port Moresby by sea.

This was the first major air movement of US troops since the war began and did much to open MacArthur to the concept of future air transport operations in the forthcoming Papuan campaign.

USAAF C-47 Linda Ann descends over Hombrom's Bluff during another transport mission to Port Moresby. Following the initial airlift of American troops from Brisbane to Port Moresby in mid-September, such missions would soon become commonplace in Papua.

CHAPTER 4

CRISIS IN PAPUA II: 17 – 24 SEPTEMBER

After their defeat at Efogi, the Australian troops on the Kokoda Track had retreated to a new defensive position at Ioribawa. Here the troops were joined by Brigadier Ken Eather's fresh 25th Brigade, another veteran AIF unit that had fought in the Middle East the previous year. Eather's men had only arrived in Port Moresby on 9 September after eight days at sea and were immediately rushed up the track. With the addition of the 25th Brigade, the Australians now possessed almost 3,000 troops at Ioribawa, outnumbering by almost two to one the IJA attack force which was some 1,700 strong.

The Japanese attack came on 14 September and after three days of fighting the Australians sustained over 200 casualties, including 49 killed, many as a result of artillery fire. In comparison the Japanese casualties were slightly lower, at around 180 with 39 killed. By 16 September the situation was at something of a stalemate with the Australian lines intact and half of the defensive force only lightly engaged. However, it was at this point that Eather decided to withdraw to Imita Ridge, which was the last defensive position in front of the roadhead at Owers' Corner.

Imita Ridge was close to supplies and the position also brought the Australian troops within the protective range of their own artillery for the first time in the campaign. However, this withdrawal provoked at electric reaction from higher command, and marked the peak of the Papua crisis. MacArthur's land forces commander was the Australian General Thomas Blamey who had just returned from a visit to Port Moresby on 12-13 September.

On 16 September Blamey made a public broadcast expressing confidence in the situation in Papua and advising that fresh troops were about to take the offensive. Just after this statement came news of Eather's withdrawal to Imita Ridge. MacArthur made clear his deep concerns to the Australian Prime Minister John Curtin about the efficiency of the Australian troops and their leadership, advising that Curtin should order Blamey to Port Moresby to personally take command and "energise the situation". When Blamey returned to Port Moresby and assumed direct command of New Guinea Force on 23 September, the move side-lined the existing commander, Lieutenant General Rowell. The two leaders were unable to reach a working arrangement, and the petulant Rowell was relieved of his command five days later. Further reliefs followed, some of which remain contentious to this day.

Against this background was a loss of confidence by MacArthur and Kenney in the Australian troops, and an urgent desire to get American land forces into action. It was in this context that the emergency airlift of the 128th Infantry Regiment to Port Moresby was undertaken, as explained in the previous chapter. The wider strategic situation was somewhat delicate too. On 18 September a crucial convoy of Marine reinforcements reached Guadalcanal (cover for which Kenney had provided the series of B-17 raids on Rabaul), but three days earlier the carrier USS *Wasp* had been sunk. This left just one USN carrier in the area, a dangerous diminution of

General Thomas Blamey, the Allied land forces commander, gives a press conference in Port Moresby on 13 September. Days later Blamey returned to Australia and expressed confidence in the situation on the Kokoda Track. However Australian forces had once again retreated, precipitating a crisis in which doubts were held over the security of Port Moresby and its invaluable airfields.

strength compared to the four carriers with which the USN had begun the Solomons campaign in early August.[1]

At this time the most forward Japanese patrols were able to glimpse the shimmering seas of the Gulf of Papua through mountain mist and gaps in the treetops. At night the most advanced detachment could see the searchlights above Port Moresby in the distance. However just when it seemed that victory was within their grasp, complex factors started to unwind at higher levels.

The Japanese commander was Major General Horii Tomitaro, and he had never received orders to advance to Port Moresby. Instead, he was to occupy a strong position from which such an advance could be made, pending the arrival of IJA reinforcements. Most of the fighting along the track, including at Ioribawa, had been made by the 144th Regiment. Horii had another relatively fresh unit on hand, the 41st Regiment. This had been in reserve behind the 144th Regiment and it was to be used to outflank the Australian positions at Imita Ridge in any future advance to Port Moresby. However, on 16 September Horii received orders to send parts of

---

I   After the loss of the *Wasp*, only the USS *Hornet* remained in the South Pacific. The *Enterprise* had just reached Pearl Harbor for repairs, and the *Saratoga* was on her way there after being torpedoed by a Japanese submarine.

41ˢᵗ Regiment back over the track to Giruwa, near Buna. This was a reaction to the feared Allied landing reported by Buna's naval commander, as noted in the previous chapter. There were in fact plans underway for such an Allied flanking movement, which would soon unfold, but these did not involve an amphibious landing. Rather Japanese intelligence had got wind of these plans via signals traffic and open discussion in the Australian media. The Japanese had then mistakenly deduced a seaborn landing to be imminent.

Additional IJA troops were *en route* to Rabaul from Korea, and Horii had expected these to be allocated for the assault on Port Moresby. However, on 13 September IJA forces had failed in their attempt to take Henderson Field on Guadalcanal, and hence these reinforcements would first be required on that front. On 19 September Horii was ordered to withdraw to a holding position deep in the mountains from where it was hoped a new attempt to take Port Moresby could be mounted in November. Another factor at play was Horii's lengthening supply lines, the logistical challenges of which limited the time he could sustain large forces in forward positions in any case.

Against this background the air war continued, including the effort the bomb Rabaul pending the landing of Marine reinforcements on Guadalcanal. On 17 September eight 93ʳᵈ BS B-17Es from Mareeba staged through Port Moresby to raid Rabaul, but one bomber soon returned to base. Late that afternoon the formation ran into bad weather, with cloud from 3,000 to 30,000 feet. Just three of the Fortresses succeeded in dropping 300- and 500-pound bombs and incendiaries near Lakunai.

No. 30 Squadron Beaufighter A19-2 at Wards 'drome on 12 September, just after its arrival from Australia. No. 30 Squadron was quick to make an impact in the theatre, with General MacArthur personally congratulating the unit after a successful barge strafing mission on 17 September.

As four of the other B-17s returned with their bombs, two of them made attacks on alternate targets at Lae and Salamaua. The B-17E (41-2650) piloted by Second Lieutenant Claude Burcky encountered cloud on approach to Port Moresby and instead Burcky set a course for Horn Island. However, he became lost over the York Peninsula, and Burcky ordered his crew to bale out at 0240 on 18 September.

An RAAF Catalina searched for the missing crew the next day and spotted a parachute on a beach on the Gulf of Carpentaria. The Catalina landed and took onboard four men who were flown to Cairns. The next day the Catalina located another four men on a mudflat in the same area and landed nearby. However, by the time they had been taken aboard the tide had gone out leaving the flying boat stranded on the mud. After waiting for the tide to come in again the Catalina was able to take-off. A ninth crewman, the navigator Lieutenant William Meenagh, was never found. As he was the first to bale out it is speculated that he came down over the ocean.

On 17 September No. 30 Squadron flew its first mission from its new base at Wards 'drome (Five-Mile). That morning a dozen Beaufighters departed for Buna and Sanananda Point, led by the squadron commanding officer, Squadron Leader Brian "Blackjack" Walker. After one of the twin engine fighters returned to base with mechanical trouble, the other eleven proceeded to the target area escorted by eight 7th FS P-40Es.

Approaching at low-level under a 5,000-foot cloud base, the Beaufighters found many barges on beaches either side of Sanananda Point and also at Buna. These were strafed with 5,000 x 20mm and 30,000 x 0.303-inch rounds of ordnance, leaving an estimated 50% of the barges seriously damaged. Three of the barges were seen burning vigorously, with several others left smoking. Fires and explosions were also seen on the shore, suggesting many stores, including fuel drums, had been offloaded from a ship overnight and had not yet been moved inland. These were possibly from the destroyer *Mochizuki* which was at Buna early that morning and embarked 98 wounded troops who were taken to Rabaul.

One Beaufighter suffered damage to its mainplane after striking a coconut palm – evidence of the extreme low-level nature of the attack. The mission was considered a great success, with MacArthur sending the squadron a message the next day via No. 9 Operational Group:

> My heartiest congratulations on yesterday's attack. It was a honey.

Six P-39s also strafed the barges on the same day.

The 17 September saw a new IJN unit arrive in the theatre. This was a detachment from No. 3 *Ku* based in the Netherlands East Indies which had been flying missions over Darwin regularly since March. No. 3 *Ku* had a similar shared history to the Tainan *Ku*, with both units having flown alongside each other in the first months of the Pacific War. Having suffered only relatively light attrition in recent months over Darwin, No. 3 *Ku*'s combat-experienced pilots would add a qualitative boost to the fighter strength at Rabaul.

The detachment was of two *chutai* plus reserves, comprising 26 pilots, 21 A6M2 Zeros and four C5Ms Babs reconnaissance aircraft which were delivered by the carrier *Taiyo* to Kavieng

A B-17E undergoes engine changes at Seven-Mile in late 1942, underlining the limited maintenance facilities available at Port Moresby.

on 17 September. Within a few days the No. 3 *Ku* aircraft had been flown to Rabaul, where the pilots flew their first CAP mission on 22 September. Overall command was vested in *hikocho* Lieutenant Commander Sakakibara Kiyoji, although operational command was the responsibility of *hikotaicho* Lieutenant Aioi Takahide. Aioi also led the No. 1 *chutai*, while the No. 2 *chutai* was commanded by Lieutenant (jg) Yamaguchi Sadao.

Also arriving at this time was a mixed detachment from the Kanoya *Ku* in Malaya. A single *chutai* of Zeros, commanded by Lieutenant Ito Toshitaka, is recorded as arriving in Kavieng two days after the Zeros of the 3rd *Ku*. However, it is probable that these two units shared the same transport. After arriving at Lakunai the Kanoya *Ku* Zero detachment was allocated to the Tainan *Ku* for command purposes. Meanwhile a single *chutai* of Kanoya *Ku* Bettys (nine aircraft plus two spares) had arrived in the theatre a week earlier and was nominally based at Kavieng.

On the night of 17 September, the Japanese planned three nuisance raids over Port Moresby in their first appearance over the town in ten days. Departing Vunakanau mid-afternoon were six Misawa *Ku* Bettys followed 90 minutes later by two No. 4 *Ku* Bettys (tail codes F-329 and F-364). However, after one of the two No. 4 *Ku* machines experienced engine trouble, both returned to Vunakanau that evening. Also unsuccessful was a third formation of nine Kanoya *Ku* Bettys. Departing from Kavieng, this formation was forced back to base by inclement weather after a flight time of only 45 minutes.

The Misawa *Ku* Bettys, each armed with 12 x 60-kilogram bombs, were led by Lieutenant Nonaka Saburo and were organised into two three-aircraft *shotai*. After passing Buna the formation ran into bad weather over the Owen Stanleys and arrived over the southern coast of Papua off course. Unable to find the target, Nonaka's *shotai* were able to land safely at Lae at 2210. After refuelling they returned to Rabaul the following day.

At least one of the bombers from the other *shotai* did arrive over the target, with an estimated 12 bombs dropped soon after 1900. The bombs landed near Seven-Mile causing slight damage to a truck and injuring six personnel. In addition the mascot of an Australian Bofors gun crew, a small dog, was killed. The anti-aircraft batteries did not open fire due to poor visibility.

None of this second *shotai* returned to base, with all three aircraft possibly flying into a mountain in the bad weather. The missing aircraft commanders were *shotaicho* pilot FPO1c Sasaki Hideo, observer FPO1c Sato Yoshio and pilot FPO2c Nishigai Mitsuo.

The following day, 18 September, saw the bad weather continue over much of Papua, and just three Allied attack sorties were completed. One B-17E dropped bombs on Salamaua, while a B-25 on reconnaissance broke through the bad weather over the mountains to find clear conditions with unlimited visibility. The crew counted 27 burnt out barges at Buna and saw four anti-aircraft guns five miles inland. They also encountered pack trains of 30-40 horses making their way along the inland Japanese supply route in daylight, an uncommon occurrence. The pack trains were strafed.

That morning seven No. 30 Squadron Beaufighters set off to attack the inland supply track running from Buna. In the face of bad weather, six of the aircraft returned with only A19-4 piloted by Wing Commander Walker persisting through to the target zone. Walker strafed trucks seen near Popondetta and a group of huts at another village.

Meanwhile six 63rd BS B-17s had staged to Waigani (17-Mile) for an expected strike against Rabaul. However, the mission was cancelled, with the crews instead standing by as an alert force.

That afternoon four Catalinas set off from Cairns and Bowen to make another night raid against Buka. Two of the flying boats dropped their bombs over the target area but could not observe the results due to darkness. The two others failed to find Buka in bad weather. One jettisoned its bombs over the sea while the other returned to base with its bombs still onboard.

Soon after dawn on 19 September Wing Commander Walker led another strike comprising seven Beaufighters against targets in the Buna-Kokoda area. Huts and structures at various villages were strafed, with 2,650 x 20mm and 17,000 x 0.303-inch rounds being expended. Buna airfield was also attacked, with an anti-aircraft position silenced and a Zero in a dispersal pen being set on fire. The IJA 47th Anti-Aircraft Battalion was responsible for defending the beachhead area and noted a number of engagements with Allied aircraft this morning. Three Beaufighters received minor damage from the anti-aircraft fire.

The morning also saw a perfectly coordinated strike on Lae 'drome by B-26s and A-20As which was witnessed by Australian soldiers manning lookout posts in nearby hills. Nine 89th BS A-20As had set out from Kila, but three returned to base with mechanical problems. The remaining six struck the 'drome and a nearby plantation at 0810, firing 4,200 x 0.50-inch and 8,000 x 0.30-inch rounds of ammunition. Moments later six B-26s of the 2nd and 408th Bombardment Squadrons raced over the runway at 6,100-feet, dropping 166 x 100-pound bombs.

Japanese groundcrew at Vunakanau manhandle 250-kilogram bombs in preparation for a Port Moresby raid by Betty bombers in late 1942. Increasingly these were in the form of night-time nuisance raids and were often affected by bad weather.

Also on this morning a B-17 flying a reconnaissance mission spotted a 2,000-ton cargo ship in the Dampier Strait off the western tip of New Britain, likely having departed Lae in the early hours. It was strafed and the 63rd BS B-17s standing by on alert at 17-Mile (Waigani) were ordered to attack it. Four of these bombers found the ship mid-afternoon and dropped 24 x 500-pound bombs from only 1,500-feet, claiming four near misses. The vessel was thoroughly strafed with 2,700 x 0.50-inch rounds, with the Fortress crews reporting that the ship's defensive guns were silenced and small fires started.

The day also saw P-40s from Milne Bay strafe a whaleboat seen near Goodenough Island. There were two Japanese aboard who were likely *Yayoi* survivors. The night of 19 September saw Port Moresby record its 81st air raid. At 2015 an unidentified aircraft reportedly dropped eight bombs five miles from 12-Mile 'drome with no damage or casualties resulting. The culprit was a *shotai* of Kanoya *Ku* Bettys which had departed Kavieng that afternoon. They dropped 19 x 60-kilogram bombs at 2007 but had been unclear of their exact position due to poor weather.

Allied aircraft had more luck with several attacks taking place in Papua. At 0715 eight 7th FS P-40Es strafed Kokoda 'drome and nearby tracks and bridges, firing 9,600 x 0.50-inch rounds. They were accompanied by four 41st FS P-400s which strafed targets along the Kokoda Track, noting a large fire at Kagi. These attacks were followed by six of nine 89th BS A-20As, which strafed and bombed supply tracks and villages inland from Buna.

In the early afternoon five No. 30 Squadron Beaufighters hunted for a reported schooner in the Huon Gulf anchored offshore from Lae, but it was not found. Instead barges and a tug on the waterfront were strafed, as well as a nearby anti-aircraft gun position. It was Wing Commander Walker's fourth mission in consecutive days.

Since his arrival in the SWPA Kenney had been keen to try the idea of "skip bombing" whereby bombs were dropped from very low altitude but did not have time to point downwards. Instead, they hit the water at a horizontal angle and with considerable forward momentum, causing them to bounce or "skip" forwards. With a suitable delayed fuse such a technique could propel bombs into the side of ships. Port Moresby had a perfect ready-made training aid for skip bombing in the form of the *Pruth*, a British cargo ship which had run onto a reef outside the harbour in 1923 but which remained largely intact.

On this morning of 19 September Kenney witnessed a B-17 of Major Bill Benn's 63rd BS engage in skip bombing practice against the *Pruth*. This was one of the aircraft that had been standing by as an alert force at Waigani (17-Mile). Some of the bombing was "especially good" with Captain Ken McCullar skipping six of ten bombs against the side of the ship. It was realised that bombs with modified five-second fuses worked best, as noted by Kenney:

> So far they worked pretty well. Sometimes they went off in three seconds, sometimes in seven, but that was good enough.

However more practice was needed before the technique could be used in combat. The following day Benn flew his contingent back to Mareeba, and the squadron further practiced the low-level bombing approaches in Australia. The 63rd BS bombers were replaced at Port Moresby on ready alert duty by seven 30th BS B-17s based at the newly completed Laloki (14-Mile). Major John Rouse was not complimentary:

> Bad field here with hills on both ends and a perpetual crosswind. Built on a swamp through a thick tall forest ... pretty dusty and dirty here. Quite a few mosquitoes and food very bad.

The loss of three Bettys to bad weather during the night raid against Port Moresby on 17 September underlined the importance of this factor. Indeed, missions launched in the face of bad weather were a poor use of precious resources, especially as alternate missions to the Solomons could have been carried out instead. In time Vunakanau would construct its own dedicated weather facility, however at this stage of the war "Weather Central" was still No. 4 *Ku* headquarters to which all information was forwarded and from which crews would collect their weather briefings.

In the light of heavy Mavis flying boat losses, it was thus not surprising that some of No. 2 *Ku's* Vals at Rabaul, lacking the range to strike Guadalcanal, were assigned an interim role of weather forecasting. Lieutenant Inoue Buntou and Lieutenant (jg) Yoshikawa Yasutoshi, a reserve officer, assumed the role of planning most of these missions. These usually departed early in the morning and focussed on assessing conditions to plan operational activity during timeframes when the weather looked most favourable.

On 20 September, Yoshikawa was tasked with taking three Vals over the northern coast of Papua to ascertain conditions for a strike against Port Moresby. The trio left before sunrise at 0535 but hit a wall of weather almost as soon as they had left. They were back at Lakunai a brief 43 minutes later. On the next day of 21 September, Yoshikawa launched the same three Vals and crews from Lakunai at 0555 and made the shoreline near Buna in clear weather. They could see that the path was clear over the Owen Stanley ranges so broadcast the good news to Rabaul to where they returned after an uneventful four-hour reconnaissance.

A substantial Japanese strike against Rorona (30-Mile) took place on 21 September following this favourable early morning weather reconnaissance mission. It comprised a mixture of three *chutai* of Betty bombers armed with 193 x 60-kilogram and 20 x 250-kilogram bombs. One *chutai* of nine Bettys was from the Kisarazu *Ku* (led by Lieutenant Tsuchiki Osamu), another *chutai* was of eight Kanoya *Ku* Bettys (after one abort) while the third was a mixed *chutai* with five bombers from the Chitose *Ku* and four from the Misawa *Ku*. These were to be accompanied by a strong escort of Zeros, comprising one *chutai* from the Tainan *Ku*, one *chutai* from the Kanoya *Ku* and three *chutai* from No. 6 *Ku*.

Overall charge of the fighters was allocated to the experienced No. 6 *Ku hikotaicho* Lieutenant Kofukuda Mitsugu, who had flown recent missions over Guadalcanal as well as one over Port Moresby on 6 September. However, this mission was plagued by bad weather from the start, with the bombers taking off from Vunakanau in heavy cloud soon after 0900. The fighters followed from Lakunai, but the six Zeros of the Tainan *Ku* soon lost contact with the remaining aircraft and returned to base.

That left Kofukuda's 36 Zeros escorting the 26 Bettys. The Kanoya *Ku* Zeros understandably stayed close to their own bombers throughout the entire mission, departing and landing with them. Of the remaining fighters, one *chutai* flew close protection while the others took defensive positions ahead of and behind the bombers. When the formation arrived over the Port Moresby area at midday it was blanketed by heavy cloud. Multiple attack runs were made over Rorona, but the bombs landed two miles from the runway in scrub country and did no damage. Some 53 fighters were scrambled from Port Moresby but there was no aerial contact in the cloudy conditions. Most of the bombers landed safely at Vunakanau at 1435, with the exception of the Misawa *Ku* contingent which followed over an hour later, indicating they likely got lost on the way home.

The weather also constrained Allied activities on 21 September, with solid overcast down to 5,000 feet. That morning two low-level strikes were successful. Eight 7th FS P-40Es dropped 500-pound bombs on bridges on the Kokoda-Buna supply route, while six 89th BS A-20s bombed the Kokoda-Efogi area.

At Milne Bay the 35th and 36th Fighter Squadrons arrived from Townsville with their P-39s to take over air defence duties from the two RAAF Kittyhawk fighter units, Nos. 75 and 76 Squadrons. Both of the Australian units commenced ferry flights to Horn Island on 22 September, with their ground personnel departing Milne Bay by ship two days later.

One final mission flown by No. 75 Squadron on 21 September was air cover for the destroyer HMAS *Stuart* which landed a company of AIF troops on Normanby Island to search for the *Yayoi* survivors. Over two days of searching eight Japanese prisoners were captured, but the main group couldn't be found. The Australian troops saw ships during the night using searchlights along the shore. These were the destroyers *Isokaze* and *Mochizuki* which had departed departed Rabaul on 22 September to search for the survivors. They found ten sailors in one of *Yayoi*'s boats south of New Britain but were unable to make contact with the main group on Normanby and returned to Rabaul.

The night of 21/22 September saw another Catalina raid on Buka by three of the flying boats. Operating from Bowen, one of the Catalinas was in the air for over 21 hours. This was considered a successful attack with a large fire started near the runway that was visible for 50 miles.

Allied aircraft were again active on the morning of 22 September. A dozen 7th FS P-40Es dropped 300-pound bombs on the wire rope pedestrian bridge over the Kumusi River at Wairopi (Neo-Melanesian for "wire rope"). This was thought to be a major choke point on the Japanese supply line from Buna to Kokoda, but in fact the IJA used several crossings along a few miles of the river where it was fordable in normal conditions. However, this bridge became a natural focus for Allied attacks as it was easily identifiable. It was knocked out on a couple of occasions but was quickly rebuilt.

Also that morning six 89th BS A-20As bombed targets near Kokoda, while four 35th FG P-39s from the Headquarters Flight strafed the Buna area. Meanwhile eight 22nd BG B-26s struck Gasmata 'drome, each armed with 2 x 1,000-pound bombs which were dropped from 5,000 feet. The runways were left badly cratered, and the crews reported leaving bombers and buildings burning. P-39s met the B-26s over Papua on the way home but no enemy fighters had been encountered.

The eight Marauder crews from the 2nd and 408th Bombardment Squadrons remained on standby at Port Moresby for the next few days, but soon returned to their base at Reid River near Townsville. This began an almost six-week hiatus of operations for the 22nd BG, which had seen six months of continuous combat in New Guinea. As a 22nd BG historian has described:

The planes and crews were worn out and no replacements were in sight. It was time for a rest.

That evening nine 28th BS B-17s attacked ships in Rabaul harbour with 20 x 500-pound bombs, claiming two probable hits. Another 5 x 500-pound bombs were dropped on Lakunai. The Fortresses were flying at only 6,000 – 8,000 feet and, illuminated by the moon, they attracted thick and accurate anti-aircraft fire. Three of the bombers were hit, including 41-24454 which had just arrived in the theatre. It was struck in the cockpit and had almost all the instruments shot away. The RAAF navigator was badly wounded, but all of the B-17s were able to return to Port Moresby. That night a B-25 made a solo armed reconnaissance of the Buna area, dropping 6 x 300-pound bombs on the airfield.

Early on 23 September, a pair of 7th FS P-40Es flown by Major Green and Lieutenant Max Wiecks in company with a pair of P-39s, strafed Taupota Mission, near Milne Bay. At the same time eight 41st FS P-39s strafed the Buna-Kokoda supply route including the Wairopi bridge.

Meanwhile six No.30 Squadron Beaufighters had taken off for a coastal sweep commencing at Paiawa (about halfway between Salamaua and Buna) and continuing eastwards to Buna. The Beaufighters were escorted by eight 7th FS P-40Es. Two small boats were strafed, as were stores and barges in the Sanananda-Buna area. Under a low cloud base of around 3,000 feet, the RAAF pilots were surprised to see six Zeros approaching Buna, with what they identified as nine dive-bombers.

The 7th FS pilots were low on fuel and could not stay and fight. The Zeros reacted quickly and dived on a lone Beaufighter, A19-50 piloted by Flying Officer DJ Moran-Hilford, who turned towards the Zeros. As they flashed past Moran-Hilford dived to sea level and powered away at 260 knots. The Zeros followed for ten miles, but the Beaufighter gradually outdistanced them.

The Japanese aircraft were in fact eighteen No. 3 *Ku* Model 21 Zeros led by Lieutenant (jg) Yamaguchi Sadao on a most unusual escort mission (see below). In the brief engagement with the Beaufighter only a relatively minor amount of ammunition was expended (140 x 20mm and 360 x 7.7mm rounds) before the Zeros returned to their core duty. This engagement is noteworthy as the first time Beaufighters and Zeros met in combat.

News of Japanese aircraft believed to be using Buna airfield brought a swift reaction. Wing Commander Walker led seven Beaufighters back to Buna at 1240, where they expected to find the Zeros on the ground. However only dummy aircraft were seen, and after noting many barges underwater the Beaufighters headed inland to Soputa village where they strafed tents and buildings. Near Buna 'drome A19-1, crewed by pilot Flight Sergeant George Sayer and observer Sergeant Archie Mairet, was hit by anti-aircraft fire and crashed with the loss of both men.

Immediately following the Beaufighters, a dozen 7th FS P-40Es also attacked Buna airfield, strafing the dispersal area and anti-aircraft positions with 7,000 rounds of 0.50-inch ammunition. Two of the P-40Es were damaged by return fire.

Meanwhile Japanese aircraft were active on relatively unusual supply dropping missions on 23 September. Horii's IJA force deep in the Owen Stanleys had been experiencing supply shortages, largely related to serious flooding of the Kumusi River two weeks earlier which had halted the movement of supplies to Kokoda for several days. At 0900 eight Misawa *Ku* Bettys led by Lieutenant Morita Rinji departed Vunakanau loaded with rations. At 1100 they were over Kokoda and subsequently spent a 20-minute period airdropping the supplies, which were manually hurled out of the bombers. The appearance of these rations gave a significant morale boost to the IJA troops in the mountains.

The eighteen No. 3 *Ku* Zeros encountered by No. 30 Squadron off Buna had in fact been tasked to escort the Misawa *Ku* Bettys on the supply drop mission. This long-range mission was a remarkable feat for a unit newly arrived in the theatre, and one of the few times that Zeros operated directly over Kokoda. After more than six hours in the air, Yamaguchi's Zeros returned safely back at Lakunai at 1420.

At midday three Kisarazu *Ku* Bettys, escorted by nine No. 2 *Ku* Zeros, dropped supplies to the marooned marines on Goodenough Island. The Bettys also spotted around ten *Yayoi* survivors on a beach on nearby Normanby Island, and these men were picked up by destroyers three days later.

That evening seven 30th BS B-17Es from the ready alert force had been detailed to bomb a battleship reported at Faisi in the Shortlands. Each Fortress was carrying a huge 2,000-pound bomb, and when the ship couldn't be seen Major Rouse led three B-17Es in bombing Buna airfield instead. Two of the huge bombs landed on or near the runway and one landed in a village nearby, although one of the bombs did not explode.

At 1933 that evening the 32nd Heavy Anti-Aircraft Battery in Port Moresby fired 11 rounds at enemy aircraft overhead. They were believed to be two Bettys but could not be observed due to clouds. Bombs fell three miles south of Seven-Mile but there was no damage or casualties. Port Moresby would now enjoy a respite from raids for over a month, the longest break the town had enjoyed since the raids began in February.

In the early hours of 24 September six B-17s from the 19th BG Headquarters Flight and the 28th BS attacked ships at Rabaul. Fortress 41-2481 *Old Topper* descended to 1,500 feet and dropped 4 x 500-pound bombs on an 8,000-ton ship. A direct hit was claimed with fires and explosions reportedly resulting. The B-17 received three hits in the wings and fuselage from anti-aircraft fire. The other aircraft dropped 7 x 300- and 16 x 500-pound bombs from the somewhat safer height of 25,000 feet. On their return to Port Moresby there was a false air-raid alarm, so the bombers diverted to Horn Island.

Also in the early hours a single No. 20 Squadron Catalina raided Buka, claiming four hits on the dispersal area with 250-pound bombs. During the mission supplies were also dropped to a coastwatcher.

At 0730 on 24 September eight 7th FS P-40Es strafed Kokoda airfield and huts in the Wairopi area, leaving one truck left burning. Thirty minutes later six 89th BS A-20s attacked Mubo village near Salamaua, dropping 8 x 100-pound and 120 x 20-pound bombs and expending 3,000 x 0.50-inch and 4,000 x 0.30-inch rounds of ammunition. Escort was provided by more 7th FS P-40s.

On 24 September Lieutenant George Newton ditched B-17E 41-9206 in Orangerie Bay some 80 miles west of Milne Bay. No one was hurt and the bomber was abandoned.

Later that afternoon six B-17s searched for ships reported off Buna, but after not finding anything 10 x 500-pound bombs were dropped on the wreck of the *Ayatosan Maru* at Gona instead. The Fortresses were accompanied by fifteen 7th FS P-40Es each armed with a 500-pound bomb. With Buna closed in by overcast, three of the P-40s found the opportunity to bomb the Wairopi bridge.

Meanwhile a 435th BS B-17E flying one of the routine reconnaissance missions had run into trouble. This was 41-9206 which had overflown Rabaul and the Shortlands where 28 Japanese vessels were noted and anti-aircraft fire from a cruiser was encountered. However, the unnamed Fortress, flown by Lieutenant George F Newton, subsequently got lost in bad weather. After spending more than 12 hours in the air Newton finally force-landed in shallow water just offshore a beach in Orangerie Bay some eighty miles west of Milne Bay on the south coast of Papua. None of the crew were injured, and the bomber was abandoned.

That evening six 93rd BS B-17s attacked shipping at Rabaul. After dropping 20 x 500-pound and four 1,000-pound bombs, a hit was claimed on a large unidentified ship.

A Model 32 Zero and Airacobra pass head-on in New Guinea skies.

CHAPTER 5

HORII WITHDRAWS: 25 – 30 SEPTEMBER

When the Australians fell back to Imita Ridge on 17 September, they were not closely followed by the Japanese. The next few days saw only minor contact as Australian patrols probed carefully forward. An attack to retake Ioribaiwa was launched on 28 September, with the Australians advancing under their own artillery cover for the first time in the campaign. However, they met no opposition, finding only empty trenches and abandoned equipment.

The Japanese main body had withdrawn from Ioribaiwa on 24 September. The bulk of Horii's force was now being redeployed between Kokoda and Buna, where there was relatively little difficulty in maintaining supplies. A rear-guard was being organised to remain deep in the Owen Stanleys. Known as the Stanley Detachment, this comprised one battalion of the 144th Infantry Regiment supported by a mountain artillery company and an engineer company.

Understandably and completely unaware of the Japanese change in strategy, the Australian advance was slow and cautious, while Horii's force retreated quickly. This meant it would be two weeks before there was another significant engagement in the mountains. Nevertheless, the fact that the Australians were advancing had a significant effect on the psyche of Allied commanders at this time. There was a feeling that the tide had turned, and with the immediate security of Port Moresby assured, planning for future offensive operations was taken with more confidence.

On 25 September an important visitor flew into Amberley to meet with Kenney. This was General Henry "Hap" Arnold, the head of the USAAF who was visiting the South Pacific. Kenney pressed Arnold on the need to relieve the long-serving 19th BG with a fresh heavy bomber group. It was agreed that it would be exchanged for the 90th BG, a B-24 Liberator unit then based in Hawaii.

Kenney also explained that many of the crews arriving from the US were "green as grass" and lacked sufficient instruction in gunnery, formation flying or night flying. Another problem was directions from staff officers in Washington which ignored local conditions; the timeworn friction of "field versus headquarters" which stems back to the Roman Empire. One good example was when Kenney had been asked why his B-26s weren't being used to attack shipping in Rabaul Harbour, as that target was within range of Port Moresby. Kenney had to explain that whilst Rabaul lay within theoretical range, restraints imposed by local conditions such as the Owen Stanley mountains the Marauders couldn't transport a meaningful bomb load to the target.

After a quick visit to Port Moresby, Arnold flew to Noumea on 28 September to attend a meeting between senior staff of the SWPA and SoPAC commands. Kenney also attended the meeting, where he was pressed by the SoPAC commander, Vice Admiral Robert Ghormley, to make raids against Rabaul his primary mission. With the situation in the Solomons still extremely precarious, Ghormley stressed the importance of pressure the Fifth Air Force could apply against the Japanese stronghold.

When Kenney made his point about the "green" crews arriving from the US, one unit he no doubt had in mind was the 38th BG. After flying its first operation on 15 September, the unit had not since managed another squadron-sized mission. The B-25 crews had been struggling with limited facilities on Horn Island where excessive dust was causing problems. However, the group had been hastily assembled and the lack of training was now being shown up, exacerbated by harsh tropical conditions for which the crews were unprepared.

To make matters worse, Horn Island was temporarily crowded with the RAAF Kittyhawks that had recently vacated Milne Bay. On 25 September B-25C #41-12910 *Suicide's Flying Drunks* of the 405th BS was taking off when a P-40E taxied onto the runway. The B-25 pilot pulled back on his stick, such that he only lightly clipped the fighter. However, the B-25 then came down very heavily and slid across the runway into some rocks. The bomber was wrecked, and one crewman suffered a fractured back.

On 25 September low cloud over much of Papua restricted Allied operations. Wing Commander Walker managed a dawn patrol of the Buna-Wairopi area in Beaufighter A19-4. No activity was seen but Walker took the opportunity to strafe a large thatched hut.

At midday eight 7th FS P-40Es set off for Wairopi, although two pilots lost contact with the formation amid the low cloud and returned to base. The other six fighters each dropped a 500-pound bomb on Wairopi bridge. One direct and two partial hits were scored, with the bridge reported as "completely destroyed".

Meanwhile six 30th BS B-17s searched for shipping reportedly anchored off Buna, but after not making any sightings their bombs were dropped on Buna airfield instead. By this time the runway had the appearance of being both unserviceable and abandoned.

In the early hours of 26 September six B-17s were sent out to raid Rabaul in the darkness. After one of the bombers couldn't find the target and returned to base, the other five dropped four 1,000-pound and 16 x 500-pound bombs over Vunakanau and shipping in the harbour. The raid was made at just 4,500-feet with a probable hit made on an unidentified ship. Several searchlights were reportedly knocked out with 0.50-inch machine gun fire. During the day three 89th BS A-20As bombed and strafed the Kokoda Track in the Ioribaiwa-Efogi area.

Neither side possessed particularly detailed charts for maritime use. A more unusual mission unfolded on 26 September when a solitary Misawa *Ku* Betty departed Vunakanau before sunrise at 0530. It headed south for a reconnaissance of the northern Papua coastline and areas approaching Goodenough Island. Aboard was the captain of submarine *I-1* taking notes and sketches of prominent shoals and reefs. Pilot FPO1c Matsuda Saburo returned the Misawa *Ku* Betty back to Vunakanau after an uneventful five-hour flight.

The *I-1* was an elderly submarine built in the early 1920s that had been withdrawn from a frontline combat role. Its deck gun had been removed and a barge was mounted abaft the conning tower with the intention of supporting commando-type landings. On the night of 2/3 October the *I-1* surfaced off Goodenough Island and made contact with the stranded Tsukioka Unit. It embarked

The wreckage of 405th BS B-25C 41-12910 Suicide's Flying Drunks at Horn Island just after its take-off accident of 25 September 1942.

71 wounded SNLF marines and delivered supplies to those remaining behind.

The No. 6 Squadron detachment of Hudsons at Milne Bay had been busy flying reconnaissance missions over both the D'Entrecasteux group and the Louisiades. However, since the sinking of the *Yayoi* a fortnight earlier there had been no contact with the enemy. Such was the boredom of these missions, often flown in foul weather, that the Louisiades were nicknamed by the aircrews as the "Lousyades".

This pattern was broken on the morning of 26 September when a small vessel was sighted west of Woodlark Island by a pair of Hudsons, A16-215 (flown by Flight Lieutenant GJ Hitchcock) and A16-229 (Flying Officer RW Shore). The Hudsons dropped eight 250-pound bombs and recorded near misses on the target. The vessel was also strafed with 3,500 x 0.303-inch rounds and was left dead in the water.

There was a ready strike force available at Milne Bay in the form of four No. 30 Squadron Beaufighters which had forward deployed from Port Moresby in recent days. While departing Wards 'drome for Milne Bay on 25 September, A19-39 collided with a truck on take-off and belly landed. It was later sent to an air depot for repairs but never returned to service and was used for parts.

Later on the morning of 26 September another Hudson, A16-211 flown by Flight Sergeant WA Wheeler, led four Beaufighters to hunt for the disabled Japanese ship. Wheeler dropped four 250-bombs on the vessel, scoring a direct hit which destroyed the bridge and main mast and blew a hole in the side of the forward hull. The Beaufighters then thoroughly strafed the cripple with 1,020 x 20mm and 10,500 x 0.303-inch rounds.

The ship was left burning and completely gutted, with questions raised as to what such a small and lightly defended vessel was doing in such a location. It was correctly believed it had a radio transmitter aboard. In fact, the vessel was a 200-ton IJN weather observation vessel, named the *Kyoei Maru No. 6*, that subsequently sank. It had been despatched to report weather conditions and aircraft movements on the approaches to the D'Entrecasteux Islands where the destroyers *Isokaze* and *Mochizuki* were *en route* to pick up further *Yayoi* survivors that night.

At 0030 on 27 September a single No. 11 Squadron Catalina raided the new target of Buin in southern Bougainville. A load of ten 250-pound general purpose bombs and ten 20-pound fragmentation bombs landed near the south-western side runway. This was in response to the recent construction activity noted at the site. A first-hand witness was Australian coastwatcher Paul Mason who reported on 23 September:

> Our scouts being employed [at] Kahili aerodrome state aerodrome is expected to be completed in a week's time. Many hundreds of natives being forced to work on aerodrome. 27 lorries, 6 motor cars, 10 horses, 6 motorcycles, 4 tractors and aerodrome working equipment at Kahili. Stores and fuel under tarpaulins spread along foreshore from mouth of Ugumo River to mouth of Moliko River. Two anti-aircraft guns near mouth of Ugumo River in fuel and ammunition dump and one anti-aircraft gun on north-western boundary of aerodrome. Wireless station on beach in front of aerodrome, also eight new iron buildings. Priests and nuns interned in iron buildings on beach. Enemy troops in green uniforms with anchor badge on arm and white hat. Scouts state 440 enemy troops but coolies too numerous to count …

Also early that morning seven 28th BS B-17s departed Port Moresby to strike Rabaul once again. However, six of the bombers turned back in the face of storms and lightning, leaving just one Fortress, 41-9015, to make a determined lone attack at 0622. Three 500-pound bombs were dropped over the harbour from 8,000-feet, with a direct hit claimed on a large transport.

Later that morning other B-17s were also active. At 0820 a lone 435th BS Fortress dropped seven 300-pound bombs on stores and buildings at Gona. After searching unsuccessfully in rain and low cloud for ships reported offshore, two 63rd BS B-17Fs dropped 20 x 500-pound bombs on barges at Buna. They experienced a moderate amount of accurate anti-aircraft fire, which damaged the right wing of Major Folmer Sogaard's Fortress, 41-24520 *Fightin' Swede*. This was a round with a five second fuse fired by the 47th Anti-Aircraft Battalion, which noted the hit drove off the B-17s.

The morning also saw formations of A-20As and Beaufighters active. Wing Commander Walker led six Beaufighters in a sweep of the coast between Salamaua and Buna. There was no activity along the coast so buildings at Buna were strafed. At the same time seven 89th BS A-20As bombed and strafed the Kokoda Track between Ioribaiwa and Kagi.

That night three Catalinas from Nos. 11 and 20 Squadrons raided Buin. Of 26 x 250-pound bombs dropped most landed on the runway. A few dozen small incendiary and fragmentation bombs were also scattered over the wider area.

Better weather enabled a good deal more activity on 28 September. The morning saw another coastal sweep by three No. 30 Squadron Beaufighters. After encountering just one loaded barge,

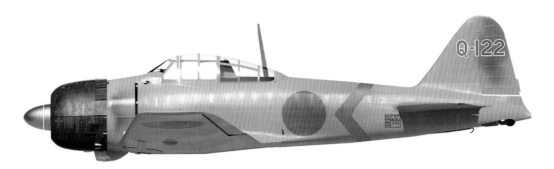

This A6M3 Model 32 Zero was among a batch of delivered to No. 2 Ku at Rabaul on 11 September. The chevron was a unique marking applied to all No. 2 Ku aircraft in late 1942.

which was claimed sunk at Buna, the Australian pilots turned their attention inland, strafing stores and buildings.

Meanwhile four 35th FS P-39s strafed Myola, claiming to have hit a newly constructed building. Shortly afterwards eight 7th FS P-40Es attacked targets at Buna and on the inland supply route, firing a total of 5,000 x 0.50-inch rounds of ammunition. During this mission Lieutenant Don Sutliff went missing, however a radio call that night indicated he was alive and well. Sutliff had got lost on the return trip and ran out of fuel. He belly landed his P-40E at an emergency grass field near Hood Point and was returned to Port Moresby by air. His Warhawk was later salvaged from the field, some 60 miles southeast of Port Moresby.

Later, Wairopi bridge was attacked by eight P-39s dropping four 100-pound bombs and four "liquid incendiaries". The latter were fuel tanks with incendiaries attached.

The day also saw a 435th BS B-17 on a reconnaissance of the Buna-Lae-Finschafen area drop three 300-pound bombs on Lae 'drome. The cloud base was reported as 15,000 feet with visibility excellent.

Meanwhile two pairs of 63rd BS B-17s had attempted to attack the Wairopi bridge but the weather in that location was too thick for the heavy bombers. The first pair returned to Waigani (17-Mile) with their bombs unexpended. The second pair meanwhile diverted to Buna, where the first B-17 bombed barges. The second bomber, flown by Lieutenant Carl Hustad was hit by anti-aircraft fire over Buna airfield. Hustad received a shrapnel wound in the heel and the aircraft's electrical system was damaged such that the bombs would not release and the bomb bay doors would not close. Despite this, Hustad made a safe return to Port Moresby.

By this time the 63rd BS was rapidly gaining in experience and had chosen to fly in pairs as its basic combat formation. This contrasted with the 19th BG which preferred to fly in threes. The choice of pairs was explained by Lieutenant James Murphy:

> We gained additional manoeuvrability, and that permitted the commander to fly his plane smoothly without worrying about which of his wingmen were going to cut off his tail. It allowed the other pilot to fly on either side, above, or below the flight commander as he saw fit or as the combat demanded.

Kenney himself was effusive in his praise of the 63rd BS commander, Major William Benn, and the unit continued to grow in confidence. This was just as well given the imminent departure of the 19th BG, and it contrasted completely with the experience of the poorly performing 38th BG which was struggling for opportunity.

On 28 September three 38th BG B-25s had the mundane duty of escorting a convoy into Port Moresby. After landing at Waigani they waited for most of the rest of their squadron to arrive for a scheduled mission. After fighting their way through rain squalls at low altitude, six Mitchells finally arrived only to be greeted by the news that the mission had been cancelled. The following morning the crews waited for permission to bomb Wairopi bridge only to have that mission cancelled also.

At 0800 on 29 September an A-20A on an armed reconnaissance had dropped 65 x 20-pound bombs over Menari on the Kokoda Track but reported all of the valleys closed in by cloud. This was likely the report which prevented the 38th BG Mitchells from taking off, and the weather meant a quiet day for the Fifth Air Force.

Towards midday a lone B-17 bombed Salamaua through cloud, an exercise more than likely meaning the bombs exploded harmlessly in the ocean or jungle. Two 435th BS Fortresses found their target of Wairopi socked in with cloud and instead bombed barges at Buna through heavy cumulus. There was just enough visibility for the bomber crews to claim six barges and an anti-aircraft position destroyed. Likewise, the 47th Anti-Aircraft Battalion was able to fire 28 rounds at the B-17s.

That night of 29-30 September saw RAAF Catalinas once again busy. Three raided Buin, reporting direct hits on the runway with a variety of ordnance that included 500-pound bombs set with 12-hour delays. Heavy and accurate fire from a nearby cruiser had the crews believing it was radar-controlled. A fourth flying boat struck Buka's runway, with ordnance including 250-pound bombs set with six-hour delays.

At 0800 on 30 September a lone P-39 dropped its belly tank on Wairopi bridge. The pilot succeeded in igniting the fuel with gunfire, but the fire soon went out. Later that morning at 1145, three 41st FS Squadron P-400s strafed huts at Menari, while two flights, each of three 89th BS A-20As, bombed and strafed targets in the same area. Four 41st FS P-400s flew as escorts.

A lone 435th BS B-17 dropped seven 300-pound bombs on Buna, although three of them struck the water. Moderate defensive fire from the 47th Anti-Aircraft Battalion was experienced.

At 1235 a pair of 63rd BS B-17s was over enemy territory. Ken McCullar and Bill Benn, in #521 *Black Jack*, and Lieutenant Byron Heichel in #356, attacked Wairopi bridge from 3,000 feet, flying just under a low cloud base. They unloaded 20 x 500-pound bombs on the target which was left "sagging but not destroyed". The bomber was then flown at just 250 feet to the coast, with crewmen machine gunning suspected targets as they went, expending 7,000 x 0.50-inch rounds of ammunition. Another pair followed on a later mission but could not see the bridge through heavy cloud. Instead, a nearby road was bombed.

While the 22nd BG was resting, one of its aircraft experienced an accident at Iron Range on 30 September. This was B-26 40-1403 *Bunagoon* which experienced brake failure while landing and ran off the runway, seriously damaging its nose. Repair of this magnitude proved impossible

From September a key target for Allied attacks was the bridge over the Kumusi River at Wairopi, partly because it was one of few identifiable targets between Buna and Kokoda. This photo was taken by an Allied reconnaissance aircraft in October by which time the bridge itself has been destroyed with only large pylons remaining on the opposing river banks. The extensive bombing and strafing has largely stripped the area of jungle foliage.

given the primitive facilities at Iron Range. It was not for another six months before the damaged aircraft was shipped to Townsville where the rear section was eventually used to put another damaged B-26 back in commission.

Meanwhile, the Japanese construction efforts at Buka and Buin were making solid progress. As early as 19 September a full *chutai* of Kanoya *Ku* Bettys was able to land at Buka after failing to push through bad weather over Bougainville *en route* to Guadalcanal. No. 2 *Ku* at Lakunai, which had been boosted by the recent delivery of ten additional Model 32 Zeros, sent its entire strength of 21 Zeros to Buka on 28 September. From this location the Model 32s were able to fly defensive patrols over the Shortlands area.

As noted in Chapter 2 the intention was for Buin to be ready to accommodate a *chutai* of dive-bombers by 20 September. To facilitate this, No. 31 *Ku* was transferred from the Philippines. This was a *kokutai* of modest size which had been established in February 1942 at Nichols Field outside of Manila operating D3A1 Vals. These dive-bombers arrived in Rabaul on 27 September where they were unloaded under the watchful eye of *hikotaicho* Lieutenant Kitamura Tensei.

Three days later, on 30 September, a single Val undertook the unit's first mission in the theatre. Sent to reconnoitre Goodenough Island, it departed at 0600 but was back on the ground 40 minutes later, a harsh lesson in the theatre's meteorology. At Rabaul Kitamura meanwhile busied himself with staff briefings and organising logistics for the unit's movements to Buin where it would finally be sent in mid-October.

B-25 Battlin' Biffy of the 405th BS being pursued by Tainan Ku fighters on 5 October as it heads at full throttle for the Owen Stanley Ranges.

CHAPTER 6

ALLIED FLANKING OPERATIONS: 1 – 10 OCTOBER

The first day of October began with a coastal sweep by six No. 30 Squadron Beaufighters. No shipping was seen, but six barges were strafed at Sanananda Point as well as buildings at Salamaua. Beaufighter A19-11 was hit by anti-aircraft fire in the starboard engine but returned to base safely on the other good engine. Four escorting P-400 Airacobras from the 41st FS strafed Menari on the Kokoda Track.

Relatively good visibility with a cloud base of 10,000 feet saw several attacks on the Wairopi bridge. The first involved a pair of P-39s from 8th FG Headquarters flying a weather reconnaissance mission which took the opportunity to drop their belly tanks, now with 4-pound incendiary devices attached, on the bridge. The pilots claimed that the resulting fires destroyed an 18-foot segment of the crossing.

A short time later, at 0930, two 63rd BS B-17s dropped 20 x 500-pound bombs on the bridge from 4,000 feet. Captain Folmer Sogaard in *Flyin' Swede* claimed two direct hits with a 30-foot section of the bridge now destroyed. Another attack soon followed after a 435th BS Fortress failed to find a ship reported off Finschhafen. Instead, seven 300-pound bombs were unloaded over Wairopi with further damage to the bridge claimed.

Two Airacobras returned to the bridge that afternoon and noted that it had been repaired with planking. It was attacked once again with incendiary belly tanks after which targets along the Kokoda Track were strafed. That night a single No. 11 Squadron Catalina dropped a mix of 250- and 20-pound bombs on Buka's runway.

At 0200 on 2 October six 63rd BS B-17s departed Seven-Mile to raid Rabaul. The pilots had been keen to debut the skip-bombing techniques they had been practicing, but Major Benn ruled against it as the five-second delay fuses were proving unreliable. Instead, this would be a conventional low-level bombing attack. Approaching the harbour at 2,500 feet just prior to dawn "as the horizon was getting light", they found it crowded with 30 ships.

Each Fortress carried five 500-pound bombs and the pilots lined up their targets separately as the harbour erupted in a blaze of anti-aircraft fire. Lieutenant James Murphy, flying B-17F 41-24543 *Pluto*, recalled:

> Everything around the harbour seemed to be firing at us. I had a good 20-second run, straight and level. The bombs went exactly as we hoped - one hit the ship directly, with the other three very close to it. Major fires broke out all over the ship.

Two of the pilots, including Murphy, claimed hits on large ships while two other pilots claimed probable hits on ships including a cruiser. The other two pilots bombed Lakunai airfield and the seaplane anchorage at Malaguna. A large explosion seen at Lakunai was believed to be an ammunition dump.

All six of the bombers were damaged by anti-aircraft fire, but there were no casualties. Two Zeros were scrambled but were unable to catch the Fortresses as they vanished into the dark western sky. Lieutenant Murphy concluded:

> Extremely low-altitude bombing was dangerous, but it worked.

On this occasion the Americans had hit the *Tenryu*, a light cruiser which had been something of a South Seas workhorse since January. One bomb landed on her stern while several others were near misses. The direct hit blew a 16-foot hole in the upper decking and peppered the aft superstructure with shrapnel, causing heavy damage. The explosion killed 22 crewmen and left another 26 wounded. Emergency repairs were quickly commenced by the repair ships *Hakkai Maru* and *Yamabiko Maru*, but the cruiser was out of action for almost three weeks. No other ships are known to have been significantly damaged in the attack, although the transport *Matsumoto Maru* suffered a near miss.

Later that morning, and despite a very low cloud ceiling of only 200 feet, three 89th BS A-20As bombed and strafed tracks at Myola. This type of flying – low ridge-running in limited visibility – was especially dangerous. However, at such low-level various signs of activity along the tracks could be seen and were targeted including numerous fires believed to indicate campsites. A short time later eight 41st FS P-400 Airacobras dropped four incendiary belly tanks on the Wairopi bridge and thoroughly strafed the surrounding area, following another pair of Airacobras that had attacked the bridge earlier.

That night a single Catalina bombed Buka 'drome, with two 300-pound bombs landing near a taxiway while 20 x 20-pound fragmentation bombs were scattered over the area. Three other Catalinas bombed Buin's airfield and a nearby ship reported as a cruiser which replied with light but inaccurate anti-aircraft fire. A fourth flying boat on the Buin raid experienced engine trouble and returned to Cairns.

Meanwhile by the last week of September No. 100 Squadron had relocated from Victoria to Bohle River airstrip, located eight miles inland from Townsville. This was a newly constructed gravel-surfaced, all-weather airstrip from where the Beauforts undertook anti-submarine patrols and convoy escort duties between Townsville, Port Moresby and Milne Bay. At this time a forward detachment of Beauforts was made ready at Milne Bay for anti-shipping duties.

On 28 September Beaufort A9-89 crashed in a swamp on the south coast of Papua while on a flight between Port Moresby and Milne Bay. The pilot, Squadron Leader Cliff Bernard, navigator Flying Officer Len Ophel and observer Pilot Officer Colin MacDonald were killed. Two other crew members suffered burns and abrasions but survived.

On 3 October No. 100 Squadron launched a daring night attack against the anchorage in the Shortlands which was regularly crowded with Japanese shipping at this time. The distance was in excess of 400 miles. Wing Commander Sam Balmer led ten Beauforts from Gurney Strip at 0100, each lugging a bulky American Mark XIII torpedo.

One of the pilots, Squadron Leader Ralph Wiley, recalled:

> On the way, we encountered a storm, which forced us to open up formation and we lost sight of two of the planes. We arrived in the Shortland Islands area and found the Japanese ships nearer Buin on Bougainville Island. It was a long harbour backed by a mountain range. The moon was obscured by cloud and visibility was poor, but I could see three cruisers and another twenty, or perhaps more, vessels in the harbour. We made a low-level attack and released our torpedo on one of the cruisers. The Japanese were taken completely by surprise and, as we swept across the stern of the cruiser, the ack-ack came too late to worry us. By getting in close to drop the torpedo it is unlikely that we missed our target. However, we did not see any explosion.

The eight Beauforts remaining together had split into two flights of four and made opposite approaches from the east and west. The pilots executed what was considered a successful surprise attack, with torpedoes dropped from 1,000 yards at stationary targets. Despite the feeling that the torpedoes "couldn't miss", no large explosions were observed as the Beaufort pilots took evasive action and fled away at low level.

It was only after the Beauforts had returned to Gurney Strip at around 0800 that it was realised that A9-60 had not returned. This was flown by Flight Lieutenant Donald Stumm who with his three crewmen were missing.

Following debriefing and an analysis of the raid it was believed the American Mark XIII torpedoes were faulty and had run too deep. This had been suspected by many in recent months including USN submarine captains. The faults were subsequently confirmed by various trials in Australia and the US, but the conclusive findings had not been forwarded to No. 100 Squadron prior to their intrepid 3 October Shortlands mission. In addition, it was believed some of the pilots may have released their torpedoes too close to their targets. To remedy this more training and the use of newly developed torpedo sights was recommended.

Later that morning eight Airacobras strafed targets along the Kokoda Track, while three 89th BS A-20As bombed and strafed the same area. Early that afternoon two 38th BG B-25Cs dropped six 500-pound bombs on the Wairopi bridge. Meanwhile a 435th BS B-17 flying a reconnaissance of the Buna-Lae-Finschafen area strafed a suspected enemy camp near the Kumusi River.

That night four Catalinas raided Buka 'drome once again, dropping a mix of 20-, 250- and 300-pound bombs from 6,000-7,000 feet. The bombs were seen to land near the runway, with one aircraft claimed destroyed. A number of fires and explosions were noted. These were tiring missions - after returning to Cairns one of the flying boats had been aloft for in excess of 24 hours.

There were few operations on 4 October, due to persistent cloud in the Papuan valleys despite a moderate overall cloud ceiling. Just one Allied air attack was recorded when eight 7th FS P-40Es strafed targets in the Myola-Kokoda-Buna area, but little activity was seen. Meanwhile nine 30th

A No. 100 Squadron Beaufort departs Gurney Strip, Milne Bay, in a spray of mud. The photo was taken around the time of No. 100 Squadron's daring raid against the Shortlands on 5 October, where a lack of results was subsequently blamed on faulty American Mark XIII torpedoes.

BS B-17Es flew up to Port Moresby from Australia to take over advanced detachment duties from the 63rd BS.

A handful of Japanese sorties were recorded. Two Vals departed Lae early that morning for a weather reconnaissance flight over the Buna area before returning to Rabaul at 0935. At the same time a Tainan *Ku* C5M Babs flew a four-hour reconnaissance flight in the opposite direction from Lakunai.

Also on 4 October an important convoy was despatched from Rabaul to Buna. This consisted of the 6,798-ton IJA transport *Yamaura Maru* escorted by two destroyers. The transport was carrying approximately 10,000 "Forty-day" ration packs which were critically needed by the IJA force in Papua. Accordingly, arrangements were made with the IJN to provide air cover for the convoy. Two *chutai* of Zeros, one from the Tainan *Ku* and one from No. 3 *Ku*, were deployed to Gasmata for this purpose. They provided overlapping patrols throughout the day, although low cloud largely concealed the convoy with the Zeros sometimes unable to find it. The *Yamaura Maru* arrived safely off Buna that evening where the rations alleviated the growing supply shortage.

The following day, 5 October, saw significantly more activity. Soon after dawn three 28th BS B-17Es dropped 20 x 300-pound bombs over Lakunai but couldn't observe the results due to bad weather. They were followed five minutes later by six 30th BS Fortresses which attacked Vunakanau with 59 x 300-pound bombs. Two other bombers lost contact with this formation on approach to the area.

However, the six Fortresses soon found themselves under attack by an estimated 25 Zeros. In fact, they encountered three separate formations of fighters. The first was a Tainan *Ku chutai* which was already in the air when the Fortresses arrived, diverting from an original intention to patrol over Buna. A second contingent was a mixed formation of five Tainan *Ku* Zeros joined with a pair from No. 3 *Ku*. The third formation was a *chutai* of seven No. 6 *Ku* Zeros.

Although the Fortresses were partly concealed by cloud, they experienced determined attacks from the Zeros over a period of 50 minutes. Major John Rouse's bombardier in B-17F 41-24403 *Blitz Buggy* recalled:

> Being in the lead of the formation we were their prime target. They made many frontal attacks on us with their small calibre machine guns and explosive cannon shells. We were badly shot up.

In fact, all six of the bombers were hit. First Lieutenant Earl Hageman's unnamed B-17E 41-9196 had an engine knocked out which was feathered and another was seen to smoke. The bomber dropped from the formation and was last seen entering cloud with Zeros in pursuit. Hageman and his eight crewmen still remain Missing in Action.

Hageman's Fortress was the only one lost although all of the other five were badly shot up, three of which suffered damaged engines. They were lucky to touch down safely at Seven-Mile by midday, all dangerously low on fuel after also battling bad weather on the return flight. One crewman, Australian navigator Flying Officer Allan Davenport was mortally wounded, dying in a Port Moresby hospital soon after returning to base. Two other crewmen were wounded. During the engagement the B-17 gunners claimed to have downed four Zeros: none were lost but four received hits.

On this same morning the *chutai* of nine Tainan *Ku* Zeros at Gasmata, led by Lieutenant Ono Takeyoshi, were aloft at 0615 to protect *Yamaura Maru* and the two destroyers which had just departed Buna. After a brief skirmish with four P-39s, the Japanese pilots pounced on two incoming B-25 Mitchells.

The Mitchells were a pair from the 405th BS flying an armed reconnaissance mission. At their mission briefing they were told that if they failed to find any shipping, they were to strafe targets of opportunity near Wairopi, bomb the bridge itself and on the way home drop medical supplies to Australian troops fighting the Japanese. They had just missed a rendezvous with their planned escort of four Airacobras, because the American fighters were busy skirmishing with the Zeros as mentioned above. The B-25s were *Battlin' Biffy* flown by Lieutenant Terrence Carey and *Tokyo Sleeper* flown by Captain William Brandon.

After conferring by radio, the two American pilots bravely decided to attack the *Yamaura Maru* which they found about 15 miles north of Buna. After dropping four 300-pound bombs which narrowly missed the transport, the two B-25s dived for sea level during which Brandon reached a top speed in excess of 400 miles per hour. Aided by the defensive fire of his upper turret, Brandon was able to outpace his pursuers which eventually broke off to return to their main convoy protection task.

Carey, however, was not so lucky with *Battlin' Biffy* shot down by Zeros and crashing near Japanese occupied territory in Papua. Most of the crew perished in the crash. Three crew survived but Carey was beheaded by a native, angry at Allied air attacks on his village. Eyewitnesses saw the other two executed by Japanese soldiers.

Meanwhile five No. 3 *Ku* Zeros led by FPO1c Iwamoto Rokuzo had launched from Gasmata to assume convoy protection duty. These encountered five more 38th BG B-25s which had launched from 14-Mile (Laloki) in response to the radio calls from Carey and Brandon. As the Mitchells made their bombing approach on descent from 10,000 feet, they spotted the Zeros climbing to intercept and wisely jettisoned their bombs and adopted a tight defensive formation.

A hard-fought running engagement subsequently unfolded, with the Zeros expending 570 x 20mm and 3,100 x 7.7mm rounds. One of the B-25s received 30 bullet hits, although the damage was repairable. Despite ambitious claims by the Mitchell gunners of seven Zeros downed, there were no Japanese losses.

Also that morning, nine No. 30 Squadron Beaufighters from Wards (Five-Mile) and six 93rd BS B-17s from Durand (17-Mile) were out hunting for the ships, but they encountered a cloud base of only 500 feet over the ocean and nothing was seen. However, the B-17s found Buna clear and took the opportunity to unload 30 x 500-pound bombs over an anti-aircraft position at the airfield. The bombing was accurate as a 5th Sasebo SNLF detachment reported losing all of its 13mm ammunition, a store of petrol and a wooden accommodation building during the raid.

At 1555 that afternoon a single 89th BS A-20A strafed barges at Sanananda Point, followed by seven more A-20As an hour later which strafed the same target and unloaded a mix of 20- and 100-pound bombs. That night three Catalinas raided Buka with bombs landing near the runway and among a stores dump area. Another Catalina made a lone raid on Buin, dropping 20- and 250-pound bombs and strafing with 400 rounds of 0.303-inch machine gun fire.

The sole remaining Tainan *Ku* Irving was active on 5 October, flying a six-hour reconnaissance over Papua, including Milne Bay, before returning over the Trobriand Islands to Rabaul.

Bad weather on 6 October saw a respite in Allied attacks, although Allied aircraft had been busy at a new location with a major airlift of troops. This was in connection with two new initiatives by Allied commanders that intertwined. The first was the obvious wish by MacArthur to outflank the IJA force in the Owen Stanleys, and the second was the development of an airfield on the northern side of the same mountain range.

Back in June an RAAF Hudson had made an emergency landing on a flat grassed area at Wanigela Mission on the north coast of Papua, roughly midway between Buna and Milne Bay. With the aid of local natives, a runway was quickly cleared which enabled another Hudson to land with fuel drums, after which both planes flew out. A month later the pilot involved, Pilot Officer Lex Halliday, flew three senior Australian and US officers back to the site to assess it for future development. However, these plans were side-lined following by the Japanese landings at Buna and Milne Bay.

However, Kenney had been intrigued by the location as he appreciated the advantage of an

B-25C Tokyo Sleeper at Hawaii while en route to Australia. One of the original 38th BG Mitchells, pilot Lieutenant Robert Herry chose the name to reflect a First-Class sleeper train ticket to Tokyo. This Mitchell became one of the longest serving in the theatre, and narrowly avoided being shot down by Zeros after attacking the Yamaura Maru on 5 October.

airfield on the northern side of the Owen Stanleys. By late September the idea of developing this site had merged with MacArthur's wish to outflank the Japanese Buna-Kokoda axis from the east. The recent quick and safe airlift of American troops into Port Moresby had convinced MacArthur to back the idea of occupying Wanigela by air, especially as any overland movements in the mountainous, jungle-clad terrain were beset with numerous difficulties.

Two Hudson night flights brought in a small party of engineers to Wanigela where, with the aid of natives, they burnt off kunai grass and cleared a larger runway. Then over the two-day period of 5-6 October, the 21st TCS flew some 60 sorties to deliver Hatforce to the location, a unit comprising the Australian 2/10th Infantry Battalion from Milne Bay alongside US engineers and anti-aircraft troops with 0.50-inch machine guns from Port Moresby. This was the first large-scale operational movement of ground troops by air in the theatre.

Meanwhile, on 6 October American troops began a slow march over the mountains. This was the 2nd Battalion of the 126th Regiment which embarked on a route parallel to the Kokoda Track but further east via Jaure. However, the progress of these troops was very slow and arduous, and even the resupply of the battalion by air proved difficult. These challenges would soon contribute to the decision to bring in further troops to Wanigela by air.

At this time the Japanese were rushing significant aerial reinforcements to Buka from where they could protect nearby shipping including at the Shortlands anchorage. As noted at the end of the last chapter, 21 No. 2 *Ku* Zeros had arrived at Buka on 28 September. On 6 October they were joined by another 23 Zeros from the Tainan *Ku*, led to Buka by the experienced Lieutenant Kawai Shiro.

However, even greater numbers of Zeros were destined for Bougainville. When a first contingent of 18 No. 6 *Ku* Model 32 Zeros had arrived at Lakunai in late August, the bulk of the unit been left behind in Japan to continue with training, led by firebrand Lieutenant Miyano Zenjiro. On the last day of September at Yokosuka, Miyano supervised the loading of three complete *chutai* of 27 Model 21 and Model 32 Zeros aboard the carrier *Zuiho*. These were subsequently flown off the carrier south of Truk for the long flight to Kavieng and then Rabaul, where they touched down on 7 October.

At 11th Air Fleet Headquarters at Rabaul, staff officers were preparing a comprehensive brief for Miyano. Upon arrival he would be ordered to prepare to conduct operations from the new airfield at Buin. Miyano's Zeros would operate alongside the newly arrived No. 31 *Ku* D3A2 Val dive-bombers.

Miyano was quick to get his contingent operational. On the morning of 8 October he led all 27 Zeros on a familiarisation flight over Rabaul, before leading them all to Buka on the same day. Now there was an impressive group of 61 Zeros at Buka from three different *kokutai*. These flew protective patrols over nearby shipping lanes and the Shortlands while they waited for Buin to become operational. This deployment meant a big portion of Rabaul's fighter strength was now almost wholly devoted to the Solomons theatre.

As these moves were taking place there were only a handful of Allied sorties on 7 October. Three 89th BS A-20As attacked the Buna-Kokoda area while two No. 30 Squadron Beaufighters from Milne Bay strafed buildings and huts at Kilia Mission on Goodenough Island. That morning three 405th BS B-25Cs reconnoitred the coast from Buna eastwards to Oro Bay. Such missions were now commonplace given the need to watch the approaches to Wanigela.

Poor weather also restricted Allied operations on the following day, 8 October, when no attack missions were launched in the morning. However early that afternoon three 13th and 90th BS B-25Ds flew an armed reconnaissance over Buna and dropped 15 x 500-pound bombs. These were among fifteen B-25s that had flown up to Port Moresby from Charters Towers the previous day. Just over an hour later three 89th BS A-20As made low-level passes over the Kokoda Track, which was bombed and strafed but no activity was observed.

The afternoon also saw a large force of B-17s concentrate at Port Moresby after arriving from Mareeba. Kenney had once again been told to apply maximum pressure on Rabaul in relation to another important operation in the SoPAC theatre. This was the landing of US Army troops on Guadalcanal to help relieve the First Marine Division. These troops were embarked from New Caledonia on 8 October and landed five days later.

That night five RAAF Catalinas raided Rabaul, dropping a mix of 250- and 500-pound general purpose bombs together with dozens of small fragmentation and incendiary bombs. Many

33rd BS B-26 Shittenengitten 40-1404 which had moved to its new base at Iron Range in late September 1942.

fires were started, and it was considered that the target was well "lit up" for the large B-17 raid which followed. Intense and heavy anti-aircraft fire was encountered from a ship and positions around the harbour perimeter. Six searchlights were also active. At the same time a sixth Catalina made a lone attack on Buka.

In the early hours of 9 October an impressive force of 30 Fortresses departed Port Moresby, the largest force of heavy bombers yet mustered in the theatre. These were a mix of machines from the Headquarters Squadron of the 19th BG as well as the 28th, 93rd and 63rd Bombardment Squadrons. After one bomber returned to base with mechanical trouble, the other 29 bombed the Rabaul town area from differing altitudes of between 4,500 – 11,000 feet in an attempt to confuse the defences. Intense anti-aircraft fire was experienced, as reported by Lieutenant James Murphy in B-17F *Pluto*:

> At 6,000 feet every searchlight in the place picked us up, and I believe every anti-aircraft battery also fired at us. With the searchlights totally blinding us except for lights in the cockpit, there was nothing else I could do except stay fixed on the instruments to fly the B-17.

However, Murphy's co-pilot panicked and grabbed the controls to commence evasive action:

> I said "You son of a bitch, get off!" … he came around almost immediately and stopped trying to take over control, and we were able to finish our bomb run and then get out of the searchlights and the anti-aircraft fire.

Parts of the town were reportedly levelled as a total of 90 x 500-pound and 207 x 300-pound bombs were unloaded. Small incendiaries were also dropped, with many fires reported including a very large one that was visible for 80 miles. In addition, Fortress gunners fired 11,400 x 0.50-inch rounds at anti-aircraft guns and searchlights. Most of the bombers received light shrapnel damage although all returned to base.

This was the first time such a large-scale raid had been launched against Rabaul itself rather than the harbour or airfields. The next day Tokyo Rose – the English-language radio propaganda broadcaster - reproved the morality of the raid, even alleging that 50 *geisha* girls lodged at the Rabaul Hotel had been killed.

At Lakunai airfield on 8 October 1942 Vice Admiral Kusaka Jinichi (left) in dress uniform walks towards the ceremonial dais where Vice Admiral Tsukahara Nishizo (right) in working IJN uniform will hand over command of the 11th Air Fleet. In the distant middle with half step is Vice Admiral Yamagata Seigo, commander of the 26th Air Flotilla.

Lieutenant Charles Mayo (left) poses with two 89th BS gunners in front of A-20A Maid in Japan 40-139 at Kila 'drome.

After daylight broke a 435th BS B-17 was over Rabaul at 27,000 feet to photograph the results of the raid. This was B-17E 41-9207 *Texas #6* flown by First Lieutenant Arnold Johnson, and it was intercepted by seven Tainan *Ku* Zeros which scrambled from Lakunai at 0800. During several attacking passes, the tail gunner, Corporal Ralph Fritz, was killed and the Australian co-pilot, Sergeant David Sinclair was wounded.

The sturdy bomber was badly shot up but continued flying, although Johnson had to shut down and feather the outer starboard engine. On approach to Townsville the other starboard engine went dead, but a safe landing was made.

The morning of 9 October saw a concerted attack against Lae airfield by nine No. 30 Squadron Beaufighters and 14 B-25s from the 13th and 90th Bombardment Squadrons. Coming in under a low cloud base of only 1,500 feet, the area was bombed and strafed. Heavy anti-aircraft fire was experienced but the crews observed no enemy aircraft present and that the runway appeared neglected. Fighter cover for the raid was provided by Airacobras of the 35th Fighter Group.

That night six Catalinas were again over Rabaul as Kenney had ordered a repeat raid by the B-17s. In conditions of good visibility, a mix of bombs was dropped included a large number of incendiaries, leaving many fires. Heavy anti-aircraft fire was experienced and nine searchlights were active.

The follow-up B-17 raid comprised 21 bombers, although one aircraft accidentally salved its bombs. The remaining 20 Fortresses unloaded 64 x 500-pound and 126 x 300-pound bombs over Rabaul township and Lakunai, together with 38 clusters of incendiaries. Once again heavy anti-aircraft fire was experienced. Some B-17s took violent evasive action, but all returned safely to Port Moresby and the raid was considered a success.

Not wanting to keep such a large concentration of heavy bombers as a ready target at Port Moresby, all were flown to Mareeba after refuelling. The crews were then granted three days leave in Cairns.

Other Allied activity on 10 October was modest. Three 89th BS A-20As attacked targets in the Kokoda-Buna area, while six 13th and 90th BS B-25s searched for a ship reported to be off Buna. They bombed a camouflaged object at the mouth of the Mambare River, thought to be a ship, and the Wairopi bridge. Meanwhile, at Horn Island 405th BS B-25D *Mississippi Rebel* crashed during a hurried take-off following a false air-raid alarm.

IJN sailors wave to a No. 2 Ku D3A1 Val from a destroyer near New Britain as the aircraft heads back to Rabaul.

CHAPTER 7

MOUNTAIN WARFARE: 11 – 20 OCTOBER

Since late September Australian forces had been advancing and probing cautiously forward along the mountain trails. During this period the Japanese rear guard, known as the Stanley Detachment, was busy constructing three lines of fortified positions between Myola and the village of Eora.

Elements of the Australian 7th Division reoccupied Myola which allowed airdrops to recommence on 11 October, although on this date one pilot reported being fired on by a light machine gun from the outer Japanese positions on an overlooking ridge. Over the next three days the Australians pushed forward on two separate axes, forcing the Japanese commander to order a withdrawal over fears of being outflanked.

Some 800 Japanese troops now occupied their main defensive position at a creek crossing known as Templeton's Two. They were outnumbered by over 3,000 Australians, most of which were directly involved in some hard fighting during 17-20 October. After a flanking movement to occupy the high ground, a final Australian assault was successful and forced a Japanese withdrawal to their third defended line at Eora. This fighting since 12 October had cost 69 Australians and 66 Japanese killed, with many more wounded on both sides.

As described in the previous chapter, the overland advance by the 2nd Battalion of the 126th Regiment to the east had been extremely slow and difficult. The objective of Jaure was not reached until 20 October. Largely because of this, a further airlift of troops to Wanigela was conducted during 14-18 October. These troops consisted of the 2nd and 3rd Battalions of the 128th Regiment as well as Australian commandos of the 2/6th Independent Company.

The development of Wanigela had been done so smoothly and efficiently that enquiries were made about other similar locations nearby. A site to the southwest of Wanigela was quickly cleared with the assistance of a missionary, Cecil Abels, and became known as Abels Field. The first C-47 landed at this airstrip on 19 October. Two other grassy airstrips nearby were soon also cleared.

With so many troops moving forward in Papua a significant increase in air transport capacity was needed, and to assist with this the 22nd Troop Carrier Squadron made the welcome move north from Essendon in Victoria to Townsville on 11 October. Meanwhile, Kenney had requested two additional troop carrier squadrons from the US, and the first of these, the 6th TCS, arrived at Port Moresby on 13 October with a strength of 13 C-47s. This was the biggest boost in air transport capacity the SWPA had received since the influx of refugee aircraft from Java back in March.

The second unit, the 33rd TCS, departed California on 18 October but did not have a smooth journey to Australia. Such was the critical need for transport pilots that several staff sergeants fresh from advanced training were rated as pilots but without the administrative and qualification paperwork (until then all USAAF pilots were officers). On arrival in Fiji one of the sergeants was mistakenly arrested for being an enlisted man attempting to fly a C-47 to Australia.

This issue was soon sorted out, but on arrival in New Caledonia on 25 October six 33rd TCS C-47s were directed to remain and assist with the resupply of Guadalcanal. These aircraft did not arrive in the SWPA until December. Meanwhile the other seven C-47s began operations from Brisbane and Cairns in late October.

However, even the transport capacity provided by these two squadrons would barely be enough to support all of the forces then concentrating in the north of Papua. Instead, it was planned to develop a coastal supply route to Wanigela using luggers and other small vessels from Milne Bay. These were small enough to safely navigate the uncharted shoal-ridden waters of the area and would hopefully avoid enemy attention, in a similar fashion to the Japanese use of barges for coastal transport.

For the past few weeks the Hudsons of No. 6 Squadron, RAAF, had been busy flying reconnaissance missions from its main base at Horn Island, with an advanced detachment operating from Milne Bay. The unit had a strength of 491 men and 18 bombers. In early October the squadron began preparing for a move to Wards 'drome, where it became operational on 11 October.

On this same date, in the early hours Flight Lieutenant L Manning, in A16-244, was one of a trio of Hudsons that had departed Milne Bay for a search of the waters near Rabaul. In St George's Channel, just north of Buka, Manning came upon what he identified as a 10,000-ton transport carrying a deck cargo of at 12 Zeros, escorted by a destroyer.

This was the auxiliary seaplane tender *Kiyokawa Maru* that in recent months had been increasingly utilised as a transport. On this voyage the ship was carrying twelve Rufe fighters from Japan to the Shortlands for use by the No. 14 *Ku* fighter wing. The main portion of No. 14 *Ku* operated flying boats in the Marshall Islands, although these were also regular visitors to the South Seas on transport flights. Also, a detachment of three No. 14 *Ku* Mavises had arrived in Rabaul on 8 October where they would be based as well as the Shortlands.

Manning dropped four 250-pound bombs on the ship from only 1,000 feet. Two of these were direct hits, with the ship swinging around in a 180-degree turn as it took evasive action. Dense smoke was then seen to rise from the decks, before the ship stopped and was rendered help from a destroyer. Two of the Rufes secured on the deck were destroyed in this attack, and the *Kiyokawa Maru* sustained damage to its engine room. However, it was soon able to get underway and continue on its voyage to the island of Poporang in the Shortlands where it unloaded the remainder of the Rufes the following day. The ship then returned to Rabaul where it was repaired by the repair ship *Hakkai Maru*.

On 11 October three 89th BS A-20s conducted an armed reconnaissance of the Kokoda-Buna area with an escort of eight Airacobras. Barges at Sanananda Point were strafed, and 80 x 20-pound bombs were dropped on a village near Wairopi.

Commandos of the 2/6th Independent Company unload from a USAAF C-47 at the newly cleared Wanigela airstrip in mid-October. The transport was named Maxine and belonged to the 6th TCS. It and was lost in a crash on 16 October, likely just a day or two after this photograph was taken.

The 6th TCS crew of C-47 41-18673 Dear Mom at Wards 'drome. The 6th TCS arrived in Port Moresby on 13 October and provided a welcome boost to Fifth Air Force transport capability.

Meanwhile Buin had finally been declared operational and on this date nine Tainan *Ku* Zeros were the first aircraft to land there, on return from a bomber escort mission over Guadalcanal.

The morning of 12 October once again saw three 89th BS A-20s, escorted by seven Airacobras, sweep over the Kokoda-Buna area at 2,000 feet. No activity was noted, and bombs were dropped on a village. An hour later three 13th and 405th BS B-25s flew a reconnaissance over the waters between the Buna-Lae coast and New Britain with three 500-pound bombs unloaded over anti-aircraft positions at Buna airfield. A similar mission by another three B-25s that afternoon met poor weather, although two 500-pound bombs were dropped on Wairopi.

The day also saw the arrival of a new player in the theatre. The seaplane tender *Sanuki Maru* dropped anchor in Rabaul harbour carrying ten Japanese Army Air Force Dinah reconnaissance aircraft as deck cargo. Further information on this deployment is provided in Chapter 9.

That night six Nos. 11 and 20 Squadron Catalinas from Cairns dropped a mix of bombs over the runway and aircraft dispersal area at Buka. Amid thick cloud and poor visibility, one large and several small explosions were noted. This raid accounted for the life of No. 6 *Ku* Zero pilot Warrant Officer Mitsuma Hirai on the ground and may have been more successful than the RAAF crews had thought as a Japanese report records the loss of ten aircraft on this date. Unfortunately, the report does not specify aircraft types or location.

Shortly after 0400 on 13 October another Fortress raid targeted Vunakanau and Lakunai. This consisted of 18 Fortresses from the 28th, 30th and 93rd Bombardment Squadrons which dropped a total of 6 x 1,000-, 20 x 500- and 154 x 300-pound bombs from heights of 6,000 to 9,000 feet. It was felt that the results were mediocre as there were problems dropping the targeting flares. One of the B-17s could not find the target and bombed Buna instead.

Later that morning three No. 30 Squadron Beaufighters flew an armed reconnaissance over the Kokoda-Buna area escorted by seven 35th FG Airacobras. Observations of Buna airfield recorded nil activity and dummy aircraft present in dispersal bays. Three "possibly serviceable" barges were strafed at Sanananda Point. On the outward flight Beaufighter A19-68 hit a mountain near Kokoda and burst into flames, with the loss of both of the crew: pilot Sergeant T Butterfield and the observer Sergeant R Wilson.

Meanwhile intelligence sources had indicated the possibility of another imminent attempt to retrieve the stranded SNLF marines on Goodenough Island. Accordingly, on 13 October three Beaufighters from Milne Bay strafed Kilia Mission, supported by 36th FS Airacobras. At 1830 that night the submarine *I-1* surfaced off Goodenough Island and launched its barge in another attempt to rescue the marines.

Two No. 6 Squadron Hudsons had been patrolling the area with one of them still present during the evening when a light was spotted on a beach. After dropping a stick of bombs inland from the light and also releasing illumination flares, nothing further was sighted. However, the activity had the desired effect, as the captain of *I-1* believed his mission was compromised and crash-dived. The *I-1* then departed the area, leaving its barge behind.

The deck of Kamikawa Maru in late October 1942 with eleven Rufes and two Petes aboard bound for the Shortland Islands. The nearest Rufe has red tail code YII-105. A sister ship, the Kiyokawa Maru, was attacked by a No. 6 Squadron Hudson south of Rabaul on 11 October whilst also ferrying Rufes to the Shortlands.

Zeros lined up on Buin's newly completed runway, which became operational on 11 October. Much of Rabaul's fighter strength was soon flying missions over the Solomons from the site.

Dawn on 14 October saw three Beaufighters strafing huts on Goodenough Island where the stranded SNLF marines were suspected of hiding. Some 700 x 200mm and 4,000 x 0.303-inch rounds were expended. A No. 6 Squadron Hudson was then active over the island taking photographs at the request of the army in preparation for an upcoming operation to eradicate the Japanese presence.

Other Allied air activity on 14 October was modest. That morning a 13th BS B-25 flying an armed reconnaissance mission dropped a 500-pound bomb on Wairopi, while late that afternoon another two Mitchells from the same unit flew another reconnaissance mission. After reporting that the runways at Salamaua and Lae appeared unusable, two 500-pound bombs were unloaded over Lae.

By mid-October the 63rd BS at Mareeba had achieved a reasonable level of combat efficiency with its B-17Es, but the other three Fortress units of the 43rd BG, the 64th, 65th and 403rd Bombardment Squadrons, had yet to fly any operations. Between 12 and 17 October these three squadrons relocated to Iron Range where the primitive tropical conditions were a big change from their previous dusty outback bases at Torrens Creek and Fenton. By this time some crews of the 64th and 403rd Bombardment Squadrons had received combat experience by flying with the 63rd BS. The 65th BS, however, was the least advanced of the group and had still not received any aircraft or crews: it consisted only of ground personnel.

At this time the Japanese were running a major reinforcement convoy to Guadalcanal, and Henderson Field was heavily bombed by IJN warships for three nights in a row between 13-15 October. It was hoped that there would be an opportunity for Fifth Air Force Fortresses to strike at Japanese shipping concentrated in the Shortlands, which was being used as a rendezvous and safe anchorage. This target was beyond the range of the SBD dive-bombers based at Henderson Field.

At 0440 on 15 October five 63rd BS B-17s departed Mareeba to be at Seven-Mile at dawn. These were followed by three more Fortresses around three hours later, and six of the bombers were soon off on armed reconnaissance flights to the Shortlands area. That afternoon Captain Kenneth McCullar in B-17F 41-24521 *Black Jack* (named because the serial number ended in "21", a winning hand in the namesake card game) came upon what was identified as a light cruiser in the Solomon Sea. It was attacked from only 1,500 feet with 4 x 500-pound bombs, and two bombs exploded close on either side of the ship. McCullar's crew believed they had sunk a light cruiser, but no ship was sunk, and the identity of the vessel attacked remains unconfirmed: it was likely a destroyer instead. Amid heavy anti-aircraft fire, *Black Jack* received a hole in an aileron. Also on this afternoon, another of the 63rd BS B-17s attacked a destroyer.

Over Papua Allied air activity was again modest. At 0830 three 89th BS A-20As escorted by seven Airacobras searched the Kokoda Track northwards from Templeton's Crossing but did not see signs of enemy activity. Later in the morning a trio of 13th BS Mitchells flew a similar mission and dropped their bombs on Wairopi.

Meanwhile in Australia Kenney attended lengthy parades of the 19th BG at Townsville and

A Rufe floatplane prepares to leave on a sortie with a 60-kilogram bomb visible under the starboard wing. The type was regularly encountered by B-17 crews in the Shortlands area who often misreported them as Zeros.

Mareeba where he handed out over 250 awards. Some crews had been in continuous combat for many months and the parades heightened rumours of an imminent return to the US. Kenney recalled with typical hyperbole:

> By the time I got through I had worn most of the skin off my thumb and forefinger of my right hand. It was a great show.

At 0730 on 16 October the regular morning patrol of three 89th BS A-20As was over the Kokoda area, and bombed bridges over the Kumusi River. Three 38th BG B-25s flew a reconnaissance of the waters between Papua and New Britain, but nothing was seen and on the return flight villages were bombed near enemy supply routes. Meanwhile 63rd BS Fortresses were ship hunting in the same area as the previous day, and a 10,000-ton transport was attacked and straddled with 500-pound bombs.

Also on 16 October the newly arrived 6th TCS sustained its first serious accident. The squadron was airdropping supplies to the Australian army in the Owen Stanleys, when C-47 41-18585 *Maxine* crashed into the jungle during a low-level drop near the village of Kagi on the Kokoda Track. The pilot, Second Lieutenant Wilson Cater, and two crewmen were killed.

At 0100 on 17 October five Catalinas raided Buna with their usual mix of ordnance. The bombs landed on the runway and amid dispersal bays and started many small fires and eight large ones which were visible for 50 miles. The crews considered this raid to be the best yet mounted against this target.

The increase in Japanese ship activity around southern Bougainville saw more B-17s from the 19th BG fly up to Port Moresby. At 0400 on 17 October seven 93rd BS Fortresses bombed the newly completed airfield at Buin for the first time. The 63rd BS was ship hunting for the third day in a row, with three B-17s searching towards the Shortlands area. At 0700 McCullar's crew bombed a ship entering Faisi harbour and claimed near misses. They expected Zeros to intercept as Buin was only 30 miles away, but no enemy aircraft were encountered. Another B-17 on a reconnaissance flight bombed a suspect aircraft carrier in Rabaul harbour.

Later that afternoon, in the only Allied air attack recorded over Papua on 17 October, three 13th BS B-25s on a reconnaissance flight dropped their bombs on a track near Salamaua.

As noted above, ten Rufes had recently been delivered to No. 14 *Ku* in the Shortlands by the *Kiyokawa Maru* where they served alongside other floatplanes, including *Kamikawa Maru* Jakes and Rufes. These aircraft had in recent days fought a number of running battles with Guadalcanal-based Fortresses, with one such battle resulting in the death of a No. 14 *Ku shotaicho* pilot. However, by 17 October a dozen Rufes and eight Jakes had been forward deployed to Rekata Bay in the Solomons, which was much closer to Guadalcanal.

This meant that by the morning of 18 October the number of floatplanes defending the Shortlands had been significantly reduced, a morning which saw another Fifth Air Force Fortress strike against Buin and ships in the nearby anchorage. These attacked in three waves. First to the target at 0335 were nine 93rd BS B-17s which dropped 44 x 500-pound bombs. They were followed 90 minutes later by six 30th BS Fortresses which unloaded a dozen large 1,000-pound bombs. Although three of these failed to explode, a cruiser was claimed as damaged.

Last on the scene were five 63rd BS B-17s which dropped four 1,000- and 14 x 500-pound bombs and claimed multiple near misses on ships. These aircraft were attacked by "Zeros" while in their attack runs. These were in fact a pair of *Kamikawa Maru* Rufes already on patrol. McCullar and his co-pilot Harry Staley saw an attack coming from head on, with four streams of tracer seemingly headed directly for their cockpit but missing. This was indicative of cautious pilots maintaining their distance from the firepower of the comparatively huge bombers, and thus opening fire from afar. McCullar responded by diving to sea level and racing away at maximum speed. The Rufes did not pursue but remained circling to continue their patrol.

Two other 63rd BS Fortresses piloted by Captain Ed Scott and Bill Thompson were flying a sea search mission when they approached the Shortlands and saw five Mavis flying boats and eight floatplanes moored below. Whilst the Americans were confident that blasts from their bombs destroyed or damaged several of these aircraft, none were destroyed although some may have received light damage.

Also on the morning of 18 October three 13th BS B-25s were flying a regular reconnaissance of the northern Papuan coast when one of the Mitchells saw a small ship to the east of Buna which they attacked with two bombs and machine guns. Unfortunately, this was a friendly vessel, one of two

20-ton luggers being used to ferry American troops and supplies from Wanigela to a new forward position at Pongani. There were several casualties, and the lugger was extensively damaged.

A wounded American serviceman is brought ashore following the incident on 18 October when a pair of B-25s attacked two luggers containing Allied troops. Note the native canoe in the background used for transport from ship to shore.

That afternoon a B-17 on a reconnaissance mission descended to 2,000-feet to strafe four schooners seen near Manus Island. Another Fortress on a reconnaissance mission bombed a twin float equipped aircraft moored near Pilelo Island, which was on the southern coast of New Britain westwards from Gasmata. Suspected troop positions inland of Salamaua near the village of Mubo were also bombed and strafed.

Despite the fighting in deep in the Owen Stanleys reaching a climax on 19 and 20 October, the mountainous conditions meant Allied aircraft could not offer direct support, save for supply dropping missions, weather permitting. As a result, no Allied daylight air attacks were recorded on these two days.

On 19 October all available Catalinas were ordered to attack shipping in the Shortlands area. In one of the strongest raids to date, four flying boats from No. 11 Squadron and three from No. 20 Squadron struck just after midnight on 19/20 October. Both Buin airfield and ships were attacked with a total of 53 x 250- and 500-pound bombs. A near miss was claimed on one transport, with anti-aircraft fire and searchlights experienced both from the ships and land positions. The transport was possibly the seaplane tender *Kamikawa Maru* which was at Buin on this date.

A No. 751 Ku Model 21 Zero, still sporting Kanoya Ku markings, intercepts a B-17E over Rabaul in late October.

CHAPTER 8

IJA DEFEAT IN THE MOUNTAINS: 21 – 31 OCTOBER

Following the Japanese defeat at Templeton's Two on 20 October, the commander of the Stanley Detachment had withdrawn his forces to the third defence line at the village of Eora. This was done in some disorder and fearing a complete collapse, Horii ordered anyone available to rush forward and man the defence line. Almost 500 men from multiple units who were resting on the northern section of the Kokoda Track answered the call and joined the subsequent battle between 22 – 27 October.

Meanwhile the commander of the 7th Division, Major General Arthur "Tubby" Allen, had been facing considerable pressure from MacArthur and Blamey about his overly cautious advance. This criticism was not without foundation, as in almost a full month since advancing from Imita Ridge, Allen's force had progressed at an average rate of not much more than a mile per day, and most of this advance had been unopposed.

Spurred to achieve quick results, Allen launched an unimaginative frontal assault against Eora on 22 October. During three days of fighting this was repulsed with heavy losses to the Australians. Further criticism came from Blamey on 26 October:

> … progress has been negligible against an enemy much fewer in number … in spite of your superior strength enemy appears to be able to delay advance at will.

Finally on 28 October the Australians moved into Eora, routing the 3rd Battalion of the 144th Infantry Regiment as they did so. The victory did not prevent Allen from being relieved of his command on 29 October, another controversy that lingers to the present day. He was replaced by Major General George Vasey.

However once again the long shadow of events in the Solomons lay over Papua. On 24-25 October newly reinforced IJA formations had failed in their attempt to overrun Henderson Field, while at the same time the Battle of the Santa Cruz Islands took place. This was a major naval engagement where both sides' carrier forces suffered heavy losses (the USS *Hornet* was sunk). The damaged Japanese carriers retreated and would no longer play a significant role in the campaign, putting an even heavier weight on the shoulders of Rabaul's land-based air power.

A consequence of these combined setbacks was that Horii could expect no reinforcements of any kind, and he was ordered to withdraw the Stanley Detachment out of the mountains to the Kumusi River. This withdrawal began on the same day as the final Australian attack at Eora. During the fighting in the week to 29 October the Australians had lost 72 killed, mainly during the initial failed assault. In comparison the Japanese lost 64 killed, half of them on the last day.

While the bulk of the Allied advance to Buna was across the mountains, a smaller force was approaching from Wanigela in the east. As noted in the previous chapter, the Australian commandos of the 2/6th Independent Company had been flown to Wanigela in mid-October, and these men immediately marched westwards along the coast to Pongani. However soon after they departed flooded rivers blocked the American 128th Regiment which was following. The American troops instead were ferried along the coast in two luggers, one of which was attacked by a B-25 in the friendly fire incident of 18 October. An airstrip was quickly cleared at Pongani, which was soon used to fly in further American troops. This was a daring initiative made right under the noses of the enemy as Pongani was only about 25 miles from Buna.

On 21 October no Allied attack missions from Port Moresby were recorded, except that three B-25s flying a routine reconnaissance strafed a small boat. That afternoon seven Catalinas departed Cairns to raid the Shortlands, encountering heavy electrical storms on the way. All aircraft reached the target area where 16 ships were seen, some of them believed to be heavy cruisers and battleships (but which were in fact destroyers). In an anti-shipping role, the flying boats dropped 28 x 250- and 19 x 500-pound semi armoured piercing bombs but failed to record any hits. Heavy anti-aircraft fire was encountered and two of the Catalinas received slight damage.

Weather was so bad over the mountains on 22 October that no missions could be launched to support the Australian troops assaulting Eora, and even the regular reconnaissance flights were cancelled. Surprisingly, a Lockheed Lodestar managed to land at Myola, the first aircraft to do so. The aircraft took off with no load and only just enough fuel to return to Port Moresby, but even that was very risky as one of the propellers was damaged after striking a tree

As well as being a centre for supply drops, Myola had become a central point for the treatment of Australian Army wounded. Efforts were underway to clear a runway and it was hoped that wounded could soon be flown directly from Myola to Port Moresby, saving four days of arduous stretcher travel over the Kokoda Track.

At 1500 that afternoon nine 63rd BS B-17s arrived at Seven-Mile from Mareeba. They were prepared for a mission, but heavy rain had made the runway too soft for fully loaded Fortresses to use.

During the day the 2/12th Battalion was embarked from Milne Bay on the destroyers HMAS *Stuart* and HMAS *Arunta*. That night the men landed at two separate positions on Goodenough Island to advance on the marooned SNLF marines known to be camped in the vicinity of Kilia Mission. However, the Japanese were prepared for the attack, and managed to repulse the Australians during two days of fighting in thick jungle.

On the afternoon of 22 October four Bettys departed Kavieng for a night raid against Port Moresby, ending a month-long period during which the Papuan capital had not been attacked. The bombers were from the newly renamed No. 751 *Kokutai* (formerly the Kanoya *Ku*; exceptionally, this unit was redesignated a month before the complete administrative restructure of the IJN air units on 1 November which saw all IJN aerial units renamed with three-digit numbers, as described in

The first airstrip at Pongani was cleared in late October and was quickly in use. Seen here are boxes of ammunition being unloaded from C-60 VHCAA (a former Dutch Lodestar).

Fifth Air Force transport capacity received a further boost in late October with the arrival of half of the 33rd TCS (the other half was held up by SoPAC). Here 33rd TCS C-47s line up to depart from Wards 'drome.

Chapter 9). This was also the first raid from Kavieng against Port Moresby, adding 200 miles to the journey as compared to flying from Vunakanau. For this reason, the bomb load was reduced from 12 down to 10 x 60-kilogram bombs per aircraft.

Shortly before dusk one of the Bettys experienced mechanical trouble, and instead diverted to Lae in company with its wingman. The remaining pair arrived over Port Moresby around

2000. One of the bombers dropped its bombs over Seven-Mile, where about 20 B-17s were assembled, and the other over Wards. However, no damage was done at either location. Both Bettys then headed for Lae where they refuelled, and all four were back at Kavieng that night.

A few hours later three formations of B-17s departed Seven-Mile to strike the shipping now concentrated in Rabaul harbour. This was something of a landmark mission as six Fortresses from Major Benn's 63rd BS would execute the first skip-bombing attack in the South Pacific. The other two formations were drawn from a dozen 30th BS B-17s which would deliver conventional low altitude bombing attacks.

At 0245 the first formation of six 30th BS Fortresses found Rabaul harbour rich with targets under a cloud base of 5,500 feet. After unloading 48 x 500-bombs they claimed several near-misses. Half an hour later the six 63rd BS B-17s arrived, with three of them making conventional low altitude attacks from 4,000 – 8,000 feet. The other three, flown by Captain Ken McCullar, Captain Franklyn Green and Lieutenant Carl Hustad, each carried four 500-pound bombs fitted with five second fuses. These pilots made multiple individual skip-bombing runs from just 200 feet. The crews jubilantly claimed hits on a cruiser, destroyers and transports in what they referred to as "jackpot night".

An hour later, seven more B-17s dropped 32 x 500-pound bombs from 4,000 to 6,500 feet, with the pilots claiming to have set a tanker on fire. It was understandably difficult to assess bombing results at night, with any explosion potentially seen by enthusiastic crews as evidence of a hit. Accordingly, the American claims proved ambitious. The only ships known to have been damaged on this date were the submarine chasers *CH-31* and *CH-32*, both of which were likely misidentified as destroyers by the American crews.

Soon after dawn on 23 October six 89th BS A-20As bombed and strafed the Kokoda Track. Further east, Japanese aircraft were active trying to support the SNLF marines on Goodenough Island. At 0715 six Zeros drawn from the Tainan and No. 3 *Ku* departed Lakunai in company with a single C5M Babs. On approach to the coast of Goodenough Island, a small vessel was encountered which fired on the Japanese aircraft. The Zeros strafed it and nearby huts seen ashore.

The vessel was the *Maclaren King*, which was one of three ketches supporting the troops of the 2/12th Battalion which had just landed on the island. It had a 0.50-inch calibre machine gun mounted on its deck which had fired on the attackers, lightly damaging two of the Zeros. The vessel was carrying wounded soldiers and four of those aboard were injured in the attack.

Meanwhile, the Babs had made contact with a group of marines and communicated with them about plans for their rescue. At 1225 the Babs returned to Rabaul accompanied by the three Tainan *Ku* Zeros. However, the No. 3 *Ku* trio had encountered bad weather on the return leg. Two Zeros eventually returned at 1500 but the Zero flown by FPO3c Koji Ikeda never made it back, becoming a victim of the elements.

In other Japanese activity on 23 October four No. 751 *Ku* Bettys departed Kavieng at 0650 for a rare daylight raid against Port Moresby. However, the bombers encountered such bad weather

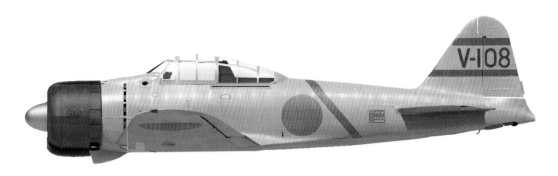

This Tainan Ku Model 21 Zero flew combat missions over New Guinea in late 1942 until it was abandoned as unserviceable at Lae (it was eventually captured by Allied forces in September 1943). The fighter was assigned to buntaicho Lieutenant (jg) Kurihara Katsumi who often shared it with Warrant Officer Yamashita Sahei.

that they diverted to Lae, where they remained until returning to Kavieng the following day.

Back at Mareeba, on this date twelve well-worn B-17Es of the 93rd BS finally departed Australia for Hawaii. The crews, overjoyed at the prospect of returning home, were accompanied by additional members of the squadron packed into the planes as passengers.

The 23 October day also saw the 38th BG lose B-25C 41-12889 commanded by Lieutenant Edward May. The bomber with four aboard left 14-Mile (Laloki) mid-morning destined for Townsville on a solo administrative flight. Townsville radar detected the Mitchell about 25 miles away over the sea, before it disappeared. Poor communications meant that the Townsville base was unaware of the impending arrival until five days later, after which an unsuccessful search was launched. The reason for the bomber's loss remains unclear.

On the morning of 24 October three 405th BS B-25Cs operating from 14-Mile flew the regular reconnaissance of the Buna-Lae-Finschhafen-Gasmata area. At 1030 *Ole Cappy*, *The Scoto Kid* and *Damn Yankee* swept over Lae at 1,100 feet and dropped six 500-pound bombs. The crews claimed to have destroyed two medium bombers and silenced an anti-aircraft position.

The day also saw the first newly cleared runway at Pongani ready to receive transports, and C-47s and C-60s began flying in American troops. Air cover was provided by 80th FS Airacobras.

That morning No. 6 Squadron recorded a "special mission" flown by Squadron Leader David Colquhoun in Hudson A16-246 to Goodenough Island. Other Hudsons were searching the waters further east, but no activity was reported by any of these flights.

During the evening of 24 October, two pairs of Beaufighters were active over Port Moresby in an unlikely night fighter role trying to intercept a Japanese reconnaissance aircraft. Although it was not picked up by searchlights, Squadron Leader Parker caught a glimpse of the aircraft before it disappeared in cloud.

During the night five Catalinas from Nos. 11 and 20 Squadrons attacked Kavieng 'drome, evidence that Allied intelligence had noted the increased recent use of this location. A sixth flying boat remained at Cairns after experiencing engine trouble prior to take-off. A mix of 20-, 250- and 500-pound bombs were dropped in what was considered a successful attack. One large bomber was claimed as destroyed and it was believed that a fuel dump was hit with fires visible for 40-60 miles.

In the early hours of 25 October eight 63rd BS B-17s flew through storms to attack shipping in Rabaul harbour. Once again, the squadron used a mix of conventional low altitude bombing and skip-bombing. A total of 61 x 500-pound bombs were dropped, a dozen of which had five second delay fuses. Heavy anti-aircraft fire was experienced which damaged three of the bombers including one that was holed 50 times. Two crewmen from Captain McCullar's *Black Jack* were wounded by shrapnel from an exploding anti-aircraft shell.

The 63rd BS was again confident of achieving results, claiming a transport and a gunboat sunk and two transports damaged. In addition, a hit was claimed on a coaling jetty with fires started. The 720-ton converted net tender *Kotobuki Maru No. 5* was sunk as a result of these attacks.

Daylight on 25 October saw efforts once again to support the Australian troops in their struggle to break the Japanese defences at Eora. Six 89th BS A-20As bombed and strafed the Kokoda Track nearby, dropping a mix of 20- and 100-pound bombs. Some 3,350 x 0.50-inch and 6,000 0.30-inch rounds of ammunition were fired.

Over Goodenough Island a Hudson was designated to support the 2/12th Battalion, spending an hour over the island but without seeing any enemy activity. A more potent form of air support in the form of six Beaufighters had been intended but these failed to reach Milne Bay after two attempts due to ongoing bad weather. Nevertheless, the troops succeeded in moving forward to Kilia Mission, passing through some elaborately constructed defences which surprisingly were unmanned. In a move not detected by the Australians, the previous night the Japanese marines had left the area and moved to nearby Fergusson Island by barge. The 2/12th subsequently remained on Goodenough Island to assist efforts to build an airfield in the Vivigani area.

That afternoon four No. 751 *Ku* Bettys departed Kavieng in another attempt to raid Port Moresby. The plan was for two aircraft to each make solo raids followed by the final pair. Only the first of these bombers arrived as planned, with the Australians recording the 85th air raid on Port Moresby at 1942 that evening. Bombs landed near Seven-Mile, but they did no damage.

The second Betty was unable to get through to the target and landed at Lae just after midnight. After taking off again the crew dropped their bombs but was unsure of the location. By 0405 they were over Milne Bay trying to find a way back through the weather, eventually landing back at Kavieng at 0700. The final pair also had difficulty in the weather, and neither succeeded in reaching Port Moresby.

Despite good weather on 26 October, Allied air activity was limited. Three 90th BS B-25s flying a reconnaissance mission took the opportunity to unload five 500-pound bombs over Lae 'drome and a wireless transmitting station at Salamaua. Anti-aircraft positions were strafed with 850

Rudimentary maintenance, Pacific style: a B-17E Fortress has a new #1 engine lifted into place with a forklift.

x 0.50-inch rounds. That afternoon two A-20As bombed and strafed targets on the Kokoda Track, with escort provided by four 49th FG P-40Es.

That night the light cruiser *Tenryu* approached the coast of Fergusson Island and made contact with the stranded 5th Sasebo SNLF marines. By 2330 some 261 men had been embarked, marking the end of a two-month period since they had first arrived on Goodenough Island on 25 August. Allied intelligence was aware that some rescue attempt was underway and at 2055 a Hudson had been despatched from Milne Bay to keep watch over Fergusson and Normanby Islands. However, no activity was noted, and the aircraft returned to base six hours later. A third Hudson later dropped two small bombs on lights seen in the area.

The following morning another three Hudsons departed Milne Bay to search the shipping lanes approaching Rabaul to try and intercept any departing ships. One of these crews sighted a cruiser and a destroyer, likely to have been *Tenryu* and an escort. However, the Hudson was unable to attack due to fuel problems. Another was drawn to the area by a radio message from the first aircraft but couldn't drop its bombs due to faulty bomb release gear. Three Zeros were seen in the distance approaching from New Britain but there was no interception and all three Hudsons returned safely to Milne Bay.

On 27 October six No. 30 Squadron Beaufighters strafed small boats, barges and anti-aircraft positions at Lae, expending 950 x 20mm and 6,000 x 0.303-inch rounds of ammunition. Fuel drums on the shore were left blazing after the attack, during which three of the attackers were hit by anti-aircraft fire. One of these aircraft, A19-49, was last seen with one engine smoking before diving into the sea half a mile from the shore. The pilot Flight Lieutenant EA Jones and the observer Flight Sergeant ER Richardson were killed.

In the early afternoon a pair of 89th BS A-20As were again active over the Kokoda Track, escorted by four P-40s. Some 60 x 20-pound bombs were dropped in the target area, but no enemy activity was seen.

Later that afternoon two Hudsons, escorted by seven Airacobras, were over Fergusson Island, with the Allies as yet unaware of the departure of all of the Japanese. A barge hidden under coconut palms on a beach was attacked with two 100-pound anti-submarine bombs and nearby native canoes were strafed.

That night five Catalinas raided Buka, with a sixth machine unable to take-off due to engine trouble. The flying boats spent two hours over the target at between 600 and 8,000 feet, dropping a mix of 250- and 500-pound general purpose and 20-pound fragmentation bombs over the runway and dispersal area. One bomber was claimed destroyed and fires were started among buildings and tents.

The early hours of 28 October saw nine 30th BS Fortresses raid Rabaul, and the crews for once experienced good weather all the way to the target. The B-17s unloaded 69 x 500-pound bombs over the harbour from altitudes between 5,000 and 9,000 feet. In the face of accurate anti-aircraft fire, a hit was claimed on an unidentified vessel.

Later that morning three 90th BS B-25s strafed a G3M2 Nell bomber at Gasmata, with one of the attackers receiving minor damage from return fire. Meanwhile a single 19th BG Fortress on a reconnaissance mission over Kavieng was repeatedly attacked by a trio of No. 751 *Ku* (former Kanoya *Ku*) Zeros. For the Japanese Zero pilots, this was a fierce fight led by *shotaicho* FPO2c Maetsuji Katsutoshi, however, the attack was caused by a comedy of errors. Maetsuji's quartet originally scrambled from Kavieng at 0610 hours following a report of 15 Fortresses in the area, likely the 30th BS B-17s which had bombed Rabaul. The quartet climbed between towering and dangerous cumulonimbus cloud to find the bombers. They were spotted in the distance, but the Zeros couldn't reach them.

Instead at 0640 they found a sole 435th BS Fortress, 41-9193 *Gypsy Rose* flown by Lieutenant Robert Irwin, on a reconnaissance flight. Curiously, number three in the formation FPO3c Echi Yuki was last seen ten minutes before the attack commenced at 0640, and it was not clear to the others what happened to him. The other three persistently attacked against the B-17 for more than 50 minutes. At 0730 Flyer1c Inetome Tsugio broke off contact when his Zero was hit, but got back safely to Kavieng at 0820, followed by Maetsuji and his wingman at 0850. Echi was never seen again, and it appears he became disorientated in cloud and spiralled out of control into the sea.

A group photo of fighter commanders at Lakunai in late October 1942. Those which can be identified are: 1. Lieutenant Commander Ito Toshitaka (hikocho Kanoya Ku and then No. 253 Ku), 2. Lieutenant Commander Aioi Takahide (hikotaicho No. 3 Ku), 3. Captain Saito Masahisa (commander Tainan Ku), 4. Lieutenant Commander Nakajima Tadashi (hikocho Tainan Ku), 5. Lieutenant Yamaguchi Sadao (chutaicho No. 3 Ku), 6. Lieutenant Baba Masayoshi (chutaicho Kanoya Ku) and 7. Lieutenant Ono Takeyoshi (chutaicho Tainan Ku). The warrior mascot on the far right was purchased from the Siwai tribe near Buin.

Diarist and pilot Captain Fred Eaton of the 435th RS, aboard as a member of Irwin's crew, later wrote:

> Over Kavieng Field and harbor at daybreak to take pictures … I watched four Zeros take off … they were at our altitude, 35,000 feet, in five minutes. They intercepted us ten minutes out of Kavieng on departure. My oxygen went out in the ball-turret and I had to come out. The only guns on the airplane that were working were one tail gun and the two waist guns. I got into the upper turret to fix those jams and got in a couple of good bursts. The crew got one Zero and one possible. This was apparently Ozanne's first combat because [co-pilot Lieutenant James Ozanne) did not know where we were when we hit a heavy fog bank and the Zeros broke off. He had put the cover over his compass, to keep the brass or empty shell casings from breaking it, ignored the time, airspeed altitude instruments, and joined the dogfight. He quickly concluded that we should circle while we climbed out of the soup. About five minutes from where we broke out, was a mountain on the heading we were on. Our plane had numerous bullet holes and one cannon hole. A "Brisbane" Colonel that we had along for a passenger, said he would recommend us for the Silver Star. What a way to celebrate my Dad's birthday.

The three Zeros had peppered *Gypsy Rose* with 193 bullet holes, but the sturdy bomber got back to Port Moresby where it landed at 1215. Their shooting was exceptionally accurate as they fired only brief bursts during their frequent attacks; an average of around 300 x 7.7 mm and 30 x 20mm rounds of ammunition per pilot. Clearly the Zero pilots engaged on their own terms and only fired when they had the Fortress in their sights.

Also on the morning of 28 October, Hudson A16-246 departed Milne Bay for a routine reconnaissance mission of the Solomon Sea. It never returned, with the loss of pilot Flying Officer DL Gorringe and his three crewmen. An explosion in cabin mounted long range fuel tanks or water contaminated fuel were considered as possible causes.

The daily reconnaissance of the Buna-Lae- Finschhafen -Gasmata area was flown by six 90th BS B-25s led by Captain Raymond Peterson. At 1515 these encountered a single Betty which had just departed Lae. Immediately upon sighting the Mitchells it descended to sea-level where a fight commenced with the Mitchells some ten miles east of Finschhafen. The Betty was well-defended by its 20mm tail gunner who damaged Peterson's Mitchell, blowing the liferaft out of its hatch and shattering one of his fins. The Mitchell briefly gyrated to a degree Peterson's wingmen were convinced he was going to crash, however he soon regained control once the flapping raft had been secured. Some 2,100 x 0.50-inch rounds were fired from the B-25s and despite many hits to the Betty it stayed airborne.

Staring at 2300 that night, three No. 751 *Ku* Bettys departed Kavieng at 20 minutes intervals to make more nuisance raids over Port Moresby. On this occasion the weather allowed the mission to unfold as planned, with crews on the first aircraft bombing Seven-Mile at 0217. These caused no damage but a stick of bombs from the second Betty landed near Bootless Inlet a short time later, killing three and wounding four personnel. The third pattern of bombs was not recorded on the ground and likely landed in the ocean. Searchlights were unable to illuminate the bombers as they were obscured by cloud, and all three had returned safely to Kavieng by 0700.

A curious footnote to this raid was tail gunner FPO1c Miyama Masayoshi in the second bomber firing 80 x 20mm rounds at two "night fighters" over Port Moresby, while the same bomber's 7.7mm gunners fired another 380 rounds. The alleged "night fighters" were in fact eight returning 30th BS Fortresses which had raided shipping in the Shortlands near Buin. Of 30 x 500-pound bombs dropped, four were seen to near-miss a heavy cruiser while others landed near unidentified vessels.

One of the bombers, however, could not find the target area and instead jettisoned its bombs before turning back to Port Moresby. This was B-17E Flying Fortress 41-9235 *Clown House* flown by Major Allen Lindberg. After becoming lost, the crew radioed Townsville which gave them a bearing for that location. However soon after dawn it was evident they were running out of fuel, and Lindberg subsequently made a safe water landing on the Great Barrier Reef, some twenty miles out to sea off Cooktown.

Two life rafts were inflated, and the crew spent two uncomfortable nights at sea before coming ashore on a reef near the coast. They were fortunate to meet a group of Aborigines on a fishing trip who guided the men to nearby Iron Range. When Lindberg and his crew were returned to Mareeba they were transferred into the 64th BS, which Lindberg would later command.

From 0935 on 29 October three 89th BS A-20As escorted by fighters attacked targets along the Kokoda Track, unloading 120 x 20-pound bombs from just 50 feet altitude. The attack was repeated by another trio of A-20As that afternoon escorted by Airacobras, with an identical expenditure of ordnance.

That night more Fortresses were sent to attack shipping in the Shortlands. The first wave comprised ten bombers, eight from the 63rd BS and two relatively inexperienced crews from the 403rd BS. Over the target area visibility was very poor with cloud layered between 1,000 to 6,000 feet, and a total of 45 x 500-pound bombs were unloaded. Most of the B-17s bombed from between 6,000 and 9,000 feet, but Captain McCullar dived to 1,800 feet to attack from under the cloud. Amid heavy anti-aircraft fire and searchlights, he was forced to make a second run after his bombs failed to release. His aircraft was hit many times and one engine was damaged, but McCullar returned safely to base as did all of the other B-17s.

A direct hit on a transport was claimed by Lieutenant Anderson, two of which were reported as beached the next day by reconnaissance aircraft. In the second attack five 30th BS B-17s dropped 21 x 500-pound bombs. Two direct hits were claimed on a possible battleship with near misses near a light cruiser and an aircraft carrier.

Also active of the night of 29/30 October was the strongest force of Catalinas yet to raid a single target. Eight flying boats, four from each of Nos. 11 and 20 Squadrons, targeted ships in the Shortlands anchorage with a mix of 250- and 500-pound semi armoured piercing bombs. A probable hit was claiming on a heavy cruiser or battleship.

Early on 30 October Wing Commander Walker led seven Beaufighters into the air from Milne Bay for what would have been their longest mission to date, a strike against the shipping in the Shortlands. However, a weather front was encountered midway to the target area and the force returned to base just over three hours later.

On this date the 90th BS lost B-25D 41-29731 *L'il De-Icer*, commanded by Lieutenant Robert Miller. Early that afternoon it departed 17-Mile for an armed reconnaissance over Lae and Gasmata returning via Hood Point. The Mitchell toted two 500-pound bombs however it was never seen again. The shattered wreckage was discovered post-war in thick jungle near Mimia village in mountains on the southern side of the Kokoda Gap. It appears that the bomber entered cloud then drove straight into the mountain. The impact detonated one or both bombs, shattering the wreckage.

On the night of 30/31 October two more formations of Fortresses were active. The first comprised eight 63rd BS B-17s which arrived over Rabaul harbour at 0230. Bad weather combined with little moonlight meant the crews spent an hour making multiple runs over the target area dropping a mix of 72 x 250-, 500- and 1,000-pound bombs. One probable hit and several near misses were claimed.

The second formation comprised nine 30th BS B-17s which continued the effort against the Shortlands anchorage. Amidst heavy anti-aircraft fire 72 x 500-pound bombs were unloaded, with three hits and multiple near-misses claimed.

Meanwhile a single Catalina flew a supply dropping mission to the north coast of New Guinea. On the return flight a nuisance raid was made at 0215, dropping small bombs over the dispersal area at Lae's airfield and strafing buildings at Salamaua.

From Kavieng three No. 751 *Ku* Bettys departed just after midnight to strike Port Moresby. However bad weather was encountered, and the trio returned to base around 90 minutes later.

On the morning of 31 October three 89th BS A-20As bombed and strafed the Kokoda area, while three B-25s on a reconnaissance mission strafed trucks south of the Buna beachhead area.

At the same time Captain Fred Eaton was flying a brand new and unnamed 435th BS B-17F on a reconnaissance mission over Rabaul. The bomber was attacked by a quartet of Tainan *Ku* Zeros, led by FPO3c Hori Mitsuo. Despite multiple attacking passes, the bomber was not hit and there were no losses to either side.

Within the space of just a few weeks the condition of the IJA force in the Owen Stanleys had deteriorated considerably. This was due to sickness and battle fatigue which contributed to a breakdown of morale. In addition, there was a growing supply crisis for the forward units. In mid-October the battle report of the 3rd Battalion of the 144th Infantry Regiment noted:

> With the unfavourable climate and severe cold, combined with the lack of supplies, casualties in the unit continue to mount. The conditions of the battle are extremely harsh.

By late October a staff communication made direct reference to the lack of supplies in relation to the decision to withdraw from Eora on 28 October:

> The strength of the force gradually deteriorated owing to the constant heavy rain and depletion of supplies … the commander realised that attacks from enemy planes had disrupted the transport of supplies further forward than the bridge at Papaki [Wairopi]. He consequently made the inevitable decision on 27 October to withdraw the force to the north bank of the Kumusi River at Papaki.

Recognising the dire need for supplies, it was decided to make another emergency supply drop at Kokoda. At dawn on 28 October a C5M2 Babs departed from Rabaul to survey the weather to the area but turned back in the face of bad weather a short time later.

However, the following day saw a *chutai* of nine Misawa *Ku* Bettys make the flight albeit without fighter escort. Such was the importance of the mission it was led personally by the Misawa *Ku hikotaicho* Lieutenant Commander Mihara Genichi. The drop of supplies and munitions was successfully made at 1335, with the force returning to Vunakanau at 1630 that afternoon. Despite the significant risks of interception by Allied aircraft, the drop was necessarily made in daylight to ensure that the majority of supplies could be retrieved.

No. 31 Ku D3A1 Val tail code 31-212 (Manufacturer's Number 2133) as it appeared at Lakunai in October 1942.

In the last months of 1942 the B-26s of the 22nd BG began to experience maintenance difficulties as the original fleet had been in constant use since April. Here the crew of a 408th BS Marauder is seen with their aircraft at Reid River in October, by which time two squadrons (the 19th and 33rd BS) had moved forward to Iron Range.

Two 76th Dokuritsu Chutai Ki-46 Dinah cruise over Rapopo airfield shortly after arriving at Rabaul in October 1942. This was the first JAAF unit to arrive in the South Pacific.

CHAPTER 9

ARRIVAL OF THE JAAF AND THE IJN RESTRUCTURE

Arrival of the JAAF

Until October all Japanese air power in the South Seas exclusively comprised IJN units. Critical aircraft losses over Guadalcanal in August and September had caused considerable angst and discussion in Tokyo, a lot of it confrontational and robust. The fallout from these discussions took the Japanese Army Air Force (JAAF) by surprise when, with no warning, political pressure demanded they contribute to the South Pacific campaign.

In Tokyo an institutional Japanese mindset prevailed that the IJN commanded the seas whilst the JAAF restricted itself to land operations. The entrenched sentiment of the times was best encapsulated by a common saying in military circles:

> If you want to see China join the Imperial Army; if you want to see the world join the Imperial Navy.

Despite crippling losses at Guadalcanal, the IJN focus remained in the Solomons with the New Guinea air campaign more or less placed on hold. Against this background the JAAF was approached to contribute to the theatre. When it finally acquiesced to deploy there, it well understood that its aircrews had limited experience to deal with long distance navigation, let alone the hostility of a tropical environment. JAAF trenchant reluctance to commit any air unit to what it termed the *Nanto homen* - the Southeast Area – mostly derived from its experience that ocean navigation was best negotiated by the IJN. Even after it was ordered there, throughout late 1942 the Southeast Area remained a low priority for the JAAF. When the JAAF fielded the original request senior JAAF officers aired the opinion among themselves that doubted whether the JAAF was really needed, as the IJN had sufficient airpower to reinforce the theatre themselves. Both these sentiments underpinned widespread IJA opposition to deploying to what the JAAF regarded as a remote and hostile theatre.

Thus, when first approached, the Southeast Area had until then barely registered on the preoccupied minds of JAAF command. JAAF units were digging in for a protracted and challenging war in Asia, and even the China front was demanding more attention. The request placed further strain on the inter-service relationship between the IJA and IJN which was lukewarm at the best of times. This would deteriorate further over the forthcoming months as Guadalcanal ground into a quagmire, and then a full retreat.

Neither were differences between the IJA and IJN confined to strategy. Their aircraft types were different designs, having evolved from completely different developmental philosophies. Aircraft parts were not interchangeable, and in most cases neither were the technical skills

Ki-46 Dinah aircrew graduate in Japan from an aviation reconnaissance school, some of whom will be posted to New Guinea with the 76th Dokuritsu Chutai.

needed to maintain them. Training and culture were different too: the IJN's officer corps looked down upon its army counterparts sometimes as intemperate thugs. These differences were exponentially more challenging than, by way of example, incorporation of RAAF units into the USAAF command structure.

Curiously, by early October, no formal agreement was drawn up between the two services as to who would do what, where and when. Caught by surprise, IJA staff officers hastily drew up a list of units which could be sent to Rabaul for the initial deployment. Initially these air and support units were directly assigned to the IJA's Southeast Area regional command, the 17th Army Headquarters at Rabaul. The units were subsequently grouped into the 6th Army Air Division which was formed on 25 November. This was commanded by General Itahana Gi'ichi who would assume a high degree of autonomy.

Then, in the first week of December 1942, a formal IJA/IJN agreement was drawn up. It authorised the JAAF to assume sole responsibility for operations in mainland New Guinea. However, the subsequent decision to withdrawal from Guadalcanal – Operation *Ke* - which also involved JAAF aircraft, saw an ongoing blurring of the New Guinea/Solomons boundary.

Immediately following the JAAF decision to deploy assets to the theatre, IJA Headquarters decided they should have their own airfield at Rabaul. This initiative was accelerated when the IJN underlined the lack of space at Vunakanau, a situation which would only worsen. As result, it was decided to build an airfield at Rapopo coconut plantation. Located southeast of Rabaul, the site offered good drainage. Construction commenced in early December of a single runway, with small tanks used to assist clearing the palm trees. It would not be operational until mid-January 1943. Before this was ready, existing IJN airfields were used (with the exception of Malahang, near Lae, which is discussed in Chapter 15).

The initial JAAF contingent for the Southeast Area was a not insignificant force, two fighter regiments, a light bomber regiment and an independent reconnaissance squadron. These air units were supported by a number of ground units, with the full list shown in the table below:

JAAF Southeast Area Deployment late 1942
(grouped into 6th Army Air Division from 25 November)

Air Units

- 12th Air Brigade, comprising Brigade Headquarters, 1st and 11th Air Regiments (*Hiko Sentai*); Ki-43-I *Hayabusa* fighters
- 45th Air Regiment (*Hiko Sentai*); Ki-48-I *Sokei* light bombers
- 76th Independent Squadron (*Dokuritsu Chutai*); Ki-46-II Dinah reconnaissance twins

Support Units
- 12th Air Sector Command
- 21st, 22nd, 47th & 48th Airfield Battalions (one company only), 33rd Airfield Company
- 5th Air Signal Regiment (Minus 1st Wire and 1st Radio companies)
- 1st Navigation Aid company
- 1st Air Intelligence Unit
- 2nd Meteorological Regiment (one company only)
- 5th, 6th and 10th Airfield Construction Units
- 81st Land Duty Company

Commanded by Captain Kirita Hideo, the 76th *Dokuritsu Chutai* was the first JAAF air unit to arrive at Rabaul. Kirita's priority task was to survey the new theatre and thus better inform Tokyo and following JAAF commanders of the conditions there. The unit arrived at Rabaul on 12 October 1942 from the Philippines, bringing ten Ki-46-II Dinahs as deck cargo aboard the seaplane tender *Sanuki Maru*. One of the unit's first missions was to reconnoitre Gasmata, which it straightaway proceeded to use as a forward base for reconnaissance missions of New Guinea.

The arrival of the nimble and high flying Dinahs was just as well, given that specialist IJN reconnaissance capability was based around the dwindling fleet of Tainan *Ku* C5Ms and a sole remaining Tainan *Ku* J1N1-C Irving. These had been augmented by a handful of No. 3 *Ku* C5Ms, although that unit would soon return to its home base in the Netherlands East Indies. While the single engine Babs had given good service, only a very small number had been manufactured and replacements were not forthcoming. Co-incidentally it was one of only two types used by both the IJN and JAAF during WWII (as the Mitsubishi Ki-15, none of which would operate in New Guinea or the Solomons). The other shared type was the Ki-46 Dinah, which would be operated by both services in the theatre.

Within a fortnight of its arrival, on 25 October the JAAF suffered its first loss in the South Pacific when 76th *Dokuritsu Chutai* commander Captain Kirita Hideo was shot down in his Ki-46 by anti-aircraft fire during a low pass over Henderson Field.

The rationale behind the selection of the 45th *Hiko Sentai* deserves special mention. In September 1940 it had replaced its antiquated Ki-32 inventory with the new Kawasaki Ki-48-I *Sokei* light bomber. Commanded by Lieutenant-Colonel Yasuoka Mitsuo, both it and its sister unit, the 208th *Hiko Sentai*, fell under the command of the Hakujoshi Operational Training School. However, the "training" designation is deceptive. Both units were *de facto* combat units, with school's role to train aircrew in long distance navigation. Hakujoshi was located on the Manchurian Plain and was thus central to extensive and featureless geography. This training was conducted over vast tracts of desert, a skill transferred to negotiating long oceanic distances. The JAAF thus earmarked these two bomber units for the Pacific, with the 45th *Hiko Sentai* slated to arrive first.

The two fighter regiments allocated to the Southeast Area, the 1st and 11th *Hiko Sentai*, faced unique challenges in their preparation for the deployment. Throughout October planners busied themselves with swapping fighter inventories between regiments to ensure the two units met newly beefed-up establishment strengths. To allow for the attrition expected in the new environment, both the 1st and 11th *Hiko Sentai* were allocated generous quotas of pilots, over 40 in each case, and above-average allocations of fighters.

To meet these substantial quotas, nearly all the *Hayabusa* allocated to both regiments were hand-me-downs from other units, mostly the 24th, 50th and 64th *Hiko Sentai*. These fighters had already seen considerable service in Indochina and Southeast Asia, and some were delayed at Truk during their delivery so they could be overhauled by service units. In return, the Southeast Asia units relieved of their older model *Hayabusa* were grateful when they received the brand-new Ki-43-II with a more powerful engine.

The next highest priority for transportation to theatre, following the aircraft and aircrews, were the airfield battalions. Their job was to maintain and guard the aircraft, with specific battalions assigned to particular air units. Each airfield battalion comprised two or more maintenance companies, one guard company, one vehicle company (with up to fifty vehicles) and a headquarters detachment.

However, a major obstacle to the deployment was a severe shortage of shipping space to deliver the JAAF aircraft to Rabaul. Whereas IJN aircraft were able to fly long oceanic delivery flights to Rabaul directly from Japan or other regional areas, the JAAF crews were unqualified for such flights. This placed even further strain on the IJA/IJN relationship. After much debate a compromise was agreed, whereupon the IJN would deliver JAAF aircraft to Truk from where ferry flights to Rabaul would proceed. However, this still imposed a serious burden on the IJN, as the JAAF bombers were too large to fit into the holds of transports. Instead, they were partially disassembled and craned onto the decks of aircraft carriers for the journey to Truk, thus sidelining the precious carriers from more essential duties.

At Truk the aircraft would be reassembled for the flight to Rabaul which involved a non-stop oceanic distance of 680 nautical miles, often with capricious weather a serious factor. Accordingly, it was agreed that IJN Ki-46 or G4M1 Betty bombers with specialist navigator crews would lead these JAAF delivery flights, some of which would later involve severe losses.

A Ki-46 Dinah is man-handled into its parking position at Rapopo, under a camouflage net. Construction of a runway at Rapopo began in December 1942 and it was ready for use in mid-January 1943.

For the voyage on the carrier decks, the *Sokei* were strapped down after the tyres were deflated. If extra deck space was available, more airframes or supplies were loaded aboard. However, again and again the JAAF found itself competing with the IJN for scarce shipping space, compounding the difficult delivery process.

Each unit had its own logistics commander of officer rank who travelled ahead to Rabaul from Truk via a Combined Fleet Mavis flying boat, with ground personnel and attached airfield units following on transports or destroyers. Newly arrived JAAF units faced huge challenges in setting up camp. Denied cooperation from the IJN, they found that even other army units refused assistance to prepare camp and other airfield facilities due to the pressing needs of their own requirements.

In the event, the 11th *Hiko Sentai* arrived at Vunakanau with 57 *Hayabusa* on 18 December 1942, with one fighter lost during the delivery flight from Truk. The 1st *Hiko Sentai* followed with 53 *Hayabusa* on 9 January 1943. Both air regiments were viewed as crack units, having excellent combat credentials from campaigns flown in both Indochina and Southeast Asia. Given that IJN fighters had virtually disappeared from mainland New Guinea, these two regiments represented a substantial reinforcement.

In contrast to the successful arrival of the fighter regiments, the problematic and delayed arrival of the 45th *Hiko Sentai* underlined the logistical challenges discussed above. By 9 December 23

Sokei had been loaded aboard the carrier *Taiyo* along with 203 men including commander Lieutenant Colonel Yasuoka Mitsuo. A further 22 *Sokei* were loaded aboard the carrier *Ryuho* with the balance of 113 personnel. *Ryuho* departed Yokohama on 11 December while *Taiyo* left on the following afternoon.

However, *Ryuho* was attacked by a USN submarine on the first day of its voyage, forcing it to return to Yokosuka, where it had to offload all the JAAF equipment including the bombers. While they waiting for shipping space to Truk to be available, the contingent moved to Hokota where they undertook further training for the next two weeks. Subsequently this contingent was loaded aboard the carrier *Zuikaku* on 31 December and arrived at Truk four days later.

Meanwhile, the other contingent on the *Taiyo* had arrived in Truk Harbour on 18 December. It took several days to offload and reassemble the *Sokei*, which then had to be test flown. Because of these delays the 45th *Hiko Sentai* would not be ready for operations from Rabaul until mid-January 1943.

Improving airfield infrastructure was a priority for the Japanese at Rabaul. Here an IJN staff car ceremoniously proceeds along the new "South Road" which led from the township to Vunakanau, in late 1942. The road is lined with soldiers from the construction unit which completed the task.

The November IJN Restructure & Reinforcement

The robust discussions in Tokyo's several military headquarters outlined above had another fallout aside from committing JAAF resources to the theatre. This matter revolved around security. The Japanese military mindset much orbited around a passion for order and numbers. For example, all aircraft and weapons were given type or model numbers, and every airframe carried a manufacturer's number, along with most associated parts. Whilst Mitsubishi and Nakajima went to considerable lengths to code airframe manufacturer's numbers for security reasons, other parts of the military had yet to catch up. When Japanese forces first swept the China theatre, the Japanese military made no attempts to hide the origins of its units, and in fact in some cases widely advertised them particularly where they were successful. For example, many IJN units were named after the bases from which the units had originally been formed, the Yokohama *Ku* being an obvious example. Other units were named after bases outside of Japan such as Tainan in Formosa (Taiwan).

However now that Japan was on the defensive it made sense to confuse Japan's enemies as to the origins of units, and their composition. IJN Headquarters drew up a scheme whereby all land-based air units would be redesignated according to the numbering scheme as outlined below. The introduction of this system had been foreshadowed back in October when the Kanoya *Ku* had been redesignated as the No. 751 *Ku* (note, not 751st which is incorrect).

The first digit was determined by the type of aircraft in the unit, whilst the second denoted the unit's original pre-war base. The third digit was a sequential allocation, i.e. the first, second, third, etc unit operating the same aircraft type from the same base. Thus, by way of example, the Tainan *Ku* which operated fighters (first digit "2"), originally from Sasebo (second digit "5"), had been the first fighter unit to originate there (third digit "1"), thus becoming No. 251 *Ku*. It is equally useful to work backwards, for example No. 802 *Ku* indicates it was operating seaplanes ("8"), and was the second seaplane unit to originate from Yokosuka ("0" and "2").

First Digit – Unit Type	Second Digit – Home Base	Third digit Sequential
2 – fighter	0,1,2 – Yokosuka	1
5 – dive-bomber	3,4 – Kure	2
7 – bomber	5,6,7 – Sasebo	3
8 – seaplane	8,9 – Maizuru	4
9 – fleet support		5 etc

This new system applied right across all land-based units in the IJN empire, not only to Vice Admiral Kusaka Jinichi's "Base Force", the 11th Air Fleet. Whilst at first glance this system appears purely administrative, it was attended by widespread personnel and unit movements and replacements, the most significant of which was the departure from the South Pacific of No. 251 *Ku*, in essence the previous Tainan *Ku*.

The departure of this veteran unit was a landmark in the history of Japanese air power in the Pacific. The number of pilots who returned to Japan from the early New Guinea campaign was only eleven, a pitiful handful from the 60-odd who had opened the Tainan *Ku*'s account in New

Guinea on 1 April 1942. No fighter unit had fought harder in 1942 than the Tainan *Ku*, which was already nearing exhaustion when it was finally crushed in the skies over Guadalcanal. Extraordinarily, despite often leading from the front, Tainan *Ku hikotaicho* Lieutenant Commander Nakajima Tadashi was among the survivors. Alongside him from the original cadre who had also survived were FPO1c Nishizawa Hiroyoshi, FPO3c Endo Masuaki, FPO3c Uehara Sadao, FPO2c Ishikawa Seiji, Lieutenant Kawai Shiro, FPO1c Okumura Takeo, FPO1c Yamashita Sadao, FPO2c Kudo Shigetoshi, Warrant Officer Ono Satoru, and Lieutenant Ono Takeyoshi. They were returned to Japan aboard the *Naruto Maru* which left Rabaul on 11 November 1942, docking at Kagoshima nineteen days later.

Just before the end of October, 27 Chitose *Ku* Bettys accompanied by their *Hikocho* Captain Ohashi Fujiro arrived at Rabaul. With these bomber reinforcements at hand, on 31 October the No. 753 *Kokutai* (previously the Takao *Ku*) returned to the Netherlands East indies, followed by the former No. 3 *Ku* Zero detachment on 8 November (now reincarnated as No. 202 *Ku*).

On 9 November the carrier *Taiyo* arrived off Rabaul ferrying a mixture of 27 Model 21 and Model 32 Zeros from No. 252 *Ku*, all of which were flown off to Lakunai. With Captain Yanagimura Yoshitane as *hikocho*, and Lieutenant Suganami Masaji as *hikotaicho*, No. 252 *Ku* would subsequently detach a *chutai* to Lae on 20 November. However, the unit would conduct its most intense fighting in the Solomons.

No. 2 *Ku* was renamed No. 582 *Ku*, nonetheless the unit's cadre continued to refer to itself as the "No. 2 *Butai*" or the "Yamamoto *Butai*" for the rest of its time in New Guinea. Commander Yamamoto Sakae remained *hikocho* and recently promoted Lieutenant Commander Shindo Saburo was appointed *hikotaicho*. Lieutenant Kurakane Yoshio and Lieutenant Sakai Tomoyasu were the next two *chutaicho* in terms of respective seniority. All of these officers were skilled and aggressive leaders.

Note it was No. 582 *Ku* alongside No. 252 *Ku* that was mostly employed for fighter operations over New Guinea, in particular the Buna area, in November and December. Henceforth detachments from these two units would rotate between Lae and Rabaul, using Gasmata as required as a halfway house.

In late September No. 31 *Ku* arrived in Rabaul (as noted in Chapter 5) where it flew anti-submarine patrols with its small fleet of Val dive-bombers. In October No. 31 *Ku* was sent forward to Buin and flew combat missions over Guadalcanal. It suffered heavy losses including four Vals shot down by Wildcats in a single mission on 16 October. On 1 November the unit was renamed No. 954 *Ku*, but little was left as it was never more than a single *chutai* strong. On 10 November the carrier *Unyo* delivered a shipment of No. 956 *Ku* D3A2 Val dive-bombers to Rabaul, and this unit replaced No. 954 *Ku*, the worn-out remnants of which were sent back to Japan.

On 8 October 1942 Vice Admiral Kusaka Jinichi replaced Vice Admiral Tsukahara Nishizo as commander of the 11th Air Fleet. This meant Kusaka now presided over all of Rabaul's air units, and thus he held a similar level of command to Kenney. Tsukahara was invalided back to Japan after the handover ceremony. Although he had only been in Rabaul for two months he had quickly acquired tropical ailments. The health of almost the entire Rabaul garrison had consistently declined since its initial occupation in 1942. The most commonplace and debilitating disease was vivax malaria which stays in the blood once contracted.

By 11 November 1942 Kusaka's Base Force (not including the floatplanes of R Area Force) rebadged administrative nomenclature appeared thus:

Old Name	New Designation	Inventory
6 *Ku*	204 *Ku*	Model 21 and 32 Zero
Kanoya *Ku* (Fighter)	253 *Ku*	Model 21 Zero
Genzan *Ku* (fighter)	252 *Ku*	Model 21 and 32 Zero
2 *Ku* (Dive-bomber)	582 *Ku*	D3A1 Val
2 *Ku* (Fighter)	582 *Ku*	Model 21 and 32 Zero
Chitose *Ku*	703 *Ku*	G4M1 Betty
Misawa *Ku*	705 *Ku*	G4M1 Betty
Kisarazu *Ku*	707 *Ku*	G4M1 Betty
Kanoya *Ku*	751 *Ku*	G4M1 Betty and Model 21 Zero
14 *Ku*	802 *Ku*	A6M2-N Rufe and Mavis
Toko *Ku*	851 *Ku*	Mavis
(nil)	956 *Ku*	D3A2 Val

From an operational perspective, on 15 November Kusaka authorised the above air units to be allocated into four forces:

Force	Commander	Units	Main Base
Flying Boat Force	*Hikocho* 851 *Ku* (Commander Ito Sukemitsu)	851 *Ku* 802 *Ku*	Rabaul & Shortlands
1st Attack Force	CO 21st Air Flotilla (Vice Admiral Ichimaru Rinosuke)	253 *Ku* 751 *Ku*	Kavieng
5th Attack Force	CO 25th Air Flotilla (Vice Admiral Uwano Keizo)	582 *Ku* (Zeros) 252 *Ku*	Rabaul Lae
6th Attack Force	CO 26th Air Flotilla (Vice Admiral Yamagata Seigo)	204 *Ku* 705 *Ku* 707 *Ku* 582 *Ku* (Vals) 956 *Ku* (Vals)	Rabaul Buin

Ballale

By mid-October with Buin airfield open for fighters and dive bombers, Rabaul's commanders coveted another base to cater for bombers, both for attack and reconnaissance purposes. The Japanese found the answer in the small island of Ballale in the Shortlands, an almost triangular island measuring about a mile across. On the island was a plantation managed by widow Edith Atkinson, who was evacuated in early 1942. Atkinson left behind copra drying sheds, living quarters for labourers and a ready-made wharf onto which military supplies could easily be unloaded. A preliminary survey conducted via an IJN launch discovered that not only was the island flat, it had hard soil, good drainage and nearby abundant supplies of coral which could be crushed to surface a runway.

On 3 November 370 men of the 18th Naval Construction Battalion landed. Commanded by Lieutenant Commander Ozaki Norihiko with orders to build an airfield, it soon became apparent that more labour was required to do the job. When Solomon Islanders refused to volunteer their labour, in late December the Japanese press-ganged 42 males which were taken to Ballale. In the event nine of these were later killed in Allied attacks, but the survivors were allowed to return home in June 1943 using two Japanese flagged canoes.

A murky and still unresolved chain of command delivered more labour in the form of British POWs. In October 1942, 600 men from the 35th Royal Artillery Regiment were shipped from Singapore to Rabaul aboard the *Kenkon Maru*. Gathering the healthiest of these, 517 POWs were on-shipped to Ballale in November. There they worked alongside Chinese prisoners from Hong Kong and the press-ganged Solomon Islanders. On the same day *Kenkon Maru* arrived, Ozaki ordered one British POW beheaded for attempting to escape by swimming. Over the next few months, the POWs crushed coral to surface the runway and taxiways, and performed hard labour to progress construction.

Many POWs died due to a lack of medical treatment, disease or injuries sustained through either beatings or as a result of Allied raids. The Japanese forbade the British from sheltering during bombing attacks, and some were executed for infractions. Alerted by locals, an Australian war graves unit arrived on Ballale on 6 November 1945, and guided by former Chinese POWs, spent the month exhuming 436 European and 14 Japanese, the latter who had died of disease. Ozaki and Captain Miyake Isamu, in charge of Ballale's anti-aircraft battery, were both arrested in Japan on 17 June 1947 in connection with the murder of the POWs. However, no charges were laid against either as the evidence presented was considered hearsay.

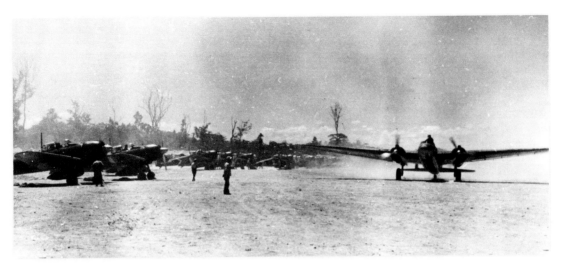

A transport Nell arrives at Buin, against a backdrop of No. 582 Ku Model 22 and 32 Zeros warming their engines. The completion of Buin allowed a large portion of Rabaul's airpower to be based there for use in the Solomons.

An IJN launch. These ubiquitous craft patrolled Rabaul's harbour area incessantly, especially following Allied air raids looking for downed crews.

Having just released a 250-kilogram bomb, a No. 582 Ku Val crosses paths with a 49th FG Warhawk over Buna. Such clashes became relatively common in the final weeks of 1942.

CHAPTER 10

KOKODA RECAPTURED:
1 – 11 NOVEMBER

After the Japanese withdrawal from Eora on 28 October, they made a complete exit from the Owen Stanleys. Horii had been ordered by 17th Army Headquarters to withdraw to the Kumusi River and make a stand in the Wairopi area (known as Papaki to the Japanese). However, this was where the main Japanese supply dumps had been built up. Reluctant to move them, Horii chose a defensive position at the village of Oivi, about ten miles forward of the Kumusi River.

In essence, Horii now chose to defend a bridgehead between the villages of Oivi and Gorari. He placed his freshest troops, the 41st Regiment, forward at Oivi, with a rear-guard provided by the 144th Regiment. In total Horii commanded a force of around 2,800 men well supported by artillery.

In comparison, Vasey's 7th Division comprised some 3,700 troops made up mostly of seven infantry battalions advancing northwards from Eora. On 2 November forward patrols entered Kokoda and found it had been abandoned. The following day Vasey held a flag-raising ceremony there with hundreds of troops present.

The Australians wasted no time in getting Kokoda's runway ready to receive transport aircraft, and the first C-47 landed at 0945 on 5 November. In the subsequent fighting the ability to quickly supply the forward troops with food and munitions by air was a crucial advantage, as was the ability to fly out the wounded.

Oivi was only ten miles from Kokoda, and it was here that the mountainous conditions ended. The area was made up of the northern foothills of the Owen Stanleys, criss-crossed by multiple tracks which for the first time in the Kokoda campaign offered the ability to manoeuvre large formations of troops.

The Australian attack on Oivi began on 5 November but after two days had made no headway against Japanese troops dug in on high ground. Vasey now made a bold move to send half of his force down a different route to attack the Japanese rear. This move succeeded brilliantly, with Gorari captured on 9 November and Horii's headquarters now cut off from his main forces.

The following day the Japanese began an immediate retreat to the Kumusi River, where their artillery was abandoned. By 11 November the Australians had won the most clear-cut victory of the entire campaign: about 440 Japanese troops were killed and many others lost their equipment in the river crossing. In comparison the Australians lost 121 killed.

⚑

In the hours before dawn on 1 November another nuisance raid against Port Moresby unfolded, with bombs falling harmlessly into the harbour and also northwest of Seven-Mile. Whilst there was no damage or casualties, this was an unusual raid insofar as it was led from Kavieng by a senior No. 751 *Ku* officer, *hikocho* Lieutenant Commander Nishioka Kazuo. Nishioka led three Bettys, each of which dropped nine 60-kilogram bombs over the target area.

Reconnaissance flights by B-17s over Rabaul and the Shortlands on 31 October reported both locations still packed with dozens of ships. Accordingly, the early hours of 1 November saw another maximum strength effort by Nos. 11 and 20 Squadrons against shipping in the Shortlands. This time nine Catalinas took part, dropping a total of 70 x 250- and 500-pound semi armour-piercing bombs. One probable hit on a warship was claimed, but results were generally unobserved.

In the same timeframe a dozen Fortresses from the 28th and 30th Bombardment Squadrons also attacked shipping in the Buin-Faisi area of the Shortlands. During co-ordinated bombing runs from 1,600 to 12,000 feet, the B-17s unloaded 44 x 500-pound and 15 x 1,000-pound bombs and the crews claimed a hit on a destroyer. In fact, the seaplane tender *Kamikawa Maru* received slight damage while the hospital ship *Takasago Maru* was near missed.

One of the 30th BS Fortresses, B-17E 41-2635 flown by First Lieutenant John Hanock, never returned from this mission. Bad weather had been experienced *en route* to the target, and Hancock was likely forced to turn back. The wreck site was not discovered until 1999, when the B-17 was found crashed on a ridgeline behind Milne Bay with two 1,000-pound unexploded bombs still in the vicinity. This was the last combat loss experienced by the 19th BG in the SWPA. Hancock and his crew were only a week away from going home.

Meanwhile the previous day a strong force of 27 Zeros had flown into Lae to provide cover for an important supply convoy running into Buna. This was the seaplane tender *Kiyokawa Maru*, being used as a transport, with the IJA transport *Yasukawa Maru* and two destroyers. The Zero force was made up of a dozen No. 251 *Ku* (ex-Tainan *Ku*) fighters led by Lieutenant Kawai Shiro with another fifteen from No. 202 *Ku* (ex-No. 3 *Ku*).

This move was not unnoticed by the Allies, being the first appearance of a sizeable formation of fighters at Lae for some weeks. The Fifth Air Force responded with an early morning strike against Lae on 1 November. This comprised 11 x 90th BS B-25s, 14 x 89th BS A-20As and six No. 30 Squadron Beaufighters, with escort provided by 16 x 8th FS P-40Es. This was among the first missions flown in the theatre by the 8th FS which had recently arrived from Darwin. After the 7th FS had begun receiving new P-40Ks, the 8th FS received hand-me-down P-40Es from that unit. The 8th FS moved into Kila 'drome, already the home of the 89th BS A-20s.

The mission was affected by the weather, with four of the B-25s turning back and only two of the Beaufighters making it as far as Salamaua where they reported heavy rain and 10/10 cloud. However, the other aircraft got through. The seven remaining B-25s dropped 40 x 500-pound bombs on the airfield from 7,000 feet, closely followed by the A-20As which bombed and strafed the same target.

Supplies are airdropped from a C-47 to 25th Brigade troops on the Kokoda Track in October. Even after the capture of the airfield at Kokoda in early November, airdropping would remain the primary method of supplying the forward Australian troops for some weeks.

Australian troops pose at Kokoda airstrip shortly after its recapture, with 6th TCS C-47 41-18697 Norma in the background.

Most of the Zeros scrambled, which were in any case preparing to take-off to patrol over the convoy as it approached Buna. A number of these managed to intercept the returning A-20As and eight escorting P-40s about ten miles south of Lae. A flight of four P-40Es led by Lieutenant Dick Dennis was bounced by an estimated 15-20 Zeros. The Americans dropped their belly tanks, before diving to gain speed and counterattacking. First Lieutenant William Day's #43 *Jerry* received three bullet hits in the first pass, while the inexperienced pilot Second Lieutenant Glenn Wohlford's P-40E was last seen trailing smoke while being pursued by two Zeros. He never returned to base and remains missing in action.

After the remaining American pilots turned into the Zeros, Day fired at a Zero from head on which burst into flames. This was No. 251 *Ku*'s FPO1c Kaneko Toshio who was killed. Seven other Zeros received minor damage while the A-20A *Little Hellion* had been damaged by anti-aircraft fire over Lae. It subsequently crash-landed at Seven-Mile but was later rebuilt as an unarmed "fatcat" aircraft, used for transport runs to Australia.

Late that afternoon three *shotai* of Zeros from Nos. 251 and 202 *Ku*, were patrolling over the ships when they spotted three 90th BS B-25s on a reconnaissance mission 20 miles northwest of Buna. A running fight began as the B-25s turned inland and sped towards Kokoda. The Zeros expended 1,200 x 20mm and 2,230 x 7.7mm rounds and made no claims, but in fact had badly damaged B-25D *The Iroquois* flown by First Lieutenant Theron Platt. Platt was forced to belly land at Kila, but when the bomber slid into a rockpile the bombs onboard detonated and only the co-pilot survived.

Just east of Buna the Zero pilots had failed to notice C-47s shuttling in and out of the new grass field at Pongani. These were escorted by 41st FS Airacobras, two of which vanished on the return flight to Port Moresby when they ran into a weather front with cloud extending from 1,000 to 26,000 feet. Two pilots, Lieutenants Joel Zabel and Thomas Ingram, likely flew into mountains and remain missing.

Meanwhile the 63rd BS was ordered up to Port Moresby to hit Lae to catch the newly arrived Zeros on the ground. However, the squadron could only marshal six Fortresses, and when these arrived they were held until daylight on 2 November to instead strike the convoy as soon as it was sighted. The resumption of Zero activity at Lae also saw the return to Port Moresby of the 22nd BG after a hiatus of several weeks, where all crews had enjoyed periods of 10-day leave in Sydney. Ten 33rd BS B-26s had flown up to 14-Mile from Iron Range.

At 0110 on the morning of 2 November a 28th BS B-17F, 41-24424 *Hell from Heaven Men* flown by Captain Richard Ezzard, was sent out to find the convoy. It was spotted by moonlight, steaming northwards from Buna. When Ezzard made a bombing run fierce anti-aircraft fire was encountered as the *Yasukawa Maru* was in fact an "anti-aircraft transport" equipped with 75mm and 20mm anti-aircraft guns. The B-17 tail gunner, Master Sergeant Robert D Chopping, was killed as a result of this fire, earning the unfortunate status of being the last member of the 19th BG to be killed in action before the group returned home to the US.

Early that morning eleven 28th BS Fortresses were first formation to attack the convoy, claiming two hits and four near misses. These were followed at 0800 by six 63rd BS Fortresses, but one of the bombers experienced an engine malfunction and returned to base with its wingman. The four remaining B-17Es found the ships about 80 miles northeast of Buna and attacked in pairs from between 4,000 – 6,000 feet. A total of 48 x 500-pound bombs was dropped but only near misses were claimed. Intense anti-aircraft fire was experienced which wounded two crewmen. With wounded onboard, the pilot of *Panama Hattie* elected to return directly to Townsville and its superior medical facilities.

By this time a complete *chutai* of nine No. 251 *Ku* Zeros from Lae had reached the convoy and engaged the bombers for almost an hour after 1000. Although the Fortress crews optimistically claimed to have downed three Zeros only one received minor damage.

Later that morning a force of seven No. 30 Squadron Beaufighters led by Wing Commander Walker was searching for the convoy but couldn't find it. They must have been close as three unidentified aircraft were sighted south of New Britain which followed them for about ten minutes before turning around. These aircraft were from one of several overlapping Zero CAPs mounted over the convoy throughout the day.

Meanwhile that afternoon another six Beaufighters led by Squadron Leader Parker were ordered to attack the ships in company with nine No. 100 Squadron Beauforts and eleven 7th FS P-40s flying as dive-bombers. However, after the three squadrons failed to rendezvous at Cape Nelson on the north coast of Papua, and with fuel consumed while waiting, the mission was abandoned. Some of these aircraft instead strafed secondary targets in the Buna area. Assigned as fighter escort to this mission was a new player: P-38 Lightnings of the 39th FS (details of their introduction into the theatre is explained in Chapter 11).

Ten 33rd BS B-26s searched for four hours for the ships without finding them. The Marauders returned to 14-Mile low on fuel, and two were written off in landing accidents. The first of these was Lieutenant Louis Ford's 40-1503 *Maybe*, which blew a tyre and the plane's nose was crushed after it skidded off the runway. The second was #40-1493 *Ole '93* which ran out of fuel on its landing approach and the pilot made an emergency belly landing.

By mid-afternoon a force of ten 90th BS B-25s had more success, attacking the ships with 33 x 500-pound bombs from 7,000 feet. Four near misses were claimed, and two Zeros made frontal attacks on the Mitchells. One of the bombers was hit many times but all returned safely to Port Moresby.

During the last two hours of daylight three more formations of B-17s reached the convoy. One of these comprised eight B-17Es from a mixed 28th and 30th BS formation, another comprised a trio of 30th BS Fortresses while several 63rd BS bombers returned for their second attack of the day. Captain Ed Scott's crew, from the 63rd BS, were likely responsible for scoring a hit on the *Yasukawa Maru* amidst many more claims of near misses.

Several Zeros intercepted the Fortresses during these attacks, damaging four of them. However, FPO1c Yasui Kozaburo from No. 251 *Ku* was hit by defensive fire from the bombers. He managed to force-land and eventually re-joined Japanese forces.

The fate of the *Yasukawa Maru* is somewhat more peculiar. After its anti-aircraft guns fought hard against the attackers throughout the day, by late afternoon the gun crews were relaxed and had begun drinking beer. The forward 75mm gunners then accidentally disabled their guns and the ship was hit, likely during Scott's attack. Bombs exploded in the No. 3 hold and the engine room, rendering the ship powerless and drifting. One crewman died in the attack, but the many wounded IJA soldiers aboard who had been evacuated from Buna were transferred to another vessel.

Australian troops won a decisive victory against the Japanese at Oivi-Gorari in early November. Here two Japanese POWs are marched to a rear area for interrogation and ultimately transport to a POW camp.

A 7th FS P-40E was lost on 2 November when Lieutenant Bryant Wesley developed engine trouble and ditched P-40E 41-5313 in Bootless Inlet. Wesley was unhurt and swam ashore.

The night of 2/3 November once again saw Catalinas from Nos. 11 and 20 Squadrons raid the Shortlands. This time six flying boats found few ships still in the area. A mix of 250- and 500-pound semi armour piercing bombs were dropped but no hits were observed.

The 3 November found the Fifth Air Force in something of a crisis. With so many B-17 sorties having been flown in recent days, and the three remaining squadrons of the 19th BG preparing to depart, Kenney's heavy bomber force was virtually limited to the 63rd BS. At this time the inexperienced 403rd BS (the only other fully combat ready 43rd BG squadron) was being used to fly the daily reconnaissance missions previously flown by the 435th BS, with a forward echelon based at Milne Bay. Note that the first B-24Ds of the 90th BG had recently arrived in Australia but were not yet ready for operations (the problematic arrival of this group is described in Chapter 11).

In fact, 3 November saw only three B-17s serviceable at Port Moresby. That morning, two of these Fortresses from the 63rd BS found the disabled and burning *Yasukawa Maru* 56 miles southwest of Gasmata. Three 500-pound bombs near-missed the ship with the American crews reporting it last seen as a solid mass of flames, with smoke rising to 4,000 feet. After drifting in the area for several days the hulk was later scuttled by a Japanese warship.

Bad weather prevented other air attacks, but that evening a single 30th BS B-17 unloaded six 500-pound bombs over the wharf area at Lae.

Clear weather on 4 November saw a resumption of the normal activity over Papua. That morning three 89th BS A-20As attacked Japanese positions at Oivi with 20-pound bombs. At 1015 three B-17s flying a daily armed reconnaissance mission of the Buna-Lae-Gasmata area found a 12,000-ton ship off Salamaua which was attacked with eight 500-pound bombs from 18,000 feet.

Three 65th BS B-17s were sent out to attack the same target. This squadron had only just become ready for operations with a transfer of three experienced crews from the 93rd BS. However, this mission was far from smooth. One bomber remained grounded due to mechanical problems, while another returned to base soon after take-off after experiencing engine trouble. The third Fortress, flown by Second Lieutenant Melville Ehlers, ran into trouble high over the Owen Stanleys when the top fuselage hatch containing the life rafts blew loose. One of the rafts inflated and became tangled in the tailplane, making the bomber difficult to control. Eventually the raft was shot away by one of the gunners, and Ehlers completed the mission by bombing a wreck near Salamaua.

Meanwhile nine 90th BS B-25Ds and nine 33rd BS B-26s searched unsuccessfully for the ship reported off Salamaua, with escort provided by seven 39th FS Lightnings. Early that afternoon Salamaua was attacked by eight B-25s of the 13th BS which dropped 30 x 500-pound bombs on the town, while six No. 30 Squadron Beaufighters were also active. These swept the coast from Buna to Salamaua searching for barges, but few targets were seen. One Beaufighter received slight damage from anti-aircraft fire while interestingly during this mission the tail of B-17E 41-2663, shot down on 12 September, was seen washed up on a beach four miles south of Buna.

Catalinas were again active in their long-range missions from Cairns on the night of 4/5 November. Five flying boats reached the Shortlands where few ships were sighted. Bombs were dropped but no results were observed in conditions of poor visibility.

During the day activity was limited. Three 13th BS B-25s on a reconnaissance mission bombed a schooner seen near Arawe on the south coast of New Britain. Near Rabaul, a lone 435th BS B-17 was attacked by six No. 251 *Ku* Zeros but sustained only minor damage. A single No. 202 *Ku* pilot also took off and attempted to intercept the Fortress but failed to make contact and landed 90 minutes later. This was the last mission in the theatre for the No. 202 *Ku* detachment which soon returned to the Netherlands East Indies.

To the east of the Kokoda Track troops of the 126th Regiment were slowly pushing overland but had experienced difficulty in co-ordinating supply drops. These had been made without parachutes, with the result that a large portion of the supplies were damaged or never recovered from the jungle. At 1010 C-47 41-38615 *The Broadway Limited* of the 6th TCS departed Wards 'drome to make the first drop of supplies using parachutes. Onboard were four crew plus four men from the 126th Regiment. Three of these acted as loadmasters, while the fourth was the regiment's commanding officer, Colonel Lawrence Quinn, who was observing the operation. Sadly, on the first pass one of the parachutes became tangled in the tail of the C-47, causing it to crash into a mountain with the loss of all eight men aboard.

Both 6 and 7 November were also relatively quiet with mainly routine reconnaissance missions flown. During one of these on 6 November a 13th BS B-25 dropped five 500-pound bombs on a destroyer seen off the southern tip of New Ireland, with the closest bomb landing 40 feet from the stern. The following day three B-25s bombed two floatplanes seen moored at Lasanga Island to the south of Salamaua, while another B-25 once again bomber a schooner near Arawe. Also on 7 November, three 89th BS A-20As bombed and strafed targets near Buna, where the airfield was reported as very muddy and half underwater.

Meanwhile on 6 November Lieutenant Nelson Brownell of the 8th FS was patrolling the Kokoda area in P-40E 41-25178 when the engine stopped. The aircraft crashed, resulting in the first fatality for the 49th FG in New Guinea. Brownell's fighter had been named *Spoddessape* meaning spotted-assed ape. This name originated from veteran pilots who joined the 49th FG in early 1942 after fighting in Java. After they were evacuated from the Netherlands East Indies a common saying was that they left "… faster than a spotted-assed ape."

It will be recalled from Chapter 2 that the 71st and 405th Bombardment Squadrons of the 38th BG had not moved to Rorona (30-Mile) as planned in September, but instead had deployed to the relative safety of Horn Island. Following the IJA retreat over the Owen Stanleys, these two squadrons moved forward to Rorona in late October. The ground component arrived by ship on 1 November but took about two weeks to unload and fully move into the base.

On paper this was an important boost to Kenney's forward air power, but there were concerns about the combat effectiveness of these squadrons. The commanding officer, Colonel Theodore Castle, had never fully recovered from a crash in Hawaii and was likely suffering from post-traumatic stress disorder. Kenney wanted experienced and aggressive leadership and so on 6 November chose the proven 22nd BG veteran Major Brian "Shanty" O'Neill to take over the 38th BG. O'Neill had led the 408th BS and was reputed as a hard-drinking and skilled pilot who quickly earned the respect of his crews. O'Neill brought in his own hand-picked team to shape up the two 38th BG squadrons, Major Melvin Offers taking over the 71st BS and Major Forrest Harsh the 405th BS.

At this time of reorganisation, the two squadrons were stood down from operations for a week. While the ground personnel were constructing a camp at Rorona, the air echelons had begun operations at Wards 'drome (Five-Mile). However, that location was becoming a busy centre for RAAF operations, with Nos. 6 and 30 Squadrons based there in addition to the newly arriving No. 22 Squadron (see below). Wards was also increasingly being used by C-47s of the 374th Troop Carrier Group (comprising the 6th, 21st, 22nd and 33rd TCS), and soon the location would become headquarters for all Allied transport units. Accordingly, the two 38th BG squadrons were directed to move to Durand (17-Mile).

At 0850 on 8 November three 89th BS A-20As bombed and strafed Oivi, but results were unobserved. An hour later a trio of 13th BS B-25s on a reconnaissance mission strafed a possible wireless transmission station seen near Gasmata. Three B-25s returned later and dropped two 500-pound bombs on the site.

Early in the afternoon Wing Commander Walker led a trio of No. 30 Squadron Beaufighters in an armed reconnaissance of the Wairopi-Buna track, with top cover provided by four P-40Es at 12,000 feet. The track appeared well used but no activity was noted, and huts in the Sanananda

C-47 41-38601 Swamp Rat seen bogged at Pongani after landing on a freshly cleared strip on 7 November. American troops of the 32nd Division subsequently dragged the transport onto dry ground.

area were strafed. Meanwhile, following engine problems Robert Howard of the 8th FS crash-landed his P-40E into trees close to the camp of 2/6th Australian Field Ambulance at Myola.

On the night of 8/9 November three Catalinas from Cairns raided Kavieng. A mix of bombs were dropped on runways and dispersal areas occupied by No. 751 *Ku*'s Bettys, but results were unobserved.

Daylight on 9 November saw conditions of good visibility and several Allied attack missions. At 0840 six 89th BS A-20As bombed and strafed Oivi, expending 239 x 20-pound fragmentation bombs together with 1,600 0.50-inch and 3,400 x 0.30-inch calibre rounds. Fifteen minutes later nine Beaufighters swept over the Kokoda-Buna area on an armed reconnaissance. Several targets were strafed with 2,650 x 20mm and 18,000 x 0.303-inch rounds in what was considered a successful attack. Light anti-aircraft fire was experienced which injured one observer and damaged two of the aircraft.

Also on this morning eight 33rd BS B-26s attacked supply dumps in the Buna-Sanananda area with 199 x 100-pound bombs. At 1030 a lone 435th BS B-17 was attacked by two Zeros over Mono Island near the Shortlands. The bomber was holed seven times before making its escape. Late in the afternoon three 13th BS B-25s on a reconnaissance mission bombed a schooner off Salamaua and a merchant ship off New Ireland, claiming a hit on the latter target.

That night a lone Catalina on a reconnaissance mission attacked a destroyer seen 54 miles southwest of Gasmata with four 250-pound bombs but all missed.

By 10 November Vasey's victory at Oivi-Gorari was apparent and the Fifth Air Force was directed to maintain pressure on the IJA troops withdrawing into the area south of Buna. At 0800 a trio of No. 30 Squadron Beaufighters strafed targets there. Fighter sweeps over the same area were conducted by 8th FS P-40s and 41st FS Airacobras but no enemy aircraft were encountered. A second Beaufighter strike planned for that afternoon was unsuccessful due to bad weather.

A No. 22 Squadron Boston at Port Moresby in October. The unit would not make its combat debut until mid-November but suffered its first loss on 10 November when a Boston exploded in mid-air during bombing practice on the Pruth wreck off Port Moresby.

At 0920 eight 33rd BS B-26s attacked anti-aircraft positions and supply dumps near Sanananda Point from 1,400 feet with 228 x 100-pound bombs. The attack was co-ordinated with three 89th BS A-20As strafing the same area and dropping 120 parafrags, reporting that anti-aircraft positions were silenced. A near-miss occurred when the A-20A crews saw one anti-aircraft gun blown out of its pit by a preceding B-26 bomb and returned to strafe it despite ground fire. Leading the 89th BS was Captain Ed Larner whose *Spook* (40-109) drove through treetops. On return to Kila both outer wing panels needed to be replaced.

Later than morning B-17F 41-24550 of the 403rd BS piloted by Lieutenant Charles Downer was flying a lone reconnaissance of the Shortlands area when he circled to photograph a large collection of ships seen below. The Fortress was then attacked by several fighters from a combined formation of a dozen No. 204 *Ku* and six *Hiyo* (land-based) Zeros. The Zeros were returning from a Guadalcanal mission and were led by No. 204 *Ku hikotaicho* Lieutenant Commander Kofukuda Mitsugu. A half-hour running battle started at 1050, with the B-17 suffering a damaged engine before losing its pursuers in cloud.

Another unit that had moved forward to Port Moresby in recent days was No. 22 Squadron which had been training on its Boston Mark IIIs in Townsville. By the end of October most of the squadron personnel had arrived at Wards 'drome and commenced constructing a camp. In early November aircraft were still arriving and the squadron would not be ready for operations until mid-November. Tragically, the squadron's first fatalities occurred before then. On 10 November Flight Lieutenant Vernon Morgan and two crewmen were carrying out bombing practice with 20-pound fragmentation bombs on the *Pruth* wreck when their aircraft, A28-12, exploded in mid-air. Further incidents of this type would follow.

Northeast over the mountains, work on a new all-weather airfield had been proceeding at Pongani. The field, on a well-drained site and covered with gravel from a nearby pit, was finished on

9 November, and was soon busily receiving transport flights from Port Moresby. On 10 November, C-47 41-18564 *Flying Dutchman* of the 33rd TCS departed Wards 'drome for Pongani flown by Second Lieutenant George W Vandervort, carrying an additional two crew and 20 American infantry troops.

Over the Owen Stanleys the aircraft experienced a severe downdraft and crashed near Mount Obree. Of those onboard, seventeen initially survived the crash which was at a height of 9,000 feet in an extremely remote area. Some soon died of their wounds or the extreme cold. Two days later a group of the healthiest survivors left to find help, but only two of these men reached an Australian outpost more than a month later. At length four others also managed to find a path out through the mountains, with those remaining behind eventually dying of hunger and exposure.

Another loss occurring on this date was that of No. 6 Squadron Hudson A16-205. This was flown by Flying Officer David Hersey, who had just taken over as commander of the No. 6 Squadron Milne Bay detachment. It had taken off from Gurney Field at 0630 on a routine patrol but crashed into coastal waters in bad weather. The location was near a coastwatching post which heard an explosion, and wreckage was recovered a few days later.

Meanwhile half of the 63rd BS B-17s had recently been sent forward to Port Moresby from Mareeba, and shortly after midnight on 10/11 November five B-17s took off to bomb the ships seen at the Shortlands the previous day. At 0415 some 20 x 500-pound bombs were dropped from 5,000 to 8,000 feet on a transport vessel, which was claimed as hit after black smoke and debris was seen.

Daylight on 11 November saw a resumption of the Allied attacks in the Buna area. Three Beaufighters strafed suspected supply dumps as well as a barge camouflaged with palm leaves discovered near the Gona wreck. Defensive fire from machine guns was encountered with the fuselage of one of the attackers holed by a single bullet. Later in the morning a trio of 89th BS A-20As bombed and strafed the Wairopi area. That afternoon Wing Commander Walker led four Beaufighters in another attack, where huts and motor vehicles were strafed.

Meanwhile the remaining three squadrons of the 19th BG were finally leaving Australia. The 64th and 65th Bombardment Squadrons moved from Iron Range to Mareeba, taking over camps previously used by the 28th and 30th BS. Together with the 63rd BS, three squadrons of the 43rd BG were now concentrated at Mareeba which was vastly more comfortable than the primitive tropical conditions at Iron Range. Meanwhile the 403rd BS was using a forward base at Milne Bay and would move there in entirety from Iron Range by 23 November.

While virtually all of the 19th BG ground personnel were being sent home, many of the aircrews whose tours had not yet expired were rapidly transferred into the 43rd BG by mid-November, as were some older B-17E Fortresses. This resulted in a week of confusion over which crews and aircraft were flying for which unit, until administrative processes caught up and restored order.

Engineers strip 89th BS A-20A Old Man Mose for parts after its emergency landing at Pongani on 21 November.

CHAPTER 11

THE BATTLE OF BUNA BEGINS:
12 – 21 NOVEMBER

By 11 November the frontline IJA force in Papua had been completely routed at Oivi-Gorari. Over the next few days a hurried and confused evacuation to the coast took place. The stragglers that emerged through the jungle represented just a fraction of the fighting strength of the proud force that had marched into the mountains with such vigour two months earlier. The about-face of Japanese fortunes was no more pronounced than in the fate of Horii himself. Wanting to find a quick way to the coast, Horii took a raft down the Kumusi River. After arriving at the mouth, he was swept out to sea and drowned.

On 16 November Australian troops crossed the Kumusi River and began an advance towards the Buna beachhead area which was just 40 miles away. This date marks the end of the Kokoda Campaign and the beginning of the Battle of Buna-Gona. At the same time American troops were advancing along the coast and on 16 November were just a few miles away from the Buna perimeter. The coastal advance was supported by luggers and small ships, which were used to transport a limited amount of heavy equipment including artillery.

Another parallel American advance was occurring a few miles inland, and on 16 November these troops had captured Dobodura. This location had excellent prospects for an airfield complex, and a company of engineers immediately set to work clearing the first landing strip.

Meanwhile the Japanese forces consolidated into three distinct beachhead areas along a coastline of about 15 miles. To the east was Buna, in the centre was Sanananda-Giruwa and to the west was Gona village. These locations were on a thin coastal strip which lay between the sea and a tidal forest swamp through which the attackers would need to approach. Japanese defensive positions had been constructed over the past several weeks and were extremely well dug in. They were occupied by around 5,500 IJA and IJN troops.

The subsequent battle unfolded in two distinct parts. From the east American troops of the 32nd Division assaulted Buna, while the Australian 7th Division force which had advanced from Kokoda (assisted by the bulk of the US 126th Regiment) attacked Gona (the 25th Brigade) and Sananada-Giruwa (the 16th Brigade). However, as will be seen the initial American advance from the east did not commence as planned.

The mid-November period also saw the last major Japanese attempt to land fresh troops on Guadalcanal to recapture Henderson Field. This led to another busy period of maritime activity in the Solomons, with the Naval Battle of Guadalcanal fought over 12-15 November. Despite significant losses, the result was an American victory which effectively secured Henderson Field.

At this time Major Bill Benn, who had so ably led the 63rd BS, was promoted to a staff position with 5th Bomber Command. He was replaced by Captain Ed Scott. Benn, who had arrived in Australia with Kenney as the general's aide, would soon ask permission on behalf of the 43rd BG for the group to adopt the name *Ken's Men*. A chuffed Kenney readily agreed. In time the name would multifariously honour not only Kenney but also the head of 5th Bomber Command, Brigadier General Kenneth Walker, as well as Ken McCullar of the 63rd BS who had helped pioneer the skip-bombing tactics.

Meanwhile Kenney's replacement for the departed 19th BG had arrived in Australia and after some delay would soon fly its first combat mission. This was the 90th BG (made up of the 319th, 320th, 321st and 400th Bombardment Squadrons) which had been created on paper in April and had in recent months undergone conversion training on B-24D Liberators in the US. In mid-September the group had arrived in Hawaii where the crews conducted navigation and formation training. By early November the first dozen B-24s had arrived in Queensland, but frustratingly for Kenney these suffered from cracked nose-wheel collars and would not be operational for two weeks. Meanwhile, another eight B-24s which had arrived in New Caledonia in late October were temporarily held by SoPAC pending the resolution of the Guadalcanal situation.

By 14 November the first of the B-24s had arrived at their designated base at Iron Range. The group's ground contingent would not arrive by ship until the last week of November, but so

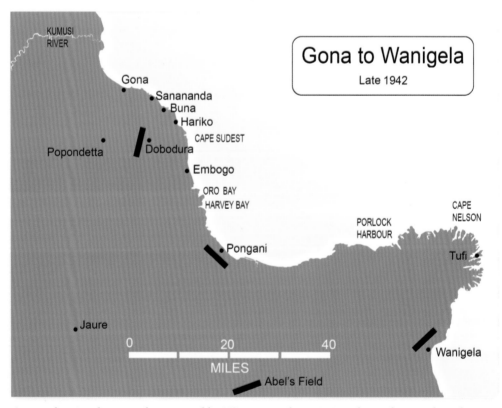

A map showing the coastal route used by US troops in late 1942 in their advance along the coast towards Buna. In addition, airfields were developed first at Wanigela and Abel's Field, then at Pongani and finally at Dobodura.

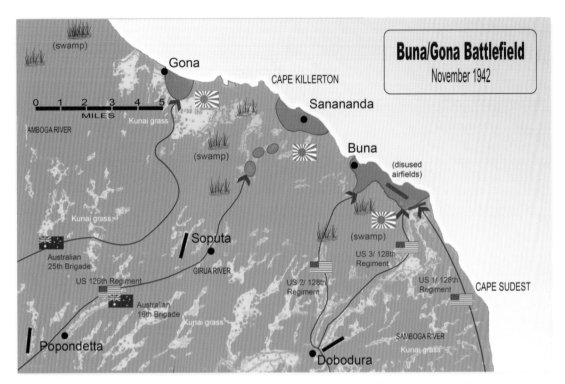

This map shows how the Battle of Buna-Gona evolved in the latter half of November, with Japanese forces concentrated in three separate Beachhead areas at Gona, Sanananda Point and Buna. The routes of the Allied advances, towards these areas are also shown. These advances, by elements of the Australian 7th Division and American 32nd Division, were supported by new airstrips quickly constructed at Dobodura and Popondetta. Another airstrip at Soputa was mainly used for airdrops.

desperate was Kenney for heavy bombers that the Liberators were rushed into action almost immediately. This hasty action would end in disaster, as will be seen.

The early hours of 12 November saw four No. 11 Squadron Catalinas raiding Buin airfield, dropping 16 x 250-pound and 12 x 500-pound general purpose bombs as well as 80 x 20-pound fragmentation bombs. Many fires were started, and it was presumed that fuel dumps had been hit. Three aircraft were claimed destroyed.

Shortly before dawn six 63rd BS B-17s raided shipping in the nearby Shortlands, dropping 29 x 500-pound bombs with the aid of illumination flares. The crews claimed two hits on two cargo vessels, one of which was a large ship estimated at 12,000-tons. In fact, the bombs had inflicted minor damage on the 15,000-ton IJN oiler *Naruto*.

The only other Allied air attack on 12 November was an early morning sweep by a trio of No. 30 Squadron Beaufighters. Two barges were strafed near Gona as were various huts and supply tracks, with a total of 1,300 x 20mm and 7,600 x 0.303-inch rounds expended.

The following day saw another pre-dawn B-17 raid on the Shortlands anchorage. Seven 63rd BS

Fortresses found a naval convoy which was attacked from 1,000 to 5,000 feet with 500-pound bombs. Hits were claimed on a light cruiser and a destroyer and other near misses on destroyers and a transport. Intense anti-aircraft fire was experienced, and B-17F 41-24384 *Pluto* had one engine knocked out and another damaged that only ran at half power. In addition, a shell had punched a hole through the plexiglass nose, so that the underpowered bomber also had to battle a loss of aerodynamics as strong air currents poured into the bomber. The pilot, Lieutenant James Murphy, recalled:

> It felt as though we were in a hurricane. Everything was flying around in the nose and up in the cockpit. We couldn't stop the air from coming in, but we did tie everything down to prevent the blowing of paper and other items.

Murphy eventually touched down at Seven-Mile two hours after the remainder of the squadron, with one of the engines windmilling when it ran dry during the landing run.

Daylight on 13 November saw an armed reconnaissance over the Buna area by a trio of Beaufighters, with barges and collapsible boats strafed. In the only other Allied air attack on this day a B-17 flying a reconnaissance mission strafed a schooner moored off Manus Island. Meanwhile another lone B-17 was attacked by four Zeros near Buin but escaped with minor damage.

At 0250 on 14 November two 65th BS Fortresses departed Seven-Mile tasked with finding a Japanese convoy leaving the Shortlands for Guadalcanal. The crews were to land at Guadalcanal if necessary or even ditch, such was the knife-edge situation in the Solomons. After observing several vessels in the Shortlands, the pair continued about one third of the way to Guadalcanal where they descended to low altitude under an intense storm. One of the pilots, Second Lieutenant John Frost II, recalled that they came down upon:

> … a whole damn ocean full of ships.

At 0740 the crews unloaded nine 500-pound bombs over a large transport packed with troops but scored only a near misses. Six Zeros then arrived forcing the Fortresses into clouds prior to making the long return flight to Seven-Mile, marking one of the longest incursions by the Fifth Air Force into the SoPAC theatre.

The morning also saw another armed sweep by three Beaufighters. Buna was not observed due to a low cloud base, but native canoes used for transporting supplies near the mouth of the Kumusi River were strafed, as were stores seen on the riverbank. The mission was repeated by four Beaufighters early in the afternoon, which strafed targets in the Buna area and the mouth of the Kumusi River.

In other activity on 14 November six 22nd BG B-26s flew two search missions for a ship reported off Buna but failed to find any sign of it. That evening a lone 13th BS Mitchell on an armed reconnaissance dropped five 500-pound bombs on supply tracks inland from Buna.

There were two Allied raids during the night of 14-15 November. The first of these was by five Nos. 11 and 20 Squadron Catalinas which dropped 100 x 20-, 16 x 250- and 18 x 500-pound bombs on Buin 'drome from 4,400 to 8,000 feet. This was considered a highly successful attack, with eight aircraft claimed destroyed and fires started at suspected fuel and ammunition dumps.

A few hours later a dozen Fortresses departed Seven-Mile to attack shipping at Rabaul, although one bomber soon returned to base and another failed to find the target. The B-17s were from the 63rd and 64th Bombardment Squadrons, this being the first bombing mission for the latter unit. A total of 78 x 500-pound bombs were dropped over ships and Rabaul itself. Ken McCullar claimed a direct hit on an unidentified vessel and could feel the explosion from 6,500 feet. This was the IJN transport *Azuma Maru* which suffered medium damage.

On the return flight B-17E 41-2662 *Spawn of Hell* ran out of fuel and Lieutenant William Compton made a safe emergency landing on a beach 100 miles southeast of Port Moresby. The aircraft was spotted by two Tiger Moths of No. 1 Rescue and Communications Squadron, and a week later fuel was delivered by a lugger permitting the B-17 to be flown out.

As noted above, the first 90th BG B-24s had just arrived at Iron Range and were immediately pressed into action despite the inexperience of their crews. Eight had been flown up to Seven-Mile where ground crews from the 43rd and 22nd Bombardment Groups prepared them for a dawn raid against shipping in the Shortlands.

However bad weather was soon experienced with three bombers turning back to base. The remaining five approaching the target area in pairs or alone at around 5,000 feet between 0530 and 0630 on 15 November. Co-pilot Lieutenant Ray Smeltzer wrote:

> One of my jobs was to ensure that the bomb bay doors did not slip towards the closed position during bombing runs. To do this, I would sit directly below the flight deck area and just forward of the bays and push on the manual lever to keep the doors from creeping toward the closed position. If they did inch forward, the bombs might not release, and thus nullify the run. As I sat there, I could hear the guns firing, and looking through the now open bays I could see far below the convoy with the wakes churning behind them trying to zigzag to avoid our bombs. Just at that moment, I caught a flash just to the side, and looked there only to see a small plane with red circles on the wings go right across our path. Well, suddenly I realized that here I was with not even a rock to throw, while this little fighter was going to shoot projectiles at me. It worried me to the extent that I immediately crossed my legs …

The fighter was one of a pair of patrolling No. 802 *Ku* Rufes which engaged the first Liberator at 0530 and claimed it as a probable kill. Meanwhile down below at Buin, alongside a No. 204 *Ku* Zero contingent, a dozen *Hiyo* Zeros led by *buntaicho* Lieutenant Kaneko Tadashi were temporarily there to support the Guadalcanal campaign. Four of these Zeros (from both units) succeeded in attacking a pair of Liberators but failed to inflict any damage.

One of the B-24s, *Lady Beverley*, was damaged by a bursting anti-aircraft shell and could not maintain altitude. Lieutenant John Warner was forced to ditch the bomber near Milne Bay, but the impact broke the fuselage in half. Of eight crewmen onboard only two were rescued by Australian soldiers.

Meanwhile *The Condor* experienced fuel transfer problems five hours after leaving the target

B-24D 41-23714 8-Ball en route to the Shortlands. This Liberator was among the first batch to arrive in Australia with the 321st BS.

area, and it became clear the bomber would not make it back to base. Lieutenant Dale Thornhill feathered all of the engines and made an emergency belly landing on a beach east of Iron Range. Despite vigorous efforts, the undamaged bomber resisted all attempts to be salvaged and its remains are still there today.

At 0850 on 15 November six No. 30 Squadron Beaufighters strafed anti-aircraft positions in the Buna area. The raid was co-ordinated with five B-26s from the 2nd and 19th Bombardment Squadrons which dropped 26 x 300-pound bombs on the same targets. The mission was repeated that afternoon by identical sized formations of Beaufighters and B-26s, with the difference that some of the Beaufighters found barges to strafe. The day also saw No. 22 Squadron make its combat debut, with three of its Bostons strafing canoes and a hut near Gona.

In preparation for the unfolding Allied ground offensive, 16 November saw a maximum strength effort by the Fifth Air Force against targets in the Buna area. This comprised 50 sorties by B-25s, B-26s, Bostons and Beaufighters, typically attacking readily identifiable targets at Buna or along the coast. During one of these missions a 90th BS B-25C, 41-12982 *Old Victory* flown by Lieutenant Richard Yeager, sustained a direct hit from anti-aircraft fire and crashed in flames near the Buna shoreline. All six crew onboard were killed.

Another loss occurred after an 89th BS A-20A, 40-155 *Abijah Gooch*, departed Cairns at 0900 for Port Moresby. The aircraft disappeared with the loss of all four onboard.

The Allied activity over the Buna area covered a movement along the coast by three small craft which were among a number purchased on the Australian civil market by the US Army Service of Supply for work in New Guinea waters. These were the *Alacrity*, *Bonwin* and *Minnemura*, in company with a captured Japanese barge, which were sailing from Oro Bay to Hariko, which was very close to the Buna perimeter. The barge carried two Australian 25-pounder field guns,

Troops of the US 32nd Division are loaded on luggers and small ships bound for Pongani. Prior to the development of Dobodura's airfield the American advance on Buna was dependent on these vessels, four of which were sunk by No. 582 Ku Val dive-bombers on 15 November.

while the other vessels were each towing a boat or pontoon and were laden with rations and ammunition for the American troops nearby. Among those aboard was Major General Edwin Harding, the commander of the US 32nd Division. At 0800 that morning, naval lookouts at Buna had spotted these vessels arriving at Oro Bay. It was the first time that the Japanese had become aware of such movements along the coast.

The reaction was swift, and at 1515 a strike force departed Rabaul comprising a dozen No. 582 *Ku* Vals each armed with a pair of 60-kilogram bombs. The dive-bombers were led by recently promoted Lieutenant Commander Inoue Buntou and were escorted by six No. 582 *Ku* Zeros led by Lieutenant (jg) Susugi Usaburo. These had no trouble finding the four vessels two and a half hours later, which made easy targets as they were slow moving and only defended by light machine guns. More importantly for the Japanese, the Allied fighter cover that had been present over the vessels during the day had just returned to base.

Soon the attackers left all four vessels blazing under palls of black smoke. Some 24 men were killed with many more wounded. The survivors, including General Harding, swam ashore. The loss of the supplies and the artillery pieces completely disrupted the American attack plans. Those troops already forward deployed would now be wholly dependent on air dropped supplies until Dobodura airfield could be used by transport planes. Other troops waiting to be ferried forward from Pongani were forced to undertake a gruelling 30-mile march over swampy terrain with full packs.

The attackers landed at Lae at 1910, except for two Zeros which made an unusual night flight to Rabaul where they touched down at 2130. Meanwhile at 1740 six No. 252 *Ku* Zeros had left Rabaul to strafe the same targets, but with dusk fast approaching they had returned to base 80 minutes later. A lone Betty surveyed the scene later that evening, noting that wrecks were visible as were another two vessels.

Also on this afternoon three No. 751 *Ku* Bettys departed Kavieng to bomb Port Moresby with a load of 33 x 60-kilogram bombs. However, on reaching the Papuan coast at 1845 near Buna the weather over the mountains had closed in, so the crews jettisoned their bombs and returned to Kavieng.

Later that evening four Nos. 11 and 20 Squadron Catalinas from Cairns once again attacked Buin 'drome, dropping a mix of 20-, 250- and 500-pound bombs from between 2,400 to 9,200 feet. In conditions of very poor visibility, hits were made on the runway and dispersal areas with one aircraft claimed destroyed.

That night the 90th BG readied for its second combat mission, a raid against Rabaul from Iron Range which included aircraft from three squadrons (the 319th, 320th and 400th BS) led by the group commander, Colonel Arthur Meehan. Shortly before midnight, twelve Liberators, including seven from the 319th BS, began taking off, each heavily loaded with 31,000 gallons of fuel and six 500-pound bombs. However, raised dust from the first bombers hampered visibility and obscured the runway lights for those following. This was in addition to confusion over the order in which the aircraft were meant to take off.

A 400th BS B-24D named *Bombs to Nippon* (41-23942) veered off the runway and exploded with the loss of all eleven onboard. The incident destroyed a 403rd BS B-17F parked alongside the runway (41-24522) and damaged three other Liberators, although all were later repaired.

Of the ten Liberators which continued with the mission, four soon returned due to bad weather and just two found the target area and unloaded their bombs from between 7,000 and 10,000 feet. One of these crews claimed to have hit a merchant ship in Rabaul Harbour, while two other B-24s bombed Lakunai and Vunakanau instead albeit through cloud. However, the lead B-24D (41-11902 *Punjab*) which was piloted by the 320th BS commander Major Raymond Morse and co-piloted by the 90th BG commander, Colonel Arthur Meehan, disappeared without trace during the mission with the loss of all ten men onboard.

The loss of Morse and Meehan was a big blow to the morale of the inexperienced group, and this compounded the disastrous first two missions which had seen the loss of four B-24s (as well as three others seriously damaged) and 27 men. When informed of the disaster, Kenney withdrew the unit from further large-scale combat missions pending further training.

At 0907 on 17 November eight B-25s swept over Lae 'drome, dropping 55 x 100-pound demolition bombs and 268 x 20-pound fragmentation bombs. They were hoping to catch the No. 582 *Ku* Vals and Zeros that had flown in the previous evening. These had already departed, including five Vals and three Zeros that were sent hunting shipping along the coast from Buna (two vessels were attacked: the *Willyama* had to be beached as a total loss while the *Two Freddies* was badly damaged). Escort for the B-25s was provided by 7th and 8th FS P-40Es,

B-24D 41-24108 is seen at an unidentified Australian airfield shortly after the arrival of the 90th BG in Australia in early November. The bomber would later be named The Butcher Boy while serving with the 320th BS.

a flight of which briefly pursued a single Zero before it was lost in cloud.

At 1000 the Vals and Zeros tangled with five B-26s from the 2nd and 19th Bombardment Squadrons that were bombing and strafing Gona Mission. One B-26 received minor damage, while one Val was damaged and ditched on its flight back to Rabaul – the crew were rescued. The remainder of the No. 582 *Ku* aircraft returned to Rabaul at 1230.

Also on this morning six No. 30 Squadron Beaufighters strafed Lae 'drome, under the protection of escorting P-40s. Activity was noted in the dispersal area, with a dozen men seen running from parked aircraft. One "Sally" and one Zero were well strafed and left burning. At 1315 that afternoon a trio of B-25s unloaded 15 x 500-pound bombs over Gasmata's runway which might have been used by the returning Japanese aircraft.

Meanwhile the 9th FS only flew its first combat mission over New Guinea on 17 November. The squadron had been struggling with low numbers of worn-out P-40Es and also malarial conditions at its base at Rorona (30-Mile). This initial mission was escorting C-47s flying supplies to Pongani. On return to Port Moresby two P-40Es got lost in overcast conditions and subsequently ditched along the Papuan coast after running out of fuel. These were 41-24821 flown by Lieutenant Floyd Finberg and 41-36166 flown by Lieutenant William Hanning: both men were unhurt and had returned to their squadron within a few days.

The 17 November also saw a convoy of five destroyers (*Kazagumo, Makigumo, Yugumo, Oyashio* and *Kagero*) depart Rabaul soon after dawn. These vessels carried some 1,000 reinforcements for Buna. Taking advantage of overcast weather, the destroyers took the direct route south of New Britain. Cover was provided by a trio of No. 582 *Ku* Zeros from Rabaul which patrolled overhead from 0930 to 1145. After refuelling at Lae the Zeros returned to Rabaul. Later that afternoon Warrant Officer Tsunoda Kazuo led a *chutai* of nine No. 582 *Ku* Model 32 Zeros from Rabaul to Lae where they landed just before sunset.

Also that afternoon three No. 751 *Ku* Bettys departed Kavieng to raid Port Moresby. In an exact repeat of the failed mission on the previous day, after encountering bad weather the crews jettisoned their bombs and returned to Kavieng.

The destroyers arrived safely off Buna late on the evening of 17 November. After offloading was completed, the ships departed at 0230 the next morning. Meanwhile a second echelon of three destroyers (*Asashio*, *Umikaze* and *Kawakaze*) had embarked 500 troops at Rabaul at midnight and set off for Buna. The following morning this convoy was covered by eight of Tsunoda's No. 582 *Ku* Zero contingent from Lae which took off at 0515 and landed at Gasmata at 0720.

The aerial activity at Lae and the naval activity off Buna were noticed by Allied forces and missions unfolded against both targets on 18 November. The first were two nuisance raids against Lae by lone B-25s at 0400 and 0447. Each aircraft dropped six 300-pound bombs, but results were unobserved.

At 0630 a combined strike by Beaufighters and B-25s covered by fighters departed Port Moresby. In a maximum strength effort by No. 30 Squadron, 11 Beaufighters led by Wing Commander Walker took off from Wards although three aircraft soon returned to base with mechanical trouble. The remaining eight strafed Lae 'drome, expending 1,100 x 20mm and 5,300 x 0.303-inch rounds of ammunition. Heavy anti-aircraft fire was experienced and two Beaufighters were damaged. Meanwhile the B-25s struck the alternative target of Salamaua with 35 x 500-pound bombs but results were unobserved due to the low cloud cover.

Eight 408th BS Marauders were ordered up to Port Moresby from Reid River. Early that afternoon they searched unsuccessfully in bad weather for the Japanese destroyers, and four of the B-26s instead dropped 16 x 500-pound bombs near Buna's airstrip.

A trio of 64th BS B-17s on a reconnaissance mission spotted the three destroyers 50 miles southwest of Gasmata soon after midday. Together with another force of four B-17s from the same squadron, the ships were attacked unsuccessfully with 56 x 500-pound bombs over a 45-minute period.

Just after a dusk a pair of 63rd BS B-17s bombed the ships as they approached Buna but were also unsuccessful. These bombers, piloted by Lieutenants Raymond Holsey and William Humrichouse, had been attacked by a patrol of six No. 582 *Ku* Zeros which had departed Lae at 1500. The Fortress crews claimed as many as seven Zeros destroyed, including one seen to crash-land on a beach (intelligence moderated this claim to two probably destroyed and one damaged). On this occasion Zero pilot FPO1c Ohara Yoshikazu failed to return with the others which landed at Lae at 1830. The B-17s probably also combatted six No. 252 *Ku* Zeros from Rabaul which patrolled over Buna from 1640 to 1715. They reported attacking one B-17 prior to landing at Lae at 1815.

The destroyers subsequently moored in the Buna anchorage and had almost completed unloading when they were found by six 64th BS Fortresses at 2120 that evening. Although there was a low 1,000-foot cloud base, a full moon made conditions ideal for skip bombing. After dropping flares the B-17 pilots made individual attacks on the destroyers, and Lieutenant Lewis A Anderson claimed a direct hit.

Anderson's bomb had hit the *Umikaze* amidships causing heavy damage. It was left dead in the water and had to be taken under tow by the *Asashio*. After emergency repairs at Rabaul the *Umikaze* returned to Japan for further repairs and did not return to service until February 1943. In addition, during this same attack the *Kawakaze* suffered damage from a near miss.

In the early hours of 19 November six Nos. 11 and 20 Squadron Catalinas made a long-range attack on Kavieng airfield. Bombs were dropped on the runway and dispersal areas in conditions of very poor visibility, with one aircraft claimed to have been wrecked. One Catalina failed to find the target and bombed Rabaul instead.

As the damaged destroyer was slowly towed back to Rabaul, it was fortunate to be shielded by poor weather and torrential rains on both 19 and 20 November which prevented any daylight Allied attack missions in the region. On the morning of 19 December six No. 582 *Ku* Zeros departed Rabaul to patrol above the ships but returned to base due to the weather. During the night a single No. 11 Squadron Catalina raided Kavieng airfield and claimed one aircraft destroyed.

The morning of 20 November saw another attempted patrol over the *Umikaze* by five No. 582 *Ku* Zeros from Rabaul which once again returned to base in the face of bad weather. Meanwhile from Lae a trio of No. 252 *Ku* Zeros departed at 0810 for a patrol over the Buna area. A short time later a single B-25 was encountered south of New Britain flying a reconnaissance mission, and in the subsequent combat a Zero was shot down. This same Zero also appears to have been claimed by a turret gunner from a B-17 in the same area, the *San Antonio Rose*.

Late that afternoon another patrol of No. 252 *Ku* Zeros from Lae met a B-17 ten miles southeast of Buna that was returning from a reconnaissance over Rabaul. Once again, the defensive gunners shot down a single Zero. The two No. 252 *Ku* pilots lost in these combats were FPO2c Gono Iwao and Leading Seaman Kanoya Yasutaka.

For the third night in a row Kavieng experienced a Catalina raid on the night of 20/21 November, albeit by a single No. 11 Squadron machine. In conditions of good visibility five bombs landed on a fuel or ammunition dump near the runway. Heavy anti-aircraft fire was experienced, with a single searchlight also active.

Clear weather on 21 November saw a resumption of normal Allied air activity. The frontline of the Buna perimeter was the eastern end of Buna's airfield, with American troops poised to advance on these positions. An air support program was planned for 0800, after which the assault would begin.

The air support comprised a dozen 89th BS A-20As which dropped 223 x parafrags from low-level over the airfield and strafed anti-aircraft positions with 6,100 rounds of 0.50-inch and 10,000 rounds of 0.30-inch calibre ammunition. Minutes later ten B-25s swept in at 6,000 feet and plastered the same area with 50 x 500-pound bombs.

However, on the ground things did not go as planned. One of the 500-pound bombs landed among American positions, killing four men and wounding another two. Meanwhile the orders to attack did not reach the relevant units until almost an hour after the air attack. Another coordinated attack was planned for 1245, but the requested air support did not materialise.

Yet another attack time was then fixed at 1545, when seven A-20As and six B-25s bombed and strafed the Buna airfield in a repeat of the morning attack. However, this time several 20-pound fragmentation bombs landed among American positions, killing six and wounding another dozen men. Not surprisingly, the subsequent attack failed to make significant progress against the Japanese positions.

During these raids a single 89th BS A-20A, 40-101 *Old Man Mose*, was damaged by anti-aircraft fire over the target. The pilot made an emergency landing at Pongani and the bomber never flew again. A crew chief later arrived from Port Moresby and spent days stripping the airframe of usable spare parts. Another loss occurred when Lieutenant BA Makowski force-landed P-40E 41-5607 at Kokoda, and the aircraft slid into trees at the end of the runway.

Meanwhile Australian troops had been advancing against stiff Japanese resistance along the Sanananda Track towards Sanananda Point. In an effort to support this movement, late on the morning of 21 November three No. 22 Squadron Bostons and three 89th BS A-20As bombed and strafed Sanananda village.

That afternoon a lone B-17 on a reconnaissance flight noted up to a dozen twin-engine bombers parked at Buka's airfield. These were strafed with 1,000 rounds of 0.50-inch ammunition, and the crews claimed to have set two of the bombers on fire.

In better news for the American troops advancing on Buna, 21 November saw the completion of the runway at Dobodura, to a length of 1,000 yards and a width of 110 feet. Transport aircraft could now fly supplies into this location which was just a few miles behind the frontlines. This did much to improve a strained logistical situation, exacerbated by the sinking of the small ships five days earlier.

Another troop convoy departed Rabaul in the early morning of 21 November, comprising four destroyers: *Kazagumo*, *Makigumo*, *Yugumo* and *Arashio*. These vessels anchored off Buna safely that evening and disembarked 800 troops.

During the last week of November all nine fighter squadrons of the three USAAF fighter groups in the SWPA were now based in Papua for the first time. This was a considerable force, comprising the 35th FG (39th, 40th and 41st Fighter Squadrons) and 49th FG (7th, 8th and 9th FS) at Port Moresby while the 8th FG (35th, 36th and 80th Fighter Squadrons) was now wholly based at Milne Bay. The 8th and 35th Fighter Groups were equipped with Airacobras while the 49th FG was equipped with P-40E/Ks, with one exception.

The exception was the 39th Fighter Squadron which was transitioning to P-38F Lightnings. It will be recalled from Chapter 1 that prior to Kenney's departure from the US in July he had requested a batch of Lightnings sent to Australia. These advanced twin-engine fighters offered superior endurance and high-altitude performance compared to the existing fleet of P-39s and P-40s.

Major George Prentice's 39th FS was the first unit scheduled to receive the new fighters. After offloading their existing Airacobras to other units, in late July the 39th FS moved to Antil Plains near Townsville in anticipation of receipt of the new type.

Not long after they first arrived at 14-Mile with their P-38Fs in October, the 39th FS crews applied shark-teeth to their mounts. Many also received names and nose-art like this example, Japanese Sandman II.

Soon the first of around 60 Lightnings arrived in Brisbane as deck cargo. They were assembled at Amberley and flown to Townsville where the 39th FS pilots underwent transition training. Within weeks squadron level exercises were underway, and on 21 September fourteen Lightnings flew into Port Moresby via Horn Island on a training flight.

However, the introduction into service of the P-38s was far from smooth. Squadron engineers soon discovered that the new fighter was technically both complex and demanding. Compared to the Airacobra, the Lightnings were a maintenance nightmare, and needed about four times the man hours to keep them airworthy. Not only was there an extra engine to maintain, the complicated airframe also boasted new technology such as control servo boosters and it took time for maintenance personnel to become familiar with such items.

The most challenging problem proved to be leaking fuel tanks, and replacements and repairs to these were commonplace. To do this, an access panel had to be removed from the lower wing to gain access to the fuel cells. Screws then had to be removed from the filler neck section inside the cell on the wing's top surface before it could be removed. In theory this sounded simple, but the only way to get sufficient leverage to remove the screws was for a mechanic to physically get his head and shoulders inside the tank. Often the petrol fumes were overpowering. Fortunately, the problem was rectified in later models, but the leaking tanks created many problems during the first months of P-38 service in the SWPA.

Finally on 18 October the 39th FS flew its first P-38s to its new operating base at 14-Mile (Laloki). In due course a handful of escort missions were flown, but the Lightnings were not destined to make their combat debut in the theatre until late November. Instead, the squadron was distracted by orders to send temporary reinforcements to Guadalcanal.

The first request came on 29 October when eight Lightnings were ordered to Milne Bay from where they would make the 600-mile ferry flight to Guadalcanal guided by a B-17. The bomber was also intended to carry maintenance personnel and spare pilots, but after it arrived two days late the operation was cancelled.

A second request soon followed, and on 14 November eight P-38s followed a B-17 to Henderson Field from Milne Bay. The following day the Lightnings strafed beached Japanese merchant ships, after which they spent several days flying patrols and escort missions but saw no further contact with the enemy. Overall the 39th FS "Guadalcanal adventure" was short-lived and viewed as an anti-climax. Seven Lightnings returned to 14-Mile on 22 November, however the eighth was left behind at Henderson Field for repair after a ground mishap.

Meanwhile two other Lightning losses had occurred on 4 November. Lieutenant Richard Cella ditched P-38F 42-12649 while returning to Port Moresby from Milne Bay. The second loss occurred when Captain Jim Porter ditched a P-38F just after take-off from Horn Island. He had departed for a delivery flight to the 39th FS at Port Moresby.

As noted in Chapter 8, during the peak of the Kokoda Campaign, Australian Army sick and wounded had been gathered at Myola where a runway was being cleared to fly these men to Port Moresby. On 1 November there were 438 patients in hospital at Myola, with most awaiting evacuation. A first case had been flown out successfully on 27 October, but there was uncertainty over which aircraft to use for the task and if operations could be conducted safely.

Myola was at a height of 6,500 feet and surrounded by high trees. The cleared strip was only 650 yards long which was equivalent to only 450 yards at sea level. While Myola is usually described as a dry lakebed, most of the area was swampy and only around the fringes was land dry enough for a runway. In addition, fickle mountain winds could produce rotor turbulence, giving an element of real danger to aerial operations at the site. A further complication was the need to make a steep climbing turn immediately after take-off to avoid a hill.

A Ford Trimotor which had originally evacuated from New Guinea in early 1942 had been impressed into service by the RAAF as A44-1. With a spacious fuselage it had been converted into an air ambulance to accommodate eight stretcher cases. Enquiries via the Department of Civil Aviation located a suitable pilot, Tom O'Dea. O'Dea was a veteran of the burgeoning 1930s civil aviation scene in New Guinea where he had flown many different types including Ford Trimotors. In modern parlance he was a highly experienced bush pilot.

O'Dea was also the owner of a DH.50 transport biplane which had an enclosed cabin for four passengers. It was agreed to replace the existing 240hp Puma engine with a 450hp Pratt & Whitney Wasp. The high-powered engine made the aircraft ideal for use from short strips, while a long-range fuel tank was also installed. This conversion was undertaken at Essendon

Airport near Melbourne in mid-November with a view to use at Myola. The aircraft was taken over by the RAAF as A10-1.

Meanwhile three Stinson O-49 Vigilant light aircraft were sourced from the USAAF and began medical evacuation operations with American markings and red crosses. They were likely operated under the auspices of No. 33 Squadron, although one of the pilots was Lieutenant RE Notestine, USAAF. Notestine began flying out one patient at a time from Myola in mid-November.

On 22 November O'Dea made his first flight to Myola in the Ford Trimotor and successfully evacuated eight patients. However, on his return flight the Ford flipped over while landing at Myola, destroying the aircraft and seriously injuring O'Dea. This was quickly followed by a crash of two of the Stinsons within a 24-hour period (one of which was later repaired). Not surprisingly Myola was subsequently deemed too dangerous and its use as a landing ground was ended. Up to this time the Stinsons had evacuated about 30 patients.

The remaining two Stinsons saw some subsequent use by No. 33 Squadron. Meanwhile the DH.50 had arrived at Horn Island. It then crashed at Kerema in southern Papua but was repaired locally by which time it was no longer needed as an air ambulance. Instead, it was fitted with a belly tank from a Kittyhawk for use as a fuel tanker, with an eye on rescuing stranded aircraft which had run out of fuel and made emergency landings. However, it does not appear to have been used regularly in this role and was soon withdrawn from use.

One of three Stinson O-49 Vigilant light aircraft which was used to evacuate sick and injured soldiers from Myola in November. This aircraft has 15 Red Cross mission markers painted on its cowl and is seen at Kokoda shortly after the Myola operations were discontinued. The use of these light aircraft in this role became redundant after airfields at Dobodura and Popondetta were opened and larger aircraft such as C-47s undertook medical evacuations.

A No. 751 Ku Betty returns to Kavieng at dawn after another night mission. The unit made regular nocturnal nuisance raids against Port Moresby in late November.

CHAPTER 12

STALEMATE AT THE BEACHHEADS: 22 – 30 NOVEMBER

Mid-November had seen the Japanese defeated in their latest attempt to land sizeable reinforcements on Guadalcanal. At this time, they also discovered the American advance along the northern coast of Papua right up to the perimeter of the Buna beachhead. These developments initiated a gradual change in Japanese strategic thinking from the desire to seize Guadalcanal at all costs, to a broader position which balanced the need to stabilise the wider Buna area. On 16 November the chief of staff of the Combined Fleet noted:

> Buna is becoming a bigger issue in this region than the problematic Solomon Islands, in terms of national defence. It is essential to nip this in the bud now, and deprive the Allies of any room for a counter-offensive.

In recognition of these new demands, on 16 November the IJA had created the 8th Area Army based at Rabaul which oversaw the 17th Army focussed on the Solomons, and the newly formed 18th Army responsible for New Guinea. As noted in the previous chapter, significant reinforcements had arrived at Buna by destroyer during 18-21 November, and follow-up convoys were planned.

Meanwhile the initial Allied attacks against the beachheads had been made in the assessment that the dispirited defenders would be quickly overwhelmed, and that haste was necessary lest fresh reinforcements arrive. However, the strength of the fortified Japanese positions had been badly underestimated, and the defenders' determination took the attackers by surprise. Lacking heavy weapons, the initial Allied attacks were easily repulsed.

Major David B Parker, an engineer observer with the US 32nd Division, described the initial attacks:

> The first opposition from the enemy here was a surprise and shock to our green troops. The enemy positions were amazingly well camouflaged, and seemed to have excellent fields of fire even in the close quarters of the jungle ... snipers were everywhere ... and they were so well camouflaged that it was nearly impossible to discern them. The enemy habitually allowed our troops to advance to very close range - sometimes four or five feet from a machine gun post - before opening fire; often they allowed troops to by-pass them completely, opening fire then on our rear elements, and on our front elements from the rear.

During the last week of November, the Allies gradually encircled the beachheads but frustratingly their attacks made no major gains. Many of the Australian formations were already significantly weakened, having been involved in the Kokoda Campaign for several weeks (where the 16th Brigade had lost a third of its strength in battle). Sickness also took a heavy toll, with both the Australian and American troops having to advance through dengue-ridden and malarial swamps. By 25 November forward medical stations were holding 638 sick men behind the Australian positions on the Sanananda Track.

The Australians gained an important advantage with the capture of Popondetta which was suitable for an airfield and was within 15 miles of the beachheads at Sanananda Point and Buna. Directed by Australian Army engineers, native labourers quickly cut a 1,600-yard swathe through a field of kunai grass. The first C-47 landed on 21 November and further improvements to the site were soon underway. Two days later broken down 25-pounder field guns were flown in, together with jeeps and ammunition, so that the troops were soon enjoying artillery support. These moves were mirrored at Dobodura, where the US 32nd Division soon enjoyed the support of Australian 25-pounders and American 105mm howitzers.

Dobodura and Popondetta were only 35 minutes flying time from Port Moresby, and during clear weather as many as 30 aircraft might be flying these routes. The bulk of these were transport aircraft, mainly the C-47s of the 6th and 33rd TCS, and some would fly as many as four or even five sorties per day. With so much activity in this area a major task of the fighter force was maintaining full squadrons flying protective patrols in relays during daylight. This was a significant burden for the relatively short-legged Port Moresby-based Airacobras and P-40s, and the area to be defended was a large one including friendly ground positions and the coastal supply route. Another complicating factor was the weather, with the fighters needing to return to Port Moresby at the first sign of the Owen Stanleys clouding over in the afternoons. Not surprisingly a number of Japanese attacking formations would successfully penetrate this air cover.

Meanwhile a major problem identified by the Australian Army during the Kokoda Campaign had been a lack of effective air support. With a thick jungle canopy and terrain which often lacked readily identifiable landmarks, direct air support missions had rarely been effective and often ran the risk of inflicting friendly casualties. Recognising this, in early October Blamey had requested an RAAF army cooperation squadron be sent to Papua.

No. 4 Squadron, equipped with Wirraways, was at this time training with Australian and American troops in Queensland. The unit was directed to move to Port Moresby even though there were justifiable concerns about the relative inability of the Wirraways to defend themselves against Japanese fighters.

The first three Wirraways, led by Squadron Leader Geoff Quinan, arrived at Berry (12-Mile) on 8 November, while the main ground party arrived five days later. By 20 November the full squadron of 18 Wirraways had arrived, and these were immediately flying daily reconnaissance sorties over the Buna-Gona area.

The first loss occurred the next day when the crew of A20-519 were trialling a landing strip cleared at Wairopi. The Wirraway touched down on a patch of soft sand, and it landed "hot" causing it to crash into trees at 80 miles per hour. The crew were slightly injured but were able

A No. 4 Squadron Wirraway forward deployed to Popondetta in late 1942, from where they routinely flew "low and slow" missions over the beachheads.

A No. 4 Squadron Wirraway crew show off a twin Vickers GO (Gas Operated) 0.303-inch calibre machine gun mounted in the rear cockpit.

to walk to Kokoda where two other Wirraways ferried them back to their squadron three days later. A20-519 was later salvaged for parts.

Soon No. 4 Squadron was working closely with ground troops on a daily basis, closely observing enemy positions and directing artillery fire by flying "low and slow" over the battlefield. On 28 November single Wirraways were permanently allocated to each of the Australian 7th Division and the US 32nd Division, being forward deployed at Popondetta and Dobodura often for several days at a time.

Poor weather on the morning of 22 November prevented Allied air attacks in Papua. However, at 0730 a formation of a dozen No. 582 *Ku* Vals escorted by a dozen Zeros (split between Nos. 582 and 252 *Ku*) departed Rabaul to strike Allied shipping near Buna. These ran into a force of a dozen 41st FS Airacobras with a pair of 39th FS P-38s also in the vicinity. The Airacobra pilots got the upper hand, claiming two Zeros destroyed and three "probables", while the Japanese made no claims. In fact, just one No. 252 *Ku* Zero was lost, that flown by Leading Seaman Maeda Tomio.

There were no Allied reports of Japanese air attacks in this area, so the Vals likely jettisoned their bombs or unloaded them harmlessly into the jungle. Interestingly, nine of the Vals lugged four 60-kilogram bombs, two on underwing hardpoints and two on centreline pylons, while the others carried three. The Vals and Zeros landed at Lae at 1150.

Despite the Zero pilots making no claims, Lieutenant Herbert Hill of the 41st FS was forced to bale out of his P-400 and parachuted into the middle of Buna's airfield. No doubt he was captured and executed. It is unclear if this was a result of the aerial combat or possibly due to anti-aircraft fire.

Just after 1100 a single B-17 dropped four 500-pound bombs on Lae 'drome, with much smoke seen after the bombs exploded near a group of green shacks. In the early afternoon the weather had cleared sufficiently for eight 89th BS A-20As to attack supply tracks near Sanananda Point at 1255. A total of 320 x parafrags were dropped, while 3,000 x 0.50-inch and 6,700 x 0.30-inch rounds were expended.

Just over an hour later six No. 30 Squadron Beaufighters strafed Lae 'drome and claimed to have hit a Zero as it was taking off. Four other Zeros were strafed on the ground, while three other airborne Zeros were noted. On the return flight while passing over Salamaua a pair of Zeros were encountered, thought to be returning from Buna. These pursued A19-26 for 20 minutes at a speed of 250 knots. The Beaufighter was hit in the wings and fuselage, with the resulting loss of hydraulic power forcing the pilot to make a belly landing on return to Wards.

A short time later, at 1428, five B-26s targeted enemy positions around Buna's airfield with 20 x 500-pound bombs. Accurate anti-aircraft fire was encountered which shattered the windscreen of one of the Marauders.

Meanwhile five No. 100 Squadron Beauforts were ordered to make a torpedo attack on the four destroyers that had disembarked troops off Buna overnight (see Chapter 11). One of the Beauforts failed to take off due to engine trouble, while the others ran into bad weather while approaching the target area two hours later and returned to base. Four other Beauforts were also readied but their mission was cancelled on account of the capricious weather.

Late in the afternoon a mixed formation of six No. 30 Squadron Beaufighters and nine 89th BS A-20As made a combined strike on aircraft at Lae 'drome and barges seen in nearby waters. Several Zeros were targeted on the ground while the Beaufighters and A-20s briefly fired on a trio of airborne Zeros. The Australians claimed one damaged and the Americans one as probably destroyed.

As the Allied bombers raced back towards Port Moresby, they were met by a protective force of 49th FG P-40s near Cape Ward Hunt. In a confusing series of engagements, the P-40s tangled with three groups of enemy aircraft comprising two Zeros and six Vals (all from No. 582 *Ku* which had departed Lae on an anti-shipping mission); three No. 252 *Ku* Zeros which departed Lae at 1525; and a pair of No. 252 *Ku* Zeros which departed Lae at 1640.

One of the No. 252 *Ku* Zeros (flown by FPO3c Oda Toru) was shot down, and the other two Zeros in his *shotai* were badly damaged. However, it was the American pilots who came out worse for wear, with three of the P-40s lost. Lieutenant Donald Dittler was last seen battling Zeros in P-40E 41-24811 and remains missing. Two other pilots tried to nurse their damaged fighters back over the ranges. Lieutenant Donald Sutliff baled out of P-40E 41-5610 near Wairopi and eventually re-joined his squadron after a 21-day ordeal in the jungle. Lieutenant Ralph Wire baled out of another P-40E near Myola. He was able to walk to Kokoda from where he was flown back to Port Moresby a few days later.

Adding to the 49th FG losses on this day, after an uneventful sweep of Buna, Lieutenant Robert McComsey's engine started to smoke near Kokoda. He subsequently baled out of his 9th FS P-40E 41-36089 and soon returned to his unit.

Late that afternoon a single B-17 came across two "destroyers" south of New Britain, which were in fact two 840-ton torpedo boats on a supply run from Rabaul to Lae, the *Hiyodori* and *Otori*. Eight 500-pound bombs were dropped, but all missed. Six 65th BS Fortresses were then sent out to search for the ships and a pair of these bombers found them at 1825 some 68 miles southwest of Arawe.

The B-17s attacked with eight 500-pound bombs but failed to inflict any damage. One of the bombers, B-17E 41-2536 piloted by Lieutenant John Frost, was hit in the radio compartment by anti-aircraft fire. The bomber caught fire and crashed into the ocean, but not before six parachutes were seen to open. At least one crewman, the Australian navigator Pilot Officer Allan Fairfax, was picked up by the *Hiyodori* but was likely soon executed as he was never reported as a Prisoner of War. All ten men aboard were listed as missing in action.

About an hour later nine B-25s found the two ships and attacked them with 44 x 500-pound bombs. One bomb was thought to have scored a direct hit on one of the ships, but without apparent effect as both were left manoeuvring at high speed and with no apparent damage.

From 2200 a B-17 and four B-25s made individual bombing runs over Lae 'drome, unloading a total of 24 x 500-pound bombs. Also during the night, a single No. 20 Squadron Catalina from Cairns bombed Kavieng's runway and dispersal area.

Meanwhile another attempt had been made to raid Port Moresby. Four No. 751 *Ku* Bettys departed Rabaul from 1920, but after encountering bad weather all had returned to base by 2330.

The following day, 23 November, was relatively quiet as Allied air support was being readied for separate Australian and American offensives against the respective beachheads in coming days.

In the morning two B-25s on a reconnaissance mission briefly fought two No. 582 *Ku* Zeros from Lae, but there were no losses to either side. Meanwhile seven 408th BS B-26s set out to raid Lae, but after climbing to 14,500 feet they could not get over a weather system and turned back. That afternoon three of the Marauders made solo attacks on enemy positions near Sanananda Point.

That evening two No. 582 *Ku* Vals, each loaded with four 60-kilogram bombs, departed Lae to attack shipping near Buna. Underlining the importance of the mission it was again led by senior officer, Lieutenant Commander Inoue Buntou. However, after encountering a single Airacobra the dive-bombers returned to Lae at 1950.

The first of the Allied offensives was launched on 24 November, when at 0800 a dozen P-40Es strafed enemy positions in front of American troops advancing on Buna along the inland track from Dobodura. However, the intended target was not hit, and the ground forces waited for a follow-up air attack. This did not unfold until the early afternoon, when an attack by eight Airacobras and four P-40s was promised.

Eventually just four P-40s showed up and these mistakenly strafed a friendly command post. Fortunately, only one man was slightly wounded, but the air support had been completely ineffective, and the American troops were disappointed that no bombers had been used. As will be seen, elsewhere in the theatre Allied air units had one of their busiest days during the Papuan campaign, with 89 aircraft involved in ground attack missions.

On this the day the bulk of air support was directed against Sanananda-Giruwa and Gona, with the latter area scheduled to receive six hours of continual attacks from 0800 until 1400. Strafing and light bombing by A-20As, B-25s and B-26s was followed by B-17s of the 63rd and 65th Bombardment Squadrons which unloaded almost 45,000 pounds of bombs on enemy positions. Many of the bombs dropped by the B-17s were 20- and 100-pounders dropped from low altitude during "gunship" passes whereby the gunners strafed enemy positions. In contrast to the aerial efforts on the American front, these attacks impressed the Australians. The 16th Brigade recorded that:

> … the ground actually shook at times with the bomb blasts.

Also involved in these missions was No. 30 Squadron, with nine Beaufighters strafing coastal positions near Sanananda Point in conjunction with an attack by eleven 89th BS A-20As. The Beaufighters expended 2,600 x 20mm and 35,000 x 0.303-inch rounds, with A19-30 receiving slight damage from anti-aircraft fire. Two hours later the attack was repeated by six Beaufighters and three A-20As. The 13th and 90th Bombardment Squadrons were also active over the Sanananda front, with their B-25s flying both morning and afternoon missions.

Meanwhile No. 4 Squadron committed virtually its full strength to missions over Gona, with a dozen Wirraways dropping 31 x 250-pounds of bombs and strafing with 17,000 rounds of 0.303-inch ammunition. As each Wirraway carried a maximum load of two 250-pound bombs, this ordnance expenditure reflects multiple sorties by some of the crews.

While engaged in one of the Buna missions, Captain William Martin of the 7th FS was hit by anti-aircraft fire in the engine of his P-40E. He forced-landed just three miles south of Buna and destroyed the instruments in his plane before setting out towards friendly positions. Even though these were relatively close, the nature of the swampy terrain and high kunai grass meant it was three days before he made contact and was flown to Port Moresby from Popondetta.

In an attempt to counter the incessant Allied attacks, at 1515 a dozen Zeros from Nos. 252 and 582 *Ku* departed Lae to patrol over Buna. Led by Warrant Officer Tsunoda Kazuo, the Japanese ran into a squadron of Airacobras which they estimated at being 21 strong. In a brief skirmish Tsunoda's pilots claimed one P-39 shot down before returning to Lae at 1800.

Just 30 minutes before these Zeros landed at Lae a small force of four No. 582 *Ku* Vals had departed for an evening raid on Dobudura, which they claimed to have attacked between 1900 and 1950. While a pair of Vals returned safely to base at 2100, the other pair got lost and had force-landed by 2215. The position of one of the Vals was 20 miles from Lae but the other location was not reported.

The ground offensives, together with the loss of several of the small ships, were putting enormous pressure on Allied air transport capacity. To augment this, Hudsons of No. 6 Squadron were used for supply dropping, with 17 such sorties to the Buna area being flown on 21 and 22 November. On 24 November A16-225 was taking off from Wards on another one of these missions with a load of 2,000 pounds of supplies and ammunition when it swung around and crashed. The Hudson caught fire and burned, although the crew escaped with minor injuries.

Meanwhile, late that afternoon Allied reconnaissance aircraft had detected five Japanese destroyers in the Vitiaz Strait, between New Guinea and the western tip of New Britain. These were the *Harusame, Shiratsuyu, Inazuma, Hayashio* and *Isonami* which had left Rabaul the previous evening on a transport run to Lae. With Allied air attack now likely, their speed was increased to 30 knots which meant the destroyers were just hours away from entering the Huon Gulf and approaching Lae.

The 63rd and 65th Bombardment Squadrons were at Seven-Mile with most crews having flown two ground attack missions that morning. A pair of B-17s departed at 1800 to shadow the destroyers and illuminate the area with flares for an attack by both squadrons. After flying through a weather front, the main formation of Fortresses spotted the destroyers' wakes easily in the Huon Gulf, with the aid of a full moon.

Among the first to attack was Ken McCullar in *Black Jack*, who made three skip-bombing runs from 200 feet before dropping his remaining bombs from 1,200 feet. However, he was only able to claim near-misses. The destroyers were all relatively modern, built in the 1930s and well-armed with 5-inch dual purpose guns and 25mm anti-aircraft guns which put up a tremendous barrage. *Black Jack* was hit multiple times with two engines being knocked out and several of the crew receiving minor injuries. McCullar was fortunately able to nurse the damaged bomber back to Seven-Mile.

Meanwhile First Lieutenant William O'Brien in *Talisman* scored a direct hit during two bombing runs from 2,000 feet on the destroyer *Hayashio*. In fact, the destroyer had been near missed in an attack by a B-17 at 1853 and suffered a loss of power from its port engine. O'Brien's attack occurred at 2100 when the ship was 35 miles northeast of Salamaua. A direct hit landed on the forward turret and soon the crew were battling dangerous fires.

The destroyer was brought to a halt in a small bay where other vessels were seen coming to lend assistance. However, the fires spread to the forward magazines which exploded, reducing the *Hayashio* to a floating wreck. At 2225 the captain gave the order to abandon ship, and those aboard were transferred to the *Shiratsuyu*. The *Hayashio* was sunk by 5-inch gunfire from the *Shiratsuyu* about half an hour later. Some 50 men were lost in the explosions and fires, an unknown amount of whom were the soldiers aboard.

Among the vessels going to the assistance of the *Hayashio* were the torpedo boats *Hiyodori* and *Otori* which had arrived at Lae the previous day. Both of these vessels got caught up in the attacks and suffered minor damage from near misses.

As well as the B-17s, other squadrons were also ordered to attack the destroyers which were considered a prime target. The two B-25 units then in Port Moresby, the 13th and 90th Bombardment Squadrons, flew through bad weather to the Huon Gulf in what was considered a highly dangerous night mission. Unlike the Fortresses which could stay aloft for many hours, the mission profile for the B-25s was a tight one with little left in reserve in case of difficulty returning in poor weather through the mountains.

A 90th BS B-25C, 41-12996 flown by Major Raymond Peterson, came across the blazing *Hayashio* and executed an attack run but the bombs failed to release. Just then the destroyer's forward magazines exploded and debris damaged the Mitchell which crashed into the ocean. Two survivors remarkably managed to reach the shore at daybreak, near Finschhafen.

The destroyers were ideal targets for No. 100 Squadron, and that night nine Beauforts were readied at Milne Bay for a strike mission, five lugging American Mark XIII torpedoes and four each carrying two 250- and two 500-pound bombs. One of the aircraft experienced an engine fire and did not take off, while the others made their way through terrible weather. Flying Officer Bill Ewing was a crewman aboard A9-42 and recalled that the weather ranked as the worst he experienced:

> The weather was absolutely atrocious, well nigh impassable, rainstorms, thunder squalls, cloud down to the deck, and just to get through necessitated changes of course every five minutes or so; less than ideal for pilot and navigator alike.

Not surprisingly, four of the Beauforts failed to sight the enemy. The remaining four all located the burning *Hayashio*, and two of the crews saw it explode. One of these Beauforts carried out a torpedo attack but without observed effect, while one other, A9-42, bombed a vessel near the burning destroyer and claimed a direct hit.

Another Beaufort, A9-82 piloted by Sergeant JR Duncan, got lost on the return flight. After being airborne for five and a half hours, the crew signalled they were force-landing in Milne Bay. In fact, they had come down in water much further west, but the crew reached shore and were able to walk to Wanigela.

Also directed to attack the destroyers was No. 6 Squadron from Wards. Six Hudsons were led by the commanding officer, Wing Commander Alexander Barlow. Barlow was a pre-war flier with

Bombs from a B-17 explode on Buin's runway. A destroyer is anchored just offshore to the bottom left of the photo.

experience dating back to 1928 and by this time he rarely flew on operations, so his leadership of the mission underlined its importance. However, after only 25 minutes in the air the starboard engine of Barlow's Hudson (A16-215) failed, and he turned back to Port Moresby. After jettisoning fuel and bombs he was approaching Seven-Mile when he was warned an air raid was in progress. Then at just 500 feet altitude the port engine began failing, and Barlow was able to make a safe belly landing. The Hudson was subsequently repaired and returned to service.

Meanwhile the other five Hudsons ran into the bad weather over the mountains and had returned to base after a flight time of around three hours. The air raid warning also affected other aircraft returning from Huon Gulf such as several of the B-17s. Three No. 751 *Ku* Bettys had departed Kavieng at lengthy intervals starting from 1630 to make solo nuisance raids over Port Moresby.

The first raid occurred at 2052 when 60-kilogram bombs did slight damage to the casualty clearing station at 17-Mile. The second raid was the one that affected the returning aircraft. A few bombs were dropped on the south end of Seven-Mile at 0032 on 25 November but did no damage. The third Betty turned back in the face of bad weather and landed at Kavieng at 0205. The 3.7-inch guns of the 32nd Heavy Anti-Aircraft Battery briefly engaged targets during both raids.

Despite being very close to their destination of Lae, the commander of the remaining four destroyers called off their mission and returned to Rabaul, where they arrived safely in the evening of 25 November. If they had unloaded at Lae they would have risked several hours of potential air attack in daylight.

The keenness of the Fifth Air Force to attack the destroyers was demonstrated by the desire to use the Lightnings of the 39th FS as dive-bombers. Eight 500-pound bombs were delivered to Schwimmer 'drome, but when the night mission was described to the pilots they were incredulous as none of them had either night or dive-bombing training or experience. Fortunately for them sense prevailed, and the mission was cancelled.

The increased Japanese destroyer activity meant that for the last week the Catalinas of Nos. 11 and 20 Squadrons had been flying night patrols of the waters between Lae and Buna and of the sea approaches to both locations. During one of these patrols on the night of 24/25 November the burning *Hayashio* was spotted by Catalina A24-2. A destroyer was attacked with four 250-pound bombs, one of which landed in the wake of the ship. Other destroyers in the area were then dispersed after flares were dropped.

Daylight on 25 November saw relative quiet after the flurry of Allied activity the previous day. At 1030 Warrant Officer Tsunoda Kazuo led a mixed formation of Zeros (six from No. 582 *Ku* and five from No. 252 *Ku*) to patrol over Buna from Lae. A pair of 39th FS P-38s was encountered, making Tsunoda's pilots the first New Guinea-based Japanese aviators to encounter the new twin-engine American fighters. However, the contact was inconclusive, and the Zeros had returned to Lae by early afternoon.

The 26 November saw another program of Allied air attacks in support of a renewed American Thanksgiving Day ground offensive at Buna. Six No. 30 Squadron Beaufighters opened the attack at 0730 against Japanese positions along the Buna airstrip. The pilots had been given a photograph of the area which enabled them to accurately target the positions which were thoroughly strafed with 2,150 x 20mm and 12,500 x 0.303-inch rounds.

The Beaufighters were followed at 0750 by fifteen 7th FS P-40s which strafed the same area with 15,000 x 0.50-inch rounds. The attackers faced defensive fire from heavy machine gun positions, and Second Lieutenant Dean Burnett in P-40E 41-24866 was shot down and crashed in flames a short distance offshore.

Just over an hour later, five No. 22 Squadron Bostons made a low-level bombing and strafing attack led by Squadron Leader Charles Learmonth. During this attack A28-22 *Retribution*, flown by Flight Lieutenant Ken MacDonald, exploded in a ball of flames. This was similar to the loss of A28-12 during bombing practice of the SS *Pruth* wreck off Port Moresby a fortnight earlier. The cause of these losses would soon be understood and is explained later in this chapter.

Learmonth's aircraft was damaged in this attack, and his rear gunner was injured. During the morning, three trios of 89th BS A-20s also raided the Buna strip area, as did five 38th BG B-25s which each delivered four 500-pound bombs. Later in the afternoon a more modest second wave of attacks took place, with three A-20s and three 71st BS B-25s involved. One of the B-25s jettisoned its bombs after seeing Zeros in the distance, while another nine 38th BG B-25s didn't participate because of bad weather.

Meanwhile a formation of four Vals and six Zeros from No. 582 *Ku* departed Lae that morning to raid Allied targets in the Buna area. These were joined by a patrol of six No. 252 *Ku* Zeros when they met a mixed formation of 8th and 9th FS P-40s. In the ensuing combat No. 582 *Ku* pilot Flyer1c Yoshio Nobuto was shot down.

At 1015 an estimated 11 Japanese aircraft bombed and strafed Dobodura, resulting in damage to C-47 41-18560 *Cheryl*. A short distance away the lugger *Helen Dawn*, which had become stuck on a sandbar earlier that morning, was strafed by Zeros and destroyed.

A more serious nightmare scenario then unfolded for the Allies when Zeros chanced upon a pair of unescorted C-47s which had taken off from Dobodura for the flight back inland to Port Moresby. These were the six No. 252 *Ku* Zeros, which were led by FPO1c Kobayashi Katsutauru. Demonstrating expert marksmanship, the Zero pilots claimed two "Daugasu" (Douglas) aircraft shot down for the expenditure of just 60 x 20mm and 360 x 7.7mm rounds. The victims were C-47s 41-38601 *Swamp Rat* (which had been the first transport to land at a new strip at Pongani a fortnight earlier) and 41-38631 *Shady Lady*. Four crewmen were lost in each crash.

During the morning Captain Bob Faurot led five 39th BS Lightnings to Lae in what would be the combat debut in the theatre for the type. Each lugged a 500-pound bomb delivered two nights earlier and dropped these on the runway at Lae. One landed in the ocean and a huge geyser of water rose just as a Zero was taking off. Some of the pilots believed the Zero had flipped over and crashed, and it was claimed as an unlikely kill. However, no Zeros were lost at Lae on this day.

At 1038 five 22nd BG B-26s bombed a wreck at Salamaua. This was likely an alternate target, and it seems the Marauders were possibly intended to raid Lae in conjunction with the Lightnings.

Another mixed Japanese strike force set out from Lae that afternoon to again strike targets in the Buna area. This comprised four Vals and two Zeros from No. 582 *Ku* accompanied by five No. 252 *Ku* Zeros. During the mission the Japanese reported encountering a B-24, a B-25 and a P-38, but no conclusive combat took place and all fighters returned to Lae by 1705.

At 0256 on 27 November a single aircraft dropped bombs between Seven-Mile and Wards, followed eight minutes later by multiple aircraft which dropped 12 bombs near Seven-Mile. The culprits were a trio of No. 751 *Ku* Bettys from Kavieng. They were engaged by 3.7-inch anti-aircraft guns which fired 87 rounds. In a copycat of these night-time nuisance raid tactics,

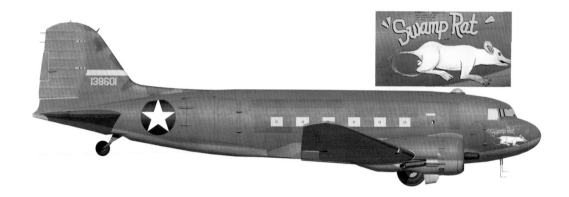

C-47 41-38601 Swamp Rat of the 6th TCS which was shot down by No. 252 Ku Zeros after taking off from Dobodura on 26 November.

two hours later a pair of B-25s dropped eight 500-pound bombs on Lae 'drome.

Also active during the night were two Catalinas. A24-25 dropped four 250-pound bombs over Buka where four warships were observed anchored offshore, while A24-24 was patrolling between Lae and Buna when it bombed a submarine as it crash-dived. This coincided with intelligence reports that Japanese submarines were being used to run supplies into Buna.

Daylight on 27 November saw three Zeros attack Dobodura at 0645. The culprits are believed to have been from No. 253 *Ku* which exceptionally had sent a small detachment forward to Lae at this time. No damage was reported from the attack.

The day also saw B-26s active in support of American troops advancing on the Buna runway. Two formations each of eight Marauders dropped a total of 64 x 500-pound bombs. However, one of the aircraft mistakenly bombed a friendly position and three men were seriously wounded.

Late that afternoon a lone B-26 dropped two 500-pound bombs into Buna's runway and reported encountering three Zeros. These were likely three No. 252 *Ku* Zeros which had joined a mixed formation from No. 582 *Ku* comprising six Vals (each carrying an unusually heavy load of five 60-kilogram bombs) and nine escorting Zeros. The latter formation attacked Soputa, which was located midway between Popondetta and Sanananda Point. It was here that a major Australian medical facility had been established, treating the sick and wounded for both the 16th and 25th Brigades. The facility was in a clearing that was devoid of cover, and unsurprisingly the attack caused heavy casualties, killing 22 Australians and wounding another 50. A witness described the scene:

> It was a scene of utter devastation; tents holed, huts keeling over, the quarter-master's-cum-dispensary store burning. Dead and wounded included patients, members of the field ambulance, natives and visitors to the hospital. In a few minutes a busy hospital was transformed into a miniature battlefield.

At an adjoining American Clearing Hospital six Americans were also killed. Some of these aircraft also strafed Allied positions near Buna, before all of the Japanese aircraft returned safely to Lae before dusk.

The Australian facility had been displaying the Red Cross when attacked, but this symbol was not as universally recognisable as it is today even among Westerners. Evidence of this lies with the American Clearing Hospital, which had removed its Red Cross after overflying transports kept mistaking it for a supply drop marking!

During the night of 27/28 November three Catalinas from Nos. 11 and 20 Squadrons raided Kavieng. A mix of 20-, 250- and 500-pound bombs were dropped on the runway and adjoining dispersal bays, with small fires being started.

Just before midnight three No. 751 *Ku* Bettys had departed Kavieng to bomb "Emo", which refers to the village of Embogo on Oro Bay but is believed to be the Japanese designation for nearby Dobodura. The Bettys returned to base before dawn after having noted that the bombing accuracy was impaired by overcast.

At dawn on 28 November three No. 582 *Ku* Vals departed Lae each carrying four 60-kilogram bombs to raid "Shinzetsuo" which was a name given to a staging point at Sumpit village, near Buna. It is possible these aircraft turned back for some reason as the flight time was very short and no raid was reported by the Allies.

At 1530 six Vals and six Zeros from No. 582 *Ku* departed Rabaul for the Buna area. These aircraft were joined by six Vals from No. 956 *Ku*, it what would be the sole mission for that unit over Papua. The dive-bombers were each carrying two, four or five 60-kilogram bombs. At 1840 that evening these aircraft attacked two RAN corvettes, HMAS *Ballarat* and *Katoomba*. The corvettes had been escorting a small cargo ship, the *Muliama*, to Porlock Harbour. That afternoon the corvettes had been sent forward to patrol off Buna overnight to counter suspected submarines running supplies.

The main weight of the attack fell on the *Katoomba*, which countered with low altitude barrage fire from its 12-pounder gun as well as close range fire from three Oerlikon 20mm guns and two Lewis light machine guns. Using full helm at its maximum speed of 14 knots, the manoeuvrability of the corvette meant that the Vals often did not release their bombs but banked away to make another run. The *Katoomba* was near missed by at least three bombs, the force of the explosions lifting the ship out of the water. This caused some machinery defects and the corvette subsequently returned to Port Moresby for repairs. The corvettes claimed to have shot down one of the attackers and damaged two others. All landed safely at Lae later that evening, although one of the No. 956 *Ku* Vals had been damaged.

Earlier Lieutenant Philip Lissner of the 8th PRS took off from 14-Mile for a reconnaissance mission in F-4 Lightning 41-2123. Following engine trouble, he feathered the right engine before crashing near 12-Mile. Lissner was killed.

At 1605 that afternoon seven 19th BS B-26s raided Buna with 24 x 500-pound bombs, while that evening A-20s and Beaufighters made a combined dusk attack on Lae, in an attempt to

8th FS P-40E-1 British serial ET618, Port Moresby, November 1942, assigned to Lieutenant William Day.

catch Japanese aircraft on the ground. Four Beaufighters made a landwards approach from the Markham Valley and targeted five fighters seen in square dispersal pens. At the same time seven 89th BS A-20As strafed and dropped small fragmentation bombs, claiming hits on two aircraft.

That night two No. 751 *Ku* Bettys set out to raid Milne Bay, each carrying 11 x 60-kilogram bombs. The aircraft were detected over the target area at 0235 on 29 November by the 33rd Heavy Anti-Aircraft Battery. For the next 50 minutes 88 x 3.7-inch rounds were fired at the intruders, both of which returned safely to Kavieng shortly before dawn. Their bombs caused no damage or casualties.

Another mission against Lae's airfield unfolded overnight with eleven 38th BG B-25s sent out in small numbers to hit the target with 1,032 x 23-pound fragmentation bombs in the two hours before dawn. After taking off from Port Moresby in terrible weather, the Mitchells flew on instruments before experiencing clearer weather on the other side of the ranges. Bombs were dropped on the runway area from medium altitude.

During the approach to Lae 405th BS B-25D 41-29699 *White Russian* piloted by Lieutenant Frank Parker was seen falling through the cloud cover, followed immediately by a bright flash as it hit the ground and exploded. The most likely cause of crash was that Parker became disorientated in the darkness and dived out of control. The wreck was located post-war high in the mountains about 20 miles southwest of Lae.

On the return flight 405th BS B-25D 41-29724 piloted by Lieutenant Willmore Pavlich experienced a compass malfunction and missed Port Moresby by a wide margin. The aircraft ran out of fuel and was ditched at Yule Island, about 60 miles northwest of Port Moresby. The crew got into an inflatable dinghy and soon reached a nearby radar station from where they were returned to their squadron.

The B-25 attacks were followed by a lone A-20 on an armed reconnaissance mission which bombed and strafed Lae 'drome at 0552 on 29 November.

Within hours Allied attention turned to Gona, where the 21st Brigade was making another assault following a program of air support. This began shortly before 0800 when six B-17s plastered the Gona Mission area with 48 x 500-pound bombs. They were followed at 0930 by eleven P-40s which dive-bombed Gona with 300-pound bombs. At 1100 three 89th BS A-20As strafed the area with 1,500 x 0.50-inch and 1,000 x 0.30-inch rounds, closely followed by a trio of Bostons again led by Squadron Leader Learmonth.

In the third tragedy to befall No. 22 Squadron in just three weeks, A28-20 piloted by Flight Lieutenant Herbert "Jimmy" Bullmore blew up in mid-air. Flying Officer Harry Craig flying A28-11 witnessed the loss:

> I watched Bullmore commence his strafing run. At the very point where I expected him to release his bombs, his Boston literally blew apart. The explosion erupted from under the aircraft's belly, blowing off the tail and completely disintegrating the fuselage.

It was realised that all three Bostons lost had been carrying 20-pound fragmentation bombs. Learmonth subsequently flew trial flights with disarmed bombs, and they were seen to tumble against one another after being released into the slipstream. Live bombs with impact fuses would have detonated, thus accounting for the losses. The use of the bombs, an old British type designed for hand dropping from slow open cockpit biplanes was discontinued.[I]

That morning a force of four Japanese destroyers was sighted steaming south through the Vitiaz Strait. This comprised the *Shiratsuyu*, *Makigumo*, *Kazagumo* and *Yugumo* which had embarked 800 IJA troops of the 21st Independent Mixed Brigade at Rabaul the previous evening for transport to Buna.

Fortresses of the 64th, 65th and 403rd Bombardment Squadrons were sent out to shadow and attack the ships. The first formation of six B-17s attacked in the early afternoon with 48 x 500-pound bombs. One destroyer was hit and was seen to list badly and stop. This was the *Shiratsuyu* which received a direct hit on the bow, causing only light casualties but resulting in serious flooding. With its speed reduced to nine knots, the destroyer limped back to Rabaul for repairs. The *Shiratsuyu* eventually returned to Japan and did not re-enter service until July 1943.

The Fortress crews claimed a second destroyer was also hit and damaged. This was the *Makigumo* which was near missed but shell splinters penetrated the hull and started a fire in one of the engine rooms. All four of the destroyers abandoned their mission and turned back. They were attacked that evening by five B-17s but this time only near misses were claimed and no damage was incurred.

The commander of the 403rd BS, Major Thomas N Charles, was aboard B-17F 41-24546 sent out to shadow the destroyers. At 1730 the crew radioed that they made contact with the convoy in the Vitiaz Strait, but they were never heard from again and no trace of the aircraft has ever been found. It may have been shot down by anti-aircraft fire from the destroyers or possibly fell

---

I   These were a different type to the USAAF 20-pound bombs.

*Among this cadre of six No. 204 Ku Zero pilots at Rabaul in late November 1942
is (circled left to right) Lieutenant (jg) Sugita Shoichi and FPO2c Banno Takao.
Sugita arrived at Rabaul with No. 6 Ku as one of Rabaul's youngest pilots. Banno's
adventures from the carrier Shoho are covered in Volume 3 of this series. He
transferred to the carrier Junyo before joining Sugita in No. 204 Ku.*

afoul of bad weather. Including Charles and the pilot Second Lieutenant John Titus, a total of
eleven crewmen were lost.

Shortly before midnight a trio of No. 751 *Ku* Bettys departed Kavieng for another nuisance
raid over Port Moresby. Bombs landed near the northern end of Seven-Mile at 0323 on 30
November, and the 3.7-inch guns of the 32nd Heavy Anti-Aircraft Battery engaged the intruders,
firing 60 rounds. One of the Bettys was slightly damaged as a result, but all had returned safely
to base by 0530.

During the night a No. 11 Squadron Catalina bombed the flying boat anchorage and IJN base
in the Shortlands but was unable to observe results. The flying boat remained in the area for
two and a half hours amidst bad weather. Meanwhile, another Catalina bombed Buin 'drome,
claiming one fighter destroyed on the ground. Then following a night reconnaissance of the
Buna area, a No. 6 Squadron Hudson made a dive-bombing attack on the Gona wreck at dawn,
claiming a hit and a near miss.

Early on the morning of 30 November five 19th BS B-26s made a rare low-level raid on Buna's
runway, dropping 20 x 500-pound bombs with delayed action fuses. This was followed that

afternoon by 17 B-25 sorties also against Buna, with the Mitchells dropping 20-, 250- and 300-pound bombs and also strafing targets with 0.50- and 0.30-inch machine guns.

Late that morning six No. 582 *Ku* Vals departed Rabaul for Gasmata where they refuelled before venturing to the Buna area in search of targets. These were escorted by a dozen No. 582 *Ku* Zeros led by Lieutenant Sakai Tomoyasu. On arrival over Buna at 1350, the Zeros clashed with a large 49th FG formation made up of sixteen 7th FS P-40s flying top cover for a dozen 8th FS P-40s on a dive-bombing mission.

The top cover P-40s were only at an altitude of 8,000 feet, and initially the Zeros got the best of them. From the 7th FS, Lieutenant John Johnson and Lieutenant Irving Voorhees were both shot down and killed, while from the 8th FS Lieutenant Bryant Wesley baled out near Dobodura. He was returned to his squadron four days later.

In a confused series of dogfights the Americans managed some revenge, shooting down two Zeros, with the leader Sakai and FPO1c Yokoyama Takashi both lost. One Val was badly shot up and was destroyed on landing at Lae, while a Zero was badly damaged. Overall, this was a significant engagement with the Zeros each expending their total supply of 1,000 x 7.7mm rounds which was their preferred weapon for air combat. Each Zero also expended an average of 110 x 20mm rounds (of 500 carried per aircraft).

The Vals lugged a heavy bomb load by their standards: most carried a single 250-pound and three 60-kilogram bombs. They claimed to have sunk six ships in the vicinity of Buna. However, the Allies didn't record any attacks on this date and possibly the Val pilots targeted the barge and small vessels sunk earlier. Probably also connected with this attack was the loss of Lodestar VHCAH (ex- Dutch LT921) which was destroyed by enemy aircraft near Buna on this date.

Just before midnight on 30 November a pair of No. 6 Squadron Hudsons carried out the first night bombing mission by the unit, dropping eight 250-pound bombs over Buna Mission.

Liberator Little Eva becomes lost over the Gulf of Carpentaria on 2 December after attempting to attack Japanese destroyers.

CHAPTER 13

GONA'S GONE! 1 – 9 DECEMBER

At the start of December, the position of the Allied ground forces was looking grim. They had been unable to penetrate the defences of the beachheads, while with every day that passed their fighting strength was sapped by sickness and casualties. The situation is explained by the Australian Army official historian:

> By this time General MacArthur was in the grip of great disquiet at Port Moresby. Nowhere round the new battlefront had his forces been able to achieve any decision. In the two weeks since they had started forward the 32nd Division had lost 492 men in battle – and had nothing to show for it. The main Japanese line was still unbreached. At Sanananda and Gona the strength of the Australians was waning fast.

In an effort to inject new vigour into the American troops Major General Harding was relieved and effectively replaced at the front by his superior, Lieutenant General Robert Eichelberger. The new commander arrived at the front on 1 December. However, a new assault on Buna four days later again ended in failure, despite the use of five Australian Bren Gun carriers. These were small, tracked vehicles with light armour plating which had arrived with some difficulty via a barge. Designed for battlefield reconnaissance and communications rather than frontal assault, all were disabled within the first half an hour of the battle.

The Allies were now forced to commit most of their available reserves which could be readily flown to the front from Port Moresby. Accordingly, the 21st and 30th Brigades, both of which had fought during the defensive phase of the Kokoda Campaign and had been resting at Port Moresby, were fully committed to the battle by 6 December. The bulk of these two brigades was employed against Gona, and this finally had a decisive effect when Australian troops entered the shattered and corpse-ridden village on 9 December. It was the commander of the Australian 39th Battalion, Lieutenant Colonel Ralph Honner, who sent out the famous message "Gona's gone!". Some 800 Japanese troops defending Gona had been annihilated.

However, a new threat now emerged in that sector, with Japanese troops having been landed to the west of Gona, near the mouth of the Kumusi River, as will be described below.

At 0845 on 1 December four 22nd BG B-26s dropped 28 x 300-pound bombs on a coconut grove near Buna suspected of concealing Japanese troops. The early afternoon saw a coordinated strike also against targets in the Buna area. First into action were 14 Airacobras which strafed machine gun positions and strong posts. These were followed by six B-25s which dropped 51 x 100-pound bombs and four A-20s which strafed and unloaded 160 x parafrags.

Meanwhile the waters north of Buna saw frenzied activity as another Japanese reinforcement convoy of four destroyers had departed Rabaul the previous evening. This consisted of the *Asashio, Arashio, Inazuma* and *Isonami* which embarked the main strength of the 3rd Battalion, 170th Infantry Regiment.

Two air units, Nos. 252 and 582 *Ku*, were tasked with providing fighter cover over the ships throughout the day. No. 252 *Ku chutaicho* Lieutenant Mitsumori Kazumasa had a dozen Zeros which he assigned into rotating patrols, the first of which departed Lakunai at 0800. Warrant Officer Tsunoda Kazuo of No. 582 *Ku* also had a dozen Zeros which he arranged into two patrols each of six fighters. The first patrol departed Lakunai at 1100. Both units had the options of using Lae or Gasmata for refuelling as required.

The destroyers were first spotted that morning near Gasmata by a 403rd BS B-17 on a reconnaissance flight. This aircraft was briefly engaged by the first No. 252 *Ku* patrol at 1133. However, two patrols from No. 582 *Ku* saw more action. The first of these engaged a formation of five 65th BS B-17s about 50 miles southwest of Gasmata at 1345. The Fortresses claimed a near miss on one destroyer after dropping 40 x 500-pound bombs.

Shortly afterwards the second No. 582 *Ku* patrol successfully thwarted an attack by four 64th BS B-17s. However, the American gunners fought back hard, hitting two Zeros. FPO2c Sekiya Kiyoshi was forced to bale out and was rescued by one of the destroyers, while the other damaged Zero was written off after returning to Gasmata.

A No. 100 Squadron Beaufort, A9-38 flown by Sergeant Reg Green, was ordered to shadow the destroyers and reported being attacked by three Zeros. The Beaufort crew claimed a Zero as probably shot down so they might also have contributed to the losses mentioned above.

Another 64th BS Fortress, B-17E 41-2645 *Miss Carriage* flown by Lieutenant Charles Crowell, had been aloft since 0600 and had since been directed to shadow the convoy. However, after a last radio transmission at 1300 nothing further was heard from it. It appears to have been shot down by Mitsumori's *chutai* of nine No. 252 *Ku* Zeros which had left Rabaul at 1345. His pilots reported knocking out one engine on a B-17 before losing the bomber in cloud. It likely crashed soon afterwards, with the loss of Crowell and his eight crewmen.

Meanwhile six 38th BG B-25s had departed Port Moresby at 1605, five from the 71st BS and one from the 405th BS. These found the convoy at 1730 about 100 miles north-northeast of Buna. From 11,500 feet 49 x 100-pound bombs were dropped with the crews claiming a single hit on a destroyer. This was the *Isonami* which suffered minor damage from a near miss.

The Mitchells were then attacked by Mitsumori's nine No. 252 *Ku* Zeros which dived on the bombers out of a cloud bank. The Zeros hit the right engine of B-25D 41-29707 *The Sunsetter's Son* flown by Lieutenant Ross Menoher. With the engine on fire the Mitchell was last seen spiralling towards the ocean. Two parachutes were seen to open but there is no evidence these men survived to be taken aboard the destroyers. Menoher and his six crewmen remain missing in action.

Another B-25 was damaged in the combat, as were two Zeros. Mitsumori led his *chutai* to Lae where they landed at 1900 that evening. Also during the evening four No. 6 Squadron Hudsons

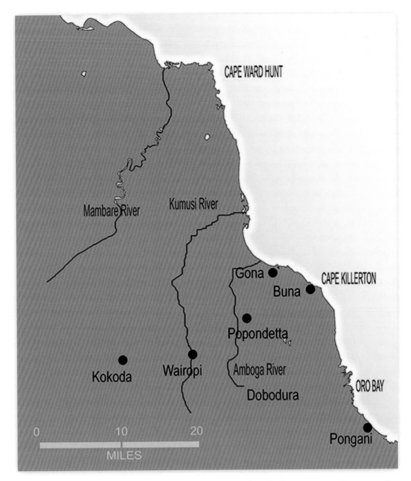

On the night of 1/2 December IJN destroyers landed troops to the west of Gona at the Kumusi River mouth. Later convoys would land troops even further west, at the mouth of the Mambare River.

raided Buna's runway, dropping 12 x 250-pound bombs with 12-hour delay fuses.

Meanwhile the Fifth Air Force launched multiple waves of night attacks against the destroyers, which unfolded shortly after midnight. In the first of these three No. 22 Squadron Bostons were led in an attack by Squadron Leader Learmonth at 0045, with bombs landing within 100 feet of one destroyer. Two other Bostons were forced to abort due to technical problems.

Six No. 30 Squadron Beaufighters were instructed to make a coordinated attack with 65th BS B-17s but had to return to base because the Fortresses did not make the rendezvous on time. Subsequently five Fortresses made attacks on the destroyers off Buna and then Gona with 40 x 500-pound bombs but scored no hits.

One of the 65th BS Fortresses, B-17E 41-9194 piloted by Lieutenant Robert Freeman, had returned to the Port Moresby circuit area when it went into a steep dive at 0215 and crashed into a hill between Five-Mile and Seven-Mile. Freeman and three crewmen were killed, while miraculously five others survived. Although no reason was given for the crash it was likely due to aircrew disorientation in the circuit area which was pitch dark at the time.

A second formation of Beaufighters, comprising four aircraft, then made an attack after a single No. 6 Squadron Hudson flown by Squadron Leader Colquhoun dropped flares to illuminate the targets. However, the attack floundered as the night vision of the Beaufighter pilots was impaired by the brightness of the flares and their own gun flashes. This meant they could not safely descend below 1,000 feet, and neither could they properly aim their guns because they couldn't ascertain their attitude nor their azimuth in reference to the horizon.

Six No. 100 Squadron Beauforts were also dispatched, three of which succeeded in making individual torpedo attacks. Two pilots dropped torpedoes at a range of 1,200 yards while a third attacked from 2,000 yards, but no hits were observed.

Six 90th BG B-24s departed Iron Range at 1600 and also searched for the destroyers, and at 1930 a pair dropped 22 x 300-pound bombs on them 40 miles north-northwest of Buna but without effect. Among the bombers which set out was 321st BS B-24D 41-23762 *Little Eva* flown by Lieutenant Norman Crosson. This bomber suffered a bomb release failure over the destroyers and instead headed for the secondary target of Lae, where the airfield was bombed amid storms and poor visibility.

Crosson subsequently crossed the Owen Stanleys flying on instruments but became lost after emerging in clear weather over the ocean while trying to find Iron Range. Running out of fuel he ordered his nine crewmen to bale out. Four of the crew were killed when the aircraft subsequently crashed near the coast of the Gulf of Carpentaria at 0245. The remainder parachuted safely and were split into two groups after landing in a desolate part of the Australian outback.

Crosson and another crewman were rescued two weeks later when they were spotted on a cattle station near Burketown. The other group of four suffered a long ordeal in the harsh environment. Only one of these men, Staff Sergeant Grady Gaston, survived after wandering onto an isolated station almost five months later on 23 March 1943.

While the Allied raids had failed to inflict damage on the Japanese destroyers, it did prevent them from offloading their troops onto barges off Buna as planned. Instead, the ships sailed west and the troops were landed in small groups on the coastline near the mouth of the Kumusi River. These Japanese troops soon began infiltrating Australian positions on the west side of Gona.

As the destroyers began their return voyage they were harassed by Allied aircraft. Two No. 20 Squadron Catalinas from Cairns were flying the nightly patrol of the waters between Lae and Buna, when at 0455 one of these attacked four destroyers sailing in a northerly direction. Four 250-pound bombs and two depth charges were dropped from 4,500 feet, but no hits were observed.

Four No. 6 Squadron Hudsons also searched for the destroyers but failed to find them. From 0645 these instead bombed Buna and the Gona wreck with 16 x 250-pound bombs. Nine B-25s, three from the 71st BS and six from the 405th BS, also failed to find the destroyers. At 0500 two of these dropped 12 x 100-pound bombs on the secondary target of Buna.

A miracle survivor from B-24D Little Eva's crew, Staff Sergeant Grady Gaston, is met at Garbutt Airfield on 13 May 1943 by Captain Milford Foster of the 90th BG. Gaston survived almost five months in the Australian bush after bailing out of Little Eva.

A pair of 64th BS B-17s was also searching for the destroyers. One of these failed to find them and instead bombed the Gona wreck. The second Fortress found the destroyers steaming northwards at 0825 and attacked them with four 500-pound bombs but no hits were scored. The bomber was intercepted by nine No. 252 *Ku* Zeros led by Mitsumori which had departed Lae at 0555 to patrol over the ships. In the subsequent combat the B-17 was hit in an engine and one Zero was damaged but there were no losses to either side. The Zeros returned safely to Lakunai mid-afternoon.

In the belief that troops and supplies had been landed at Buna overnight, dawn on 2 December saw five No. 30 Squadron Beaufighters making a coastal sweep. They found two barges each filled with 20 Japanese troops about two miles from the Gona wreck which were strafed and sunk. The Gona wreck was observed with derricks and ropes on one side indicating use by the barges. It was also thoroughly strafed.

At 0710 four Airacobras strafed Buna, followed by six 89th BS A-20s which also dropped 229 x parafrags over Buna's runway area. All were hit by anti-aircraft fire. Later that morning another formation of six 89th BS A-20s bombed and strafed the coastal area between Gona and Sanananda Point. Two No. 4 Squadron Wirraways on reconnaissance and artillery spotting missions also strafed coastal targets in this area.

The following day, 3 December, saw a similar pattern of Allied attacks against the beachheads. At 0800 a dozen P-40Es strafed Sananando Point. These were closely followed by six 89th BS A-20s which strafed the same area with 4,400 x 0.50-inch and 2,250 x 0.30-inch rounds as well as dropping 141 x parafrags. Approximately ten minutes later four No. 22 Squadron Bostons also joined in, unloading a mix of 250- and 300-pound bombs.

Over Buna, a dozen Airacobras strafed and dive-bombed enemy positions with 500-pound bombs. Five 89th BS A-20s strafed the Buna Mission area and also dropped 172 x parafrags, closely followed by a trio of B-25s which unloaded 15 x 500-pound bombs.

Also during the morning five No. 30 Squadron Beaufighters hunted barges between Sanananda Point and Buna under friendly fighter cover. Amid many wrecked barges four that might have been operational were strafed, as was the Gona wreck.

Late that morning Mitsumori led a formation of 14 No. 252 *Ku* Zeros which departed Lakunai to patrol over Buna. However, these missed the morning's Allied air activity and after experiencing no encounters all had returned to Rabaul at 1610.

Meanwhile a trio of No. 252 *Ku* Zeros was scrambled from Rabaul at 1120 to intercept an Allied aircraft, likely a reconnaissance B-17. During a brief combat FCPO Yoshihashi Shigeru's Zero was badly shot up and he was killed while attempting to land. The culprit may have been the same B-17 that reported briefly strafing a submarine 73 miles southeast of Rabaul that morning before it crash-dived.

The day also saw the loss of C-47 41-18571 *Johnny Reb* which crashed and was destroyed by fire at Popondetta due to pilot error. Another loss on 3 December was Anson DJ437 from No. 1 Rescue and Communications Flight which crashed on the newly cleared Vivigani strip on Goodenough Island.

That evening a Japanese cruiser was reportedly sighted off Buna and nine 63rd BS B-17s took off from Seven-Mile to search for it. Despite clear weather in the area nothing was sighted, and over a period of three hours from 2225 the Fortresses instead bombed the alternate targets of the 'dromes at Lae and Salamaua. However, over these targets the weather was poor, with low cloud and thunderstorms.

B-17F 41-24429 *Dumbo* piloted by Lieutenant Lewis Anderson never returned from this mission, with another Fortress reporting to have seen a dull explosion near Finschhafen. That was likely the crash of the missing bomber as the wreck was found in the same area in 1946. A wristwatch found among the crew remains had stopped at 0042 which was likely the time of the crash. Nine crewmen including Anderson were killed.

For a two-hour period from 2315 five Nos. 11 and 20 Squadron Catalinas from Cairns raided Kavieng. A mix of 20- and 250-pound bombs were dropped from heights between 2,500 to 9,200 feet with intense anti-aircraft fire experienced in conjunction with searchlights. An estimated 18 bombers were seen near the runway and some of these were left burning.

The following day, 4 December, was relatively quiet. At 0900 six No. 582 Ku Zeros departed Rabaul on a shipping patrol. After landing at Lae at 1115 they refuelled and had returned to Rabaul mid-afternoon without encountering any Allied aircraft. Meanwhile two No. 582 *Ku* Zeros had scrambled at 1130 to try and intercept a lone B-17 on a reconnaissance mission. They spotted it at 19,000 feet but were unable to engage the bomber and landed at 1330.

In the early afternoon four Beaufighters strafed barges and land targets at Sanananda Point with 1,500 x 20mm and 19,000 x 0.303-inch rounds. The mission was coordinated with an attack by five No. 22 Squadron Bostons which bombed and strafed the same area.

Meanwhile No. 4 Squadron Wirraway A20-551 was flying a reconnaissance and artillery

This Val dive-bomber (MN 3125) was among the first batch of D3A2s assigned to No. 582 Ku in late 1942. The yellow chevron, a No. 582 Ku marking, was replaced with a vertical band sometime in early 1943.

spotting mission over the beachheads when it landed at Popondetta to refuel. While taking off the aircraft struck a concealed rock which wrecked the starboard landing gear. The aircraft was damaged beyond repair and was later salvaged for components.

By this time the Japanese garrisons were beginning to experience supply difficulties. While destroyers could quickly disembark troops, they had no time to properly unload supplies and ammunition due to the threat of Allied air attack. In response, a relatively rare Japanese air supply mission was flown on 4 December when three No. 701 *Ku* Nells flew food provisions from Vunakanau to Lae.

No. 701 *Ku* was previously known as the Mihoro *Ku* and had been based in the Marshall Islands. Equipped with antiquated G3M2 Nells, the unit arrived in Rabaul on 1 December. This move was driven by the appalling ongoing attrition suffered by the land-attack units at Rabaul which had lost 20 Bettys over Guadalcanal during November alone. No. 701 *Ku* immediately began flying sector searches from Rabaul and would soon fly its first combat mission from the new base before the end of the first week of December.

Meanwhile a number of 71st, 90th and 405th BS B-25s had concentrated at Port Moresby to raid Buna on 5 December which was the date of the planned American assault supported by Australian Army Bren Gun carriers. However, these missions got off to a bad start when Lieutenant Charles Richards of the 90th BS took off from 17-Mile for a pre-dawn raid at 0300. The B-25 failed to get over a hill at the end of the runway, with his bomb load exploding as a result of the crash. The force of the explosion was terrific with the wreckage and crew remains spread over a 100-yard radius.

It was instead six 89th BS A-20s that bombed and strafed Buna at 0815 just prior to the ground assault. Two hours later nine Mitchells dropped 43 x 500-pound bombs over Buna Mission, in an attack coordinated with nine P-40Es. The mission was repeated by a second wave of Mitchells that afternoon.

However, there were two losses from the afternoon mission. B-25C 41-12907 *The Happy*

Legend piloted by First Lieutenant Wilson L Pinkstaff never returned. It flew into mountains near Myola shortly after it entered cloud en route to the target, with the wreckage first located in 1943. All seven crew were killed.

A second bomber, B-25C 41-12911 *Per Diem* of the 405th BS, was hit by anti-aircraft fire over Buna. During an emergency landing at Seven-Mile the landing gear collapsed. The crew were unhurt, but the B-25 was written off.

In other activity on 5 December seven No. 582 *Ku* Zeros attempted to intercept a lone B-17 over Rabaul, but the encounter was not recorded by Allied sources. The B-17 was likely *Tuffy* flown by Captain McCullar (his *Black Jack* was undergoing repairs) who noted a number of fighters crowded at Lakunai below. McCullar and his crew then had a hairy return to base after a supercharger exploded. Red hot shrapnel was showered in all directions, some of which penetrated the fuselage and narrowly missed a waist gunner.

Earlier, a pair of 90th BG B-24Ds made good use of their long-range capabilities with an early morning raid over Kavieng where they dropped 240 x 20-pound fragmentation bombs over the runway and dispersal area. This was a new tactic in dropping such light bombs from heavy bombers and would be repeated the following day.

Following McCullar's report of aircraft at Lakunai, a pair of 63rd BS B-17s tried to catch them on the ground with a pre-dawn raid at 0515 on 6 December. Some 240 x 20-pound fragmentation bombs were dropped over the runway area, while ten clusters of incendiaries were dropped into Rabaul township.

Further missions against Buna were planned for the morning including a coordinated raid involving three Beaufighters and six B-25s. However, the mission was cancelled due to bad weather and nothing else eventuated in the area during the day.

Among the fighters spotted at Lakunai were 20 No. 252 *Ku* Zeros which took off at 0930 to patrol the Buna area. These were led by Ensign Shibata Chiyoyuku, and in a 20-minute period from midday they recorded combat with two Liberators. The Zeros expended a significant amount of ammunition, 880 x 20mm and 4,400 x 7.7mm rounds before returning to Rabaul at 1440. Allied sources recorded a single B-24 being attacked by 14 Zeros near Gasmata, but despite the usual ambitious claims, there were no losses to either side.

Also departing Rabaul that morning was a mixed No. 582 *Ku* formation of nine Vals and a dozen Zeros led by Val pilot Lieutenant Commander Inoue Buntou. These attacked an Australian medical facility at Popondetta at 1315 Allied time, but the bombs fell wide and there was only one casualty, a native who was killed. This was fortunate as over 400 patients were crowded into the facility awaiting aerial evacuation to Port Moresby. This had been held up for 48-hours because of the crashed Wirraway with a collapsed undercarriage that was obstructing the airstrip.

Twenty minutes later Inoue's formation bombed and strafed small ships in Porlock Harbour, where the ketch *Hilda Norling* was damaged and run aground. It was later repaired and returned to service. Nonetheless, two crewmen were killed in the attack.

A second No. 582 *Ku* formation of four Vals and eight Zeros departed Lae at 1515 and soon found the 285-ton *Kurimarau* six miles northeast of Porlock Harbour, towing a barge carrying two 25-pounder guns. The *Kurimarau* was one of the larger of the "small ships" recently acquired in Australia by the Americans and before the war it had been a trading vessel in the Solomon Islands. It was damaged by near misses which killed two men aboard including an RAN officer.

The attackers returned to Lae at 1800, and in an effort to catch them at 1940 six B-25s dropped 72 x 100-pound bombs over Lae 'drome. Although the crews claimed that most of the bombs landed on the runway area, the attack was probably not successful as an intelligence report dryly noted that:

Results not observed through weather and darkness.

The night of 6/7 December saw four Nos. 11 and 20 Squadron Catalinas raid Kavieng's wharf and jetties, dropping 48 x 20-pound and 30 x 250-pound bombs. Following a large explosion at a suspected bomb dump, smoke from a large fire rose to 5,000 feet. Heavy anti-aircraft fire and searchlights were experienced.

Daylight on 7 December saw two B-17s bomb the Gona wreck. At 1050 three No. 30 Squadron Beaufighters strafed anti-aircraft positions at Buna in an attack coordinated with six 38th BG B-25s which unloaded 65 x 100-pound bombs over Buna Mission. Two of the Beaufighters received minor damage from ground fire while the pilots witnessed nearby aerial combat between Airacobras and Japanese aircraft as described below.

At 1223 eight No. 4 Squadron Wirraways began bombing enemy troop positions south of Gona, with each unloading two 250-pound bombs. However, most bombs fell amid friendly positions. As it was felt that this forewarned the enemy of a new assault the attack was postponed until the following day.

Meanwhile Lieutenant Commander Inoue Buntou led six No. 582 Ku Vals from Lae that morning to bomb targets near Buna with a close escort of six No. 582 *Ku* Zeros led by Lieutenant (jg) Matsuki Usaburo. These were followed by a separate formation of eleven No. 582 *Ku* Zeros led by Lieutenant (jg) Asano Mitsuru.

Allied spotters near Lae gave advance warning of the incoming formation. This enabled the cancellation of transport flights and for fighter cover from the 35th, 36th and 40th Fighter Squadrons to be ready and waiting over the Buna area. However, this failed to prevent the Japanese aircraft attacking an American Field Hospital near Buna at 1120. The Vals each dropped two 60-kilogram bombs and expended approximately 4,000 x 7.7mm rounds strafing.

Shortly afterwards the attackers were spotted by the American pilots, and some two dozen P-39s tore into the Japanese formation from above. Within ten minutes the Americans had optimistically claimed four Vals and five Zeros destroyed. In fact, the American pilots downed two Vals plus a Zero flown by FPO2c Uematsu Nau.

The remaining Vals were then scattered as the Zeros tried to protect them. Inoue subsequently

A film cannister is unloaded from 8th PRS F-4 Lightning 41-2144 at 14-Mile Drome.

made an emergency landing in his damaged Val at Salamaua where it was written off. Two other Vals and three Zeros received combat damage. In comparison the only damage to the Americans was a single bullet to 40th FS pilot John Watson's Airacobra, placed there by a Val rear gunner.

On this anniversary of the Pearl Harbor attack, it was fitting that one of the key American pilots involved in this combat was Lieutenant George Welch who had flown a P-40B over Pearl Harbor. Welch chased a Zero inland that he claimed, and hence was likely responsible for the demise of Uematsu. Welch was awarded ace status after also being credited with two Vals, although his true score is unclear.

Meanwhile, two other substantial formations of Japanese aircraft had departed Rabaul earlier that morning. The first comprised eighteen No. 701 *Ku* Nells led by *hikotaicho* Lieutenant Iwaya Fumio. Each of these bombers carried ten 60-kilogram bombs destined for Allied targets near Buna. Departing ten minutes later were eighteen No. 252 *Ku* Zeros led by Warrant Officer Kojima Shizuo. The faster Zeros arrived over the Buna area first and reported encountering nine P-39s, although contact was limited due to the Airacobra's low fuel status from the previous combat.

By the time the Nells arrived over Buna at 1300, the Airacobra combat air patrol had been replaced by 7th and 9th Fighter Squadron P-40Es. However, the Nells managed to unload their bombs over the same American Field Hospital targeted earlier by the Vals, the large tents presenting the most obvious Allied target in the area. As a result of both attacks seven men were killed and another 30 wounded.

A flight of four 7th FS P-40s was then able to attack the Nells without interference from the

Zeros. The American pilots made a frontal attack which they closed to close range as the Nells had no forward-facing defensive armament. This was devastatingly effective and three Nells fell in flames in short order, those flown by Ensign Shirai Senjo, FCPO Agui Yoshihito, and FCPO Sakamoto Yoshikane.

Protective Zeros were then able to fend the P-40s away from the bombers, although a new threat emerged five miles north of Buna when a flight of 9th FS P-40s also joined the fight. Despite American claims of six Nells downed the actual score remained at three, but eight of the remaining fifteen bombers received combat damage.

Meanwhile four 63rd BS B-17s had been despatched to Gasmata to attack a tanker reported offshore. The B-17s dropped 32 x 500-pound bombs, which missed a ship and landed on Gasmata's runway close to where Zeros were seen. These were eight Zeros from No. 582 *Ku* which had been over Buna earlier but had returned to Gasmata instead of Lae.

Six of these pursued the B-17s which adopted a tight defensive formation low over the water. In attacks which began at 1310, one of the Zeros was badly shot up and the pilot was treated for injuries on return to Gasmata. At 1400 the B-17s ran into a larger group of Zeros which was the No. 252 *Ku* formation that had been defending the Nells over Buna. There were no further losses to either side although the B-17 gunners expended 11,900 x 0.50-inch rounds during these combats and the bombers each received minor damage.

Keen to try and catch freshly returned aircraft on the ground at Lae, six Beaufighters strafed Lae 'drome at 1430. The pilots saw many wrecked aircraft and they found it difficult to distinguish serviceable ones. However, one Zero was claimed as destroyed and a Val as damaged. Some personnel spotted on the ground were also targeted. Two hours later six B-25s bombed the same target and were briefly challenged by two airborne Zeros.

That evening three No. 100 Squadron Beauforts were ordered to attack the enemy ship reported off Gasmata. On arrival the crews found the area obscured by heavy cloud and rainstorms and they returned to base after a flight time of over four hours.

At 0335 on 8 December a No. 11 Squadron Catalina flying a regular reconnaissance mission between Lae and Buna took the opportunity to attack Gasmata. Despite heavy cloud cover four 250-pound bombs were dropped over the runway from 3,000 feet which resulted in a large explosion. The crew then descended to 1,500 feet and strafed the area with 600 rounds of 0.303-inch ammunition.

Following the frenzy of activity over Papua the previous day, 8 December saw a relatively modest number of Allied missions. At 0915 four 89th BS A-20As strafed anti-aircraft positions at Buna. One of the attackers, A-20A *Mike* III, was damaged by gunfire and subsequently made an emergency belly landing at Seven-Mile, although it was repaired and would later serve with the RAAF as A28-40. Following the strafers were eight B-25s which unloaded 432 x 20-pound and 24 x 100-pound bombs over Buna Mission. At 1105 two P-38s dive-bombed the Gona wreck but scored no hits.

Meanwhile an IJA infantry battalion bound to reinforce Buna had been loaded aboard six destroyers which departed Rabaul early that morning. This was the 1st Battalion of the 170th Infantry Regiment together with support troops who were embarked on the *Asashio, Arashio, Kazagumo, Yugumo, Inazuma* and *Isonami*.

Both Nos. 252 and 582 *Ku* were tasked with providing covering patrols during the day. Leading the No. 252 *Ku* contingent was the newly promoted Ensign Wajima Yoshio who had arrived in the theatre with No. 2 *Ku* in August and who had subsequently earned a fine fighting reputation over Guadalcanal. An early patrol departed Rabaul at 0700 and orbited over Buna without incident before refuelling at Lae and returning to Rabaul at 1230. However, several other patrols saw action closer to Rabaul.

At 0955 a B-17 began a long running flight with an estimated eight to ten Zeros near Vunakanau. A single No. 252 *Ku* Zero was shot down with the loss of Leading Airman Echi Horoshi, while the Fortress reported the sighting of the six destroyers leaving Rabaul. Then at 1020 a lone B-24 spotted the six destroyers further along the south coast of New Britain. The crew claimed a hit on one destroyer after dropping four 500-pound bombs prior to skirmishing with two Zeros.

As a result of these reports two formations of B-17s were sent out to hunt the destroyers. The first of these comprised four 63rd BS Fortresses which dropped 28 x 500-pound bombs. The first to attack was Lieutenant James Murphy in *Lulu Belle* who claimed a hit on the stern of a destroyer at 1456. Murphy's aircraft was immediately swarmed by an estimated dozen Zeros and a 30-minute running battle began.

Murphy dove to just 50 feet but the Zero attacks succeeded in disabling one engine and wounding his co-pilot. A second Fortress, Lieutenant Sogaard's *Fightin Swede*, joined formation with *Lulu Belle* and their combined defensive fire eventually drove the Zeros away. Another B-17, *Tuffy* (again flown by Captain McCullar), was peppered with 109 bullet holes during this combat but all four of the bombers returned to base safely.

Just over an hour later seven 65th BS B-17s found the destroyers in the vicinity of St George's Channel near Rabaul. The early detection of this convoy had forced it to turn around and abandon the mission. The 65th BS Fortresses unloaded 56 x 500-pound bombs over the destroyers, with a near miss appearing to cause one of the vessels to list.

These B-17s also faced around a dozen Zeros, but the American crews felt that the Japanese pilots did not press home their attacks and that some of them appeared inexperienced. These observations appear valid as the overall Japanese ammunition expenditure was paltry given the number of aircraft involved. Despite this, one of the 65th BS Fortresses was holed 75 times.

There were no losses to either side from these engagements although the B-17 gunners optimistically claimed seven Zeros destroyed plus additional "probables". As a result of near misses two of the destroyers, the *Asashio* and the *Isonami*, received minor damage.

A final mission on 8 December was carried out by a formation of six 90th BG B-24Ds when they unloaded 60 x 500-pound bombs over Gasmata's airfield.

Just after 0900 on 9 December, three 89th BS A-20s bombed and strafed Buna, closely followed by a formation of seven B-26s which unloaded 49 x 300-pound bombs. Flying as a co-pilot in one of the B-26s was the commander of the 22nd BG, Colonel Dwight Divine. This was the first Marauder mission after the 19th and 33rd Bombardment Squadrons had been stood down for a week due to a lack of spare parts. While providing fighter cover for these missions, Lieutenant John Hall baled out of his 40th FS Airacobra due to engine trouble but soon returned to duty.

At 1035 a dozen P-40Es dive-bombed targets in the Sanananda area with 300-pound bombs. However, an ambitious follow-up campaign was called off after one of these bombs almost demolished a Salvation Army coffee stall positioned a mile behind the Australian lines.

This 49th FG P-40E Warhawk has a pair of 300-pound bombs fitted at 14-Mile for a fighter-bomber mission against Japanese positions.

A 49th FG Warhawk and a No. 582 Ku Zero tangle over the swampy lowlands behind Buna.

CHAPTER 14

MADANG MOVE: 10 – 20 DECEMBER

After the fall of Gona on 9 December, Australian troops in the area were occupied with the enemy infantry battalion which had been landed near the Kumusi River and was advancing eastwards. It took a week for this threat to be neutralised, with hundreds of Japanese troops killed. Others were evacuated by sea and transferred to the Sanananda beachhead, however a further landing of Japanese troops even further west at the mouth of the Mambare River would soon occur.

On the Buna front the 127th Regiment, which was the third regiment of the 32nd Division, arrived at Dobodura by air on 9 December and joined the frontlines two days later. Further reinforcements soon arrived in the form of the Australian 18th Brigade. This unit had been at Milne Bay from where the first of the battalions was brought along the coast to Oro Bay by Australian corvettes on 15 December. Importantly, these troops were accompanied by eight M3 Stuart light tanks.

These tanks had first arrived at Milne Bay on 10 November, but as they each weighed 14 tons, getting them forward to the Buna area proved a major challenge. The first attempt involved the use of a captured Japanese barge, but when the tank was driven onto the barge both sank, although the tank was soon retrieved with a ship's derrick. Eventually the tanks were loaded onto a small ship and then loaded onto larger barges for transfer to a beach near Buna. However, this was a precarious process with the barges having only two inches of freeboard under the weight of the tanks.

With the tanks in the vanguard, on 18 December the fresh Australian troops gained substantial territory between the airfield and the coast. Although this was won at the significant cost of 171 men lost, it was the first major incursion into the Japanese positions at Buna and marked the end of weeks of ineffectual stalemate.

Meanwhile in the Solomons the Japanese were facing increasing difficulty in supplying their forces on Guadalcanal by destroyer. Submarines were being used to run supplies and commencing on 16 December the Japanese would use submarines to run supplies to Buna as well. However, submarines could only provide a tiny fraction of the transport capacity needed to sustain their forces at Guadalcanal and Buna. Faced with competing and unworkable scenarios, the Japanese began debating the future of both forces with evacuation now considered an option.

Despite these stressful dynamics, remarkably the IJA was simultaneously making plans to occupy Madang and Wewak on the northern New Guinea coast, as well as constructing an airbase at Cape Gloucester on the western tip of New Britain. All of these locations possessed overgrown airfields constructed before the war, and Madang and Wewak also boasted excellent ports. Soon the IJA would issue a bold plan called Operation *Hei* which included transporting a force of two IJA divisions to Wewak.

However initial plans sending more modest forces to occupy these locations were issued on 12 December and involved the following:

Wewak	3rd Battalion, 11th Infantry Regiment
Madang	3rd Battalion, 21st Infantry Regiment
	2nd Battalion, 42nd Infantry Regiment
Cape Gloucester	One company, 31st Field Road Construction Unit

Detachments from the 58th Field Anti-Aircraft Artillery Battalion and the 6th Airfield Construction Unit, together with signal units, were distributed between the Wewak and Madang forces. In addition a token IJN detachment, the 9th Base Unit, would operate two E13A1 Jake seaplanes from the new bases. These forces departed Rabaul on 16 December, and the movements and vessels involved are described below.

The afternoon of 10 December saw six No. 22 Squadron Bostons bomb and strafe Buna's muddy runway area in what was otherwise a very quiet day for air operations.

Underlining the seriousness of the Japanese supply situation, a relatively rare air transport mission was flown. Seven No. 705 *Ku* Bettys departed Vunakanau at 1220 and arrived over Buna two hours later where they spent 12 minutes airdropping supplies before returning to base late that afternoon. Nearby Allied observers counted 125 packages being dropped. Escort was provided by nine No. 582 *Ku* Zeros and six from No. 252 *Ku*, but there was no contact with Allied aircraft. A few days later No. 705 *Ku* flew their Bettys to Truk for some well-earned rest: they would not fly another combat mission until 1 January 1943.

Further south No. 7 Squadron suffered two Beaufort losses on 10 December. In the first of these Beaufort A9-161 force landed in the sea near the Palm Islands north of Townsville. The crew took to their emergency dinghy and were rescued by a merchant ship 32 hours later. The second loss was also a force landing in the sea, by A9-119 shortly after take-off from Horn Island. The crew were unhurt.

At 0930 on the morning of 11 December six 22nd BG B-26s struck the Buna area with 63 x 300-pound bombs. Large fires were started as a result. Later that morning six No. 4 Squadron Wirraways took off from Berry (12-Mile) to attack suspected storehouses near Buna. In cloudy conditions over the Owen Stanleys the formation was separated and two Wirraways, A20-51 and A20-485, went missing. No trace of A20-485 has been found and it doubtless flew into mountains in cloud. The crew of A20-51 baled out but only the pilot, Flying Officer Arthur Dineen, survived. Meanwhile the other four aircraft each bombed the targets with two 250-pound bombs.

A reconnaissance photo taken after the morning strike on Buna 'drome by six B-26s on 11 December. The area is peppered with bomb craters following weeks of attacks.

Late that afternoon the weather cleared sufficiently for two formations of bombers to raid Lae 'drome. The first consisted of six 19th BS B-26s escorted by 39th FS P-38s, while the Marauders unloaded 108 x 100-pound bombs causing one aircraft seen on the ground to explode. These were followed by six B-25s which dropped 30 x 500-pound bombs with the crews claiming to have silenced an anti-aircraft position.

Earlier on 11 December a large formation of Zeros departed Rabaul for a fighter sweep over the Buna area. This comprised 18 Zeros from No. 252 *Ku* led by Lieutenant Kagi Yu'uzo accompanied by a *chutai* of nine from No. 582 *Ku*. No Allied aircraft were encountered; however, this intrusion was fairly accurately reported from Dobodura as a "raid" by 29 Zeros at 1315. In fact, such incursions were conducted with ease during many afternoons when the Owen Stanleys clouded over and Allied fighter patrols were forced to remain south of the mountains.

At 1025 on 12 December five No. 30 Squadron Beaufighters strafed the Buna Mission area in an operation coordinated with six No. 22 Squadron Bostons. Buildings at Buna Mission were bombed and strafed but with no activity observed both formations also attacked targets at the mouth of the Kumusi River, including a large barge that was thoroughly strafed.

Further activity followed that evening. At 1700 three B-17s bombed the Salamaua runway while at 1815 three 89th BS A-20s strafed barges off Sanananda Point. Two hours later seven Fortresses unloaded 56 x 500-pound bombs over Lae 'drome, while a single No. 6 Squadron Hudson dropped two 250-pound bombs on Salamaua.

At 0900 on 13 December four No. 30 Squadron Beaufighters departed Wards to strafe targets at the mouth of the Kumusi River. However, one of the aircraft aborted due to technical difficulties and landed six minutes later, leaving the other three to complete the mission. Two barges were well strafed although one was assessed to be the same one targeted the previous day.

At 1000 several bombers (the type is unreported but probably B-25s) dropped 15 x 500-pound bombs over Buna Mission, while a short time later six 89th BS A-20s struck targets at Cape Killerton, midway between Gona and Sanananda Point. The A-20s expended 4,100 x 0.50-inch and 950 x 0.30-inch rounds and dropped 420 x 20-pound fragmentation bombs.

Two separate *chutai*, each of nine No. 252 *Ku* Zeros, patrolled over the Buna area during the afternoon but did not encounter any Allied aircraft. The first of these formations landed at Lae mid-afternoon while the second *chutai* encountered very bad weather on the return flight to Rabaul, although all had landed safely by 1800 that evening.

Late that afternoon five 2nd BS B-26s raided Gasmata, targeting grounded aircraft with 161 x 100-bombs although the crews believed the runway was unserviceable. Anti-aircraft fire struck the cockpit of one of the bombers and wounded the navigator.

Of key interest to the Fifth Air Force was further signs of Japanese naval activity in the area. At 1022 a 90th BG B-24D spotted a lone destroyer south of New Britain which was unsuccessfully attacked with four 500-pound bombs. However, of more importance was a convoy described as one cruiser and four destroyers seen by another B-24D, 86 miles north-northeast of Madang at 1425. The Liberator dropped six 300-pound bombs, two of which landed near the largest vessel.

This convoy had departed Rabaul the previous night and was made up of five destroyers, the *Arashio, Kazagumo, Yugumo, Inazuma* and *Isonami*. These carried the same reinforcements who had been forced to turn around south of Rabaul on 8 December: the 1st Battalion of the 170th Infantry Regiment together with support troops. This time the convoy had taken a route to the north of New Britain and via the Admiralties to try and avoid detection, whilst also taking advantage of the cover of bad weather.

A formation of six No. 582 *Ku* Zeros departed Kavieng at 1100 to provide fighter cover over the convoy. Also departing Kavieng two hours earlier at 0858 was the first of four No. 751 *Ku* Bettys. With take-offs staggered about an hour apart, these bombers would conduct anti-submarine patrols for the convoy in operations that were affected by bad weather.

The Zeros and the first Betty encountered a lone Liberator 82 miles north-northwest of Madang at 1155. The Liberator crew reported being attacked by five Zeros and one Betty, in fact flown by Lieutenant (jg) Kitazawa Kichinosuke. Two and a half hours later, another Liberator battled Zeros and a Betty in a position 86 miles north-northeast of Madang. This was the B-24 which bombed the convoy unsuccessfully at 1425, as noted above.

During this encounter the B-24 crew claimed a Betty as destroyed. This bomber was flown by FCPO Kouno Harumi which indeed was hit by the Liberator's gunfire and damaged, wounding two crew. Kouno subsequently ditched safely near Cape Lambert, not far from Vunakanau.

P-38F 42-12627 Loi of the 39th FS, assigned to Captain Charles Gallup and based at 14-Mile in December 1942.

The crew came ashore and was collected by vehicle two days later and driven to Rabaul, before being flown back to their base at Kavieng.

Meanwhile B-17s of the 43rd BG were sent to hunt the destroyers although some failed to find them due to the stormy weather. The first attack occurred at 1750 when three Fortresses found the destroyers off the northern New Guinea coast east of Madang. The Fortresses dropped 24 x 500-pound bombs and claimed two near misses close to the stern of one destroyer. These bombers were intercepted by a second patrol of nine No. 582 *Ku* Zeros which had departed Rabaul at 1430, but there were no losses to either side.

At 1915 a formation of six B-17s found the destroyers in the same location and attacked them with 48 x 500-pound bombs, claiming a hit on the stern of a destroyer. Later in the evening another three Fortresses bombed Salamaua, likely an alternate target after failing to find the convoy.

Meanwhile at 2000 a single No. 751 *Ku* Betty departed Kavieng bound for Port Moresby carrying 11 x 60-kilogram bombs. For around an hour from 2355 the bomber made three runs over the target area, with two small patterns of bombs landing near Wards 'drome but doing no damage. The bomber was engaged by anti-aircraft guns and searchlights, with 177 rounds being fired. On the return flight the Betty made a final radio transmission at 0150 but never returned to base. FCPO Shibada Yago and his crew doubtless fell victim to the bad weather, but where they crashed remains open to speculation.

That night the Japanese convoy made its run south toward Papua, but instead of landing near the beachheads, the ships anchored in the mouth of the Mambare River, near Cape Ward Hunt and about 50 miles northwest of the Gona-Buna area. Unlike the coastline near Buna there were no offshore reefs so the destroyers could approach close to shore, which greatly facilitated unloading. Between 0200 and 0400 all the troops were successfully disembarked, together with several barges and launches to enable the troops to make their way to the beachheads.

The night raid by Shibada's Betty meant runway lights at Port Moresby were kept turned off and aircraft were prevented from departing for some hours to search for the Japanese destroyers. Among those that eventually took off in the early hours were 38th BG B-25s which searched the Papuan coast with the aid of flares but soon returned to Port Moresby in the face of ongoing bad weather.

Five No. 100 Squadron Beauforts did take off from Milne Bay in the early hours of 14 December to attack the convoy, but these aircraft also failed to find the target amidst the poor visibility. Meanwhile a single No. 11 Squadron Catalina found the convoy around midnight as it approached the Papuan coast. It was shadowed for over two and a half hours before the flying boat was forced to return to base due to engine trouble. Four 250-pound bombs were dropped from 6,500 feet just as the destroyers entered a cloud bank, and the results were unobserved.

Dawn on 14 December saw the first of many attacks against the troops landed overnight and the destroyers. At 0600 seven No. 30 Squadron Beaufighters were led by Wing Commander Walker on a barge hunt. Operating under fighter cover, near the Mambare River mouth the crews found a dozen barges and four boats pulled up on the beach amidst piles of stores. Three barges were seen a mile offshore loaded with troops, and all targets were strafed with 2,500 x 20mm and 15,000 x 0.303-inch rounds.

The No. 30 Squadron crews witnessed a B-17 attack on the destroyers which were only five to fifteen miles from the coast. This was by a trio of 43rd BG Fortresses which unloaded 24 x 500-pound bombs, with the crews claiming a near miss. In addition, at 0730 a lone B-25 on a reconnaissance mission dropped a single 500-pound bomb near a destroyer.

Also making early morning attacks at the Mambare River were three 2nd BS B-26s and five No. 22 Squadron Bostons. The latter formation also attacked the destroyers and although two bombs landed within ten yards of a target no damage was observed. Some of these aircraft raced back to Port Moresby to quickly refuel and rearm so they could return to the Mambare River, a pattern which would be repeated throughout the day. Further sorties were flown by Beaufighters (another 15 in total), Bostons (7), P-39s (3), A-20s (23), B-25s (27) and B-26s (4).

Lieutenant Garrett Middlebrook was onboard one of the 38th BG B-25s:

> We went back next morning early … the convoy was gone but we found that they had put troops ashore near the Mambare River mouth … we strafed the area until we ran out of ammo. Then we discovered hundreds of buoys floating a mile or so off the coast, each with a little Japanese flag attached to the top of the buoy stem. Upon closer examination, we could see that each buoy had containers attached with supplies inside.

The floating supplies were hundreds of drums pushed off the destroyers that could be picked up later or would float into shore, a technique invented during supply runs to Guadalcanal. Most of these attacks involved the bombing and strafing of stores and barges on the shore, by which time the troops had dispersed inland. A few barges or boats were sunk in the early missions as later crews saw floating bodies and troops wearing life jackets in the water. The Japanese recorded the loss of 51 men during these attacks, leaving a total of 591 troops ashore.

B-24D 41-24047 Moby Dick was among the first 90th BG arrivals to Australia. The shark teeth markings were applied at Iron Range and would soon appear on other 320th BS Liberators.

Between 18 and 25 December many of these made their way eastwards by barge to join friendly forces in the Sanananda Point beachhead area.

During one of these missions A-20A *Pride of the Yankees* was damaged by shrapnel from its own fragmentation bombs. The pilot, Captain Edward Larner, made an emergency belly landing at Soputa where the aircraft was written off. Larner was among the last of a dwindling 8th BS contingent still serving with the 89th BS after the latter squadron took over the operational A-20A inventory of the 8th BS in early September (see *Volume 4* of this series). Larner was a rising star within the 3rd BG and in 1943 would be later given command of the 90th BS.

A peculiar incident occurred during one of the dawn missions when a pair of No. 22 Squadron Bostons became separated from its formation in bad weather. The pair subsequently mistook Cape Endiaidere, east of Buna, for Cape Ward Hunt, a critical navigational error of more than 50 miles! Several barges were then bombed and strafed carrying Allied troops. Fortunately, the bombs missed but the strafing disabled three of the barges and wounded seven soldiers.

Meanwhile Kenney considered the 90th BG was ready for squadron-sized strike operations after having been effectively stood down for additional training for four weeks (although this training included flying operational armed reconnaissance missions). This enabled rest for the hard-worked 43rd BG B-17s, which returned to Mareeba. Accordingly, the morning of 14 December saw 23 Liberators sent out to strike the Japanese convoy.

The first formation to attack the destroyers was six B-24s at 0905, which dropped 47 x 500-pound bombs but failed to score a hit. These B-24s were intercepted by two separate Zero patrols: six from No. 252 *Ku* which left Rabaul at 0550 and then eight more from No. 582 *Ku* which left Lae at 0530. Defensive fire from the bombers shot down No. 582 *Ku* pilot Leading Airman Sato Toshimi. Two other pilots from Sato's *shotai* were wounded. Earlier, at 0730, a single B-25 had been engaged over Cape Ward Hunt by the No. 582 *Ku* Zeros, which they misidentified as a B-17.

During a two-hour period in the middle of the day a further four formations totalling 15 Liberators attacked the destroyers south of Gasmata, dropping 53 x 100-, 48 x 300- and 100 x 500-pound bombs. Once again no hits were claimed, and the bombers were intercepted by Zeros. These were from a second No. 252 *Ku* patrol led by Lieutenant Kagi Yu'uzo which departed Rabaul 0820. The Zeros recorded a high ammunition expenditure indicating sustained combat. Three Zeros were damaged by defensive fire from the B-24s, and one pilot was injured.

Additionally, that morning one B-24 bombed Lae and in the evening another B-24 bombed Gasmata. Both locations were likely secondary targets after the crews failed to locate the convoy. While none of the destroyers was damaged in these attacks, Kenney considered the experience had been an excellent morale booster for the 90th BG. The crews claimed to have destroyed eleven Zeros, with others probably shot down or damaged. In fact just one Zero was shot down, and five were lightly damaged by gunfire, underlining the persistent over-claiming by all Fifth Air Force turret and side gunners at the time.

During the day B-17F 41-24550 *The Stingaree No. 2* of the 403rd BS departed Seven-Mile on a transport flight to Milne Bay. While climbing through 300 feet, three engines cut out. The pilot, Lieutenant Ealon Hocutt made an emergency water landing close to the shore in Bootless Inlet, and the crew was able to reach the shore using life rafts. The accident was blamed on poor fuel management.

The evening saw another nuisance raid over Port Moresby by a solitary No. 751 *Ku* Betty. It made two runs over the target area with bombs landing near Berry 'drome but not inflicting any damage. The guns of the 32nd Heavy Anti-Aircraft Battery fired 154 rounds at the intruder.

The following day, 15 December, was quiet with the Allies only managing a handful of attack sorties. Three No. 30 Squadron Beaufighters strafed targets along the Mambare-Kumusi coast but no activity was seen, and the targets were thought to be unserviceable barges or burnt-out stores. That afternoon a trio of A-20As bombed and strafed a village on the Mambare River, while a B-24 dropped bombs on the Gona wreck.

Five 90th BS B-25s departed Port Moresby to return to Charters Towers, but midway during the flight bad weather was encountered forcing the crews to fly on instruments. One of the B-25s, 41-13091 *Stinky Pinky*, separated from the others and never arrived at Charters Towers. The wreckage was not found until July 1943, in remote mountains about 100 miles northwest of Townsville. Eleven men died in the crash, including three passengers.

That evening two No. 751 *Ku* Bettys departed Kavieng for Port Moresby which they bombed at 2132 and 2250. One pattern of bombs landed in an American camp between Wards and Seven-Mile, injuring five personnel. The Bettys were illuminated by searchlights enabling the 32nd Heavy Anti-Aircraft Battery to fire 254 rounds. One of the Bettys was claimed as destroyed by the gunners, but both returned to base.

The 16 December saw three A-20As strafe targets near the Kumusi River in the morning, while another three bombed and strafed the same area late in the afternoon. In the early afternoon three B-26s dropped 18 x 300-pound bombs over Buna, while two No. 4 Squadron Wirraways strafed a machine gun position in the same area. This was likely because a Wirraway on an artillery spotting mission had been damaged by ground fire the previous day. Then at 1430 four No. 30 Squadron Beaufighters strafed huts and stores on the coast east of Gona under friendly fighter cover.

Earlier two P-39Ks were lost on a return flight from Buna after encountering solid cloud over the Owen Stanleys. Lieutenants Robert Tucker in 42-4362 and Alexander Currie in 42-4346 were last sighted at 17,000 feet over the Kokoda Gap. Currie's Airacobra went into an uncontrolled spin and when he emerged from the cloud in a valley, he baled out from only 1,500 feet. Currie then walked downstream for six days and eventually reached Popondetta. Tucker, however, was never seen again.

The day also saw three convoys depart Rabaul for Madang, Wewak and Cape Gloucester with the occupation forces mentioned at the start of this chapter. The largest force was bound for Madang and was loaded aboard the armed merchant cruisers *Aikoku Maru* and *Gokoku Maru*. Escort was provided by the light cruiser *Tenryu* and the destroyers *Isonami*, *Inazuma*, *Suzukaze* and *Arashio*. The Wewak force was transported by the armed merchant cruiser *Kiyosumi Maru* escorted by the destroyers *Yugumo*, *Kazagumo*, *Makigumo* and *Akizuki*. The much smaller Cape Gloucester force was sent aboard the destroyer *Tachikaze* and patrol boat *PB-39*.

As will be seen, Allied intelligence was aware of this impending movement, and reconnaissance aircraft were keeping a keen watch. At 1020 a B-24 spotted a cargo vessel in the Bismarck Sea to the west of Kavieng which was strafed. This vessel was unrelated to the impending movements, so was another collection of ships spotted by another B-24 that morning off the New Britain coast south of Rabaul.

This was reported as one destroyer, two cargo ships and two tankers which were attacked unsuccessfully with eight 500-pound bombs. The "tankers" were likely surfaced submarines as several were now active in the area preparing for supply runs to Buna, including the *I-4* which departed Rabaul on this day.

Dawn on 17 December saw the first of the assault convoys arrive at its destination. This was the destroyer *Tachikaze* and patrol boat *PB-39* which put a modest force of 350 troops ashore at Cape Gloucester. This force immediately occupied and started clearing the former Australian airfield which was termed the No. 1 Airfield. A few weeks later they built a second strip nearby, termed East Field or No. 2 Airfield.

Meanwhile between 1101 and 1130 three No. 30 Squadron Beaufighters made a coastal sweep of Buna's beachheads and strafed nearby supply dumps. Aircrews witnessed fires started after a pair of 2nd BS B-26s had unloaded 12 x 300-pound bombs there at 1120. A third B-26, 40-1529 *Fury*, had taken off with the others from Berry 'drome but was last seen flying through broken cloud over the Kokoda Gap. The pilot, First Lieutenant Franklin Anderson, and his six crewmen (including an RAAF co-pilot) were declared missing in action.

Other Allied attack activity on 17 December was limited to a No. 4 Squadron Wirraway strafing barges off Sanananda Point, however Japanese aircraft were active during the evening. Two No. 751 *Ku* Bettys had departed Kavieng to bomb "Emo" each carrying 11 x 60-kilogram bombs.

Allied sources recorded a raid at Dobodura at 2145 when three bombs were dropped but there was no damage or casualties.

Meanwhile nine No. 701 *Ku* Nells had departed Vunakanau for a night raid over Port Moresby. Split into three groups, all of these became confused of their position over the target area due to bad weather. At 0035 two aircraft were detected over Port Moresby by the 32nd Heavy Anti-Aircraft Battery. However, searchlights couldn't pick up the intruders in the heavy cloud and just 12 rounds were fired in the direction of the aircraft sound. Seven bombs landed a few hundred yards from one of the gun batteries, but no damage was incurred.

The morning of 18 December saw three 89th BS A-20As bomb and strafe targets near Buna. This was the day of the Australian assault using tanks, and two 71st BS B-25s were given a strange mission. This was to fly over Buna at a very low height with the engines making as much noise as possible, in an effort to mask the approaches of the tanks to the battlefield. Other aircraft were allocated leaflet dropping duties to persuade the Japanese garrison to surrender.

During one of these flights B-25 *Madam X* hit a tree which battered the wings and engines of the bomber and ruined its flying characteristics. Unable to climb, the pilot limped around the coast at less than 200 feet before making an emergency landing at the mission airfield at Dogura, near Milne Bay.

At 1255 four 8th FS P-40Es departed Port Moresby to patrol over the Cape Ward Hunt area, likely in conjunction with a bomber raid over Lae that was cancelled. On the return flight Lieutenant Richard Dennis went missing. He was last seen in the vicinity of Kokoda at 1430, undoubtedly another victim of entering instrument conditions in mountainous terrain, or mechanical failure.

Meanwhile the Madang convoy was nearing its destination and had been detected by Allied reconnaissance. It was first bombed by a single B-24 northwest of the Admiralty Islands early on 18 December which claimed a near miss against a transport.

The convoy was next attacked by six B-17s from the 63rd BS. These unloaded 32 x 500-pound bombs over the ships but scored no hits. The crews were distracted in their bombing runs by six No. 252 *Ku* Zeros which had departed Kavieng at 1125. The Zeros knocked out the engine of Captain Sogaard's *Fightin Swede* and forced him to jettison his bombs. Two other Fortresses were also damaged before they were able to adopt a tight defensive formation and fend off the attackers. In return, three of the Zeros were damaged but they all landed at Kavieng safely.

That afternoon five 90th BG B-24Ds departed Iron Range on a strike mission against the convoy led by Captain Roy Taylor. However, the formation experienced heavy cloud and severe turbulence over the Owen Stanleys and became separated. Just one B-24 located the convoy, which was bombed unsuccessfully before the bomber was chased away by nine No. 582 *Ku* Zeros which had departed Rabaul at 1430. The Zeros reported encountering two other B-24s before landing at Lae that evening.

Meanwhile one of the other B-24s aborted the mission and landed at Milne Bay, while another

B-25D Madam X on 18 December after it hit trees when strafing Buna and subseuqently made an emergency landing at Dogura Mission.

bombed the secondary target of Lae. The 320th BS B-24D flown by Lieutenant Harold Adams, 41-23835, was last seen in cloud over the Owen Stanleys but never returned to base. The wreckage was subsequently found high in the mountains near Bulldog, scattered over a wide area. Adams and his eight crewmen had been killed instantly.

That evening another formation of five 90th BG B-24s bombed the airstrip at Alexishafen, a short distance north of Madang which had not yet been occupied by the Japanese. This was likely a secondary target. However, a flight of five 63rd BS B-17s had more luck making individual attacks on the ships with 40 x 500 -pound bombs between 1950 and 2045. Some of these were skip-bombing attacks made with the aid of flares dropped by other aircraft. The pilots, including Captain McCullar, claimed four hits on a transport. McCullar's Fortress was damaged by anti-aircraft fire during the low-level attacks.

The *Gokoku Maru* was hit in the bow which started a small fire. The ship's derricks were also damaged in these attacks which meant it could not offload heavy construction equipment such as rollers. Subsequently the construction of JAAF airfields in the Madang area proceeded only slowly with light equipment.

Allied intelligence was aware of the destination of the convoy and a submarine, the USS *Albacore*, had been directed to patrol off Madang. That evening it fired a spread of three torpedoes at the *Gokoku Maru*, but they missed and instead two hit the stern of the light cruiser *Tenryu*, killing 23 of the crew. The *Tenryu* sunk two hours later with its remaining crew rescued by the destroyers. This was a nostalgic loss for the IJN, for the cruiser had been something of a stalwart of virtually all the South Pacific campaigns since the start of the year.

That evening six No. 701 *Ku* Nells departed Vunakanau to raid Port Moresby and the Buna area. Flying in staggered pairs the bombers ran into bad weather, with the first pair unloading its bombs over Port Moresby and the last two pairs over Buna. However, two of these pairs were likely off target, as Allied sources recorded only one raid. This was at 2120 when five bombs were dropped over Pongani but without doing any damage.

Later that night two No. 11 Squadron Catalinas were flying the regular patrol of the Lae-Buna area when they encountered two destroyers 53 miles north-northwest of Finschhafen. These were likely the *Mochizuki* and *Asashio* which had transported troops from Rabaul to Finschhafen the previous day. Six 250-pound bombs were dropped at 0315, but the closest landed 150 yards in front of the destroyers.

At 0502 on 19 December two B-25s made a pre-dawn raid on Lae 'drome, dropping 10 x 500-pound bombs over the target area but results were unobserved. However, following the major gains made at Buna the previous day the main weight of air attack fell on that front. At 0650 Buna was pounded by nine B-25s dropping 26 x 100- and 30 x 500-pound bombs, with the gunners also strafing anti-aircraft positions during the bomb runs. This was followed an hour later by a rare full squadron-sized raid by the 89th BS when 13 A-20As expended 7,800 x 0.50-inch and 13,400 x 0.309-inch rounds strafing as well as unloading 476 x 20-pound fragmentation bombs.

Meanwhile, other Allied aircraft were searching for the Japanese ships at sea. At 0852 a B-24 unsuccessfully bombed what the crews described as a cruiser 60 miles north of Finschhafen. A more definitive report of the convoy that had departed Madang arrived at 0929 when five 90th BG B-24s sighted four destroyers and two transports 85 miles north-northwest of Finschhafen. Subsequently 48 x 500-pound bombs were dropped over the vessels but there were no hits.

The B-24s were intercepted by six No. 582 *Ku* Zeros led by FCPO Takemoto Masami which had departed Lae at 0650. During a ten-minute period of combat the Zero flown by FPO2c Morioka Tatsuo was hit, however he baled out successfully and was rescued by one of the destroyers.

Less than an hour later, at 1020, five 43rd BG B-17s attacked the same convoy, now described as 47 miles northwest of Madang. No hits were observed after 33 x 500-pound bombs were dropped. The Fortresses were then intercepted by Takemoto's Zeros, which reported driving off the American bombers before landing at Rabaul around midday.

At 1100 three more 43rd BG B-17s arrived over the Madang area but couldn't find the convoy. Instead, 24 x 500-pound bombs were dropped over the Madang wharf, with four hits claimed.

Meanwhile further west the Wewak convoy had arrived at its destination on 19 December, and that morning six No. 582 *Ku* Zeros led by Ensign Asano Mitsuru departed Rabaul on a mission described as "strategic defence" of the Madang area. At 1250 319th BS B-24D 41-23709 piloted by Lieutenant Elmo Patterson was intercepted by Asano's Zeros over the Bismarck Sea while about 90 miles northeast of Madang. Chasing the Liberator at low level, the Zeros shot it down after expending 260 x 20mm and 1,200 x 7.7mm rounds.

Around 30 minutes later the Zeros encountered another B-24 in the same area but were unable to shoot it down. Wary of fuel limitations, the Zeros returned to Rabaul where they landed at 1630. Meanwhile the B-24 dropped four 500-pound bombs over the convoy which had departed Madang but without scoring any hits.

Late that afternoon another formation of four 90th BG B-24s searching a similar area of the

In the early hours of 19 December 1942 Lieutenant Robert Herry flew B-25C 41-12901 Stinky in an unsuccessful shipping search from Dobodura. After returning to Port Moresby the undercarriage would not lower, so Herry proceeded to Seven-Mile where there was a crash strip and nearby medical assistance. After circling Port Moresby until daybreak, the bomber came in hot and made a rough landing.

Bismarck Sea came upon a "light cruiser" north of New Britain. This was attacked by four of the Liberators with 40 x 500-pound bombs, two of which landed close to the vessel. This was the destroyer *Mochizuki*, on its way back to Rabaul from Finschhafen, which suffered minor damage from these near misses. Likely because of a faulty bomb release, the fifth B-24 dropped its ten 500-pound bombs over Lae 'drome on the return flight.

Also on 19 December, RAAF P-40E A29-137 ditched in Milne Bay. The fighter had previously crash-landed there in early September and was being flown out after being repaired.

The following day, 20 December, saw a resumption of the Buna attack missions albeit on a smaller scale. At 0630 three B-25s dropped 15 x 500-pound bombs over the Buna coast, while early that afternoon six 89th BS A-20As bombed and strafed the same area.

That morning 400th BS B-24D BS 41-23766 piloted by Lieutenant John Rafferty departed Wards for an armed reconnaissance mission over the Wewak area. Towards evening, the aircraft radioed an arrival time and requested that runway lights be turned on when they were approaching the Port Moresby area. However, the aircraft never arrived with Rafferty and his nine crewmen declared missing in action. The wreckage of the bomber was not discovered until 1984, on a mountainside at 2,800 feet altitude around 40 miles southwest of Lae.

Meanwhile seven 90th BS B-25Ds were moving from Charters Towers to form a permanent forward detachment at Port Moresby. These had left the Australian coast north of Cairns when they encountered a rain squall and proceeded in single file. B-25D Mitchell 41-29706 *Lola* flown by Lieutenant Donald Emerson was last seen trying to fly under the squall when a wing clipped the water and the bomber crashed into the ocean. Another B-25 circled the crash site but there was no sign of survivors. Emerson and ten passengers and crew were killed.

Another B-25D loss occurred some hours later after 13th BS B-25D 41-29709 *Eight Ball Esquire* departed Cooktown at 1710 for a flight to Port Moresby. After an oil pressure failure the pilot, Lieutenant William Hellriegel, feathered the left engine and turned back to Cooktown. However, the bomber could not maintain altitude and it ditched about 25 miles north of Cooktown. The 12 men aboard made it to the beach safely although several were injured. After two men walked south to Cooktown, the remainder were rescued by a boat on 23 December.

Yet another loss in this area on 20 December was an 8th FS P-40E piloted by Lieutenant King Pipes which went missing while flying on a delivery flight between Townsville and Port Moresby.

At 2235 that night a No. 11 Squadron Catalina patrolling the Lae-Buna area encountered a 400-ton motor vessel off the south coast of New Britain. The vessel was attacked with four 250-pound bombs and two depth charges from 3,000 feet but it took evasive action and there were no hits. The flying boat crew then strafed the vessel with 2,000 x 0.303-inch rounds from 1,200 feet.

The Allied offensive against the beachheads had been made possible by the intensive use of air transport. By early December the wear and tear on the transport fleet was causing Kenney serious concern, especially as replacements were sparse and there had been regular losses. Such was the emergency that several Australian civilian airliners were mobilised to assist, namely three DC-3s, a DC-2, two Stinson Trimotors, two Lockheed Model 10s, one Lockheed Model 14 and two DH-86s. Most of these aircraft were used on the busy Townsville-Port Moresby route, while the DH-86s were used between Port Moresby and Bena Bena in the New Guinea Highlands.

In addition, fifteen Hudsons and a DC-2 used for RAAF training in Australia were sent to Port Moresby for use as transports. Most of the Hudsons were from No. 1 Operational Training Unit based in Bairnsdale, Victoria, and many of the crews were seasoned veterans, having flown operational tours with frontline Hudson squadrons in the first months of the Pacific War. By 12 December a dozen Hudsons had arrived in Port Moresby where they were stripped of doors, escape hatches and many interior fittings to permit the maximum possible loading, usually around 2,500 pounds of supplies.

The first missions began on 14 December, and tragically the first Hudson was lost the next day. This was A16-36, flown by Squadron Leader William Pedrina, which was flying its fourth flight of the day, airdropping supplies to Australian ground troops at Soputa. At 1515 it banked away from the area when it was hit by ground fire and crashed. Miraculously the turret gunner, Flight Sergeant Leo Callaghan, was thrown clear and survived. However, Pedrina[I] and two other crewmen were killed.

In a reflection of the general pressure on transport squadrons at this time, on their first two days of operations the Hudsons recorded 81 flights. Due to losses of supplies from airdropping, from 24 December the Hudsons began landing at Dobodura which also enabled them to load sick and wounded soldiers for the return flight back to Port Moresby. As will be seen, some of these flights came into contact with enemy aircraft.

I   Pedrina was one of the RAAF's most experienced Hudson pilots and was a veteran of the early New Guinea operations. He had flown with No. 24 Squadron at Rabaul and then with No. 32 Squadron at Port Moresby and had been awarded the Distinguished Flying Cross.

While the No. 1 OTU Detachment was only meant to be a temporary expedient of around ten days duration, it remained at Port Moresby for four weeks. It was eventually ordered back to Bairnsdale at the end of the first week of January 1943.

By December 1942 the war in the New Guinea area was more than twelve months old but surprisingly it was only at this late juncture that the first surface-surface naval contact between Japanese and Allied vessels occurred. This resulted due to submarine transport missions to the Buna beachheads, which occurred on the surface at night. The submarines generally only submerged during daylight hours, or when there was a threat of air attack.

To combat these submarines regular night reconnaissance missions were flown by Catalinas of Nos. 11 and 20 Squadrons and also Hudsons of No. 6 Squadron. Some of the Catalinas were equipped with an early type of ASV (Air-to-Surface-Vessel) radar. This was not always serviceable, but on occasion it picked up surfaced submarines which would usually crash-dive with the approach of an aircraft. The aircrews had to flash recognition lights before attacking any unidentified vessels because friendly USN submarines and surface craft were also operating in the area.

Meanwhile the motor torpedo boat tender USS *Hilo* arrived in Milne Bay on 17 December, bringing four PT boats in which were quickly deployed to patrol off the Buna area at night. At 0120 on 19 December *PT-121* and *PT-122* came upon the submarine *I-4* at the mouth of the Mambare River. Two torpedoes were fired but these failed to leave the tubes of the torpedo boat and the *I-4* withdrew from the area. It returned a few hours later but failed to make contact with Japanese troops ashore, so the captain decided to abort the supply mission and return to Rabaul.

The following night the submarine *I-25* was in the same area and had unloaded eight tons of food when the mission was cut short after two PT boats appeared. One of these launched two torpedoes but they missed the submarine.

Other submarines known to be involved in the Buna transport missions at this time include the *I-32* and *I-121*. On the night of 27 December, the *I-25* arrived at the Mambare River mouth during its second Buna mission but was forced to retreat after PT boats were sighted. It returned the following night but also failed to make contact with the Japanese forces ashore.

Two of these PT boats were involved in a friendly fire incident at 2030 on 23 December when they came upon the schooner *Eva* unloading stores on a beach at Cape Sudest east of Buna. Presuming it to be an enemy vessel, the USN crews opened fire with their machine guns. Partially loaded with ammunition, the *Eva* burst into flames and was destroyed. The schooner's crew took cover on the beach, but and at least one man was wounded by the gunfire.

A 39th FS P-38F warms up at Port Moresby before heading for Lae.

CHAPTER 15

ENTER THE JAAF: 21 – 31 DECEMBER

Following the breakthrough on the Buna front on 18 December, in the following days Allied ground forces made steady gains amid much hard fighting. By 27 December most of the Buna airstrip and adjoining dispersal areas had been captured, with the remaining Japanese forces concentrated in a narrow coastal pocket around Buna Mission. At 0530 on 28 December a final message was sent from the Buna naval garrison:

> The garrison is being gradually destroyed by concentrated enemy fire. Our troops repeatedly mount counterattacks, often inflicting heavy casualties on the Allies in hand-to-hand combat. Our assessment of the overall situation is that we will be able to hold the garrison until tomorrow morning. On reflection, in over 40 days of battle, all the men, whether naval personnel or labourers, have given all that could be asked of them.

Orders were then issued by both Admiral Kusaka Jin'ichi and the commander of the 18th Army for the remaining IJN and IJA forces at Buna to withdraw to the Sanananda beachhead. While there was still much difficult fighting ahead, particularly on the Sanananda front, the close of 1942 saw the Allies on the brink of victory in Papua.

Meanwhile at Rabaul a series of robust discussions in the last half of December had led the IJN and IJA to jointly agree there was no option but to withdraw from Guadalcanal. Tokyo had reached the same conclusion and on the final day of 1942, Japan's most senior navy officer, Marshal Admiral Nagano Osami, Chief of Navy General Staff, briefed the emperor alongside his army equivalent, General Sugiyama Hajime, Chief of Army General Staff. Both were of large stature with broad faces, lending authority to the solemn presentation which the emperor approved. The two senior officers humbled themselves at the end of the audience with an undertaking to greater attentiveness in future military operations. With secrecy utmost, the plans to evacuate Guadalcanal in the pretext of "revised orders" would be conveyed to Truk by a Combined Fleet Mavis, personally delivered by the Chief of Staff of the Combined Fleet, Rear Admiral Fukudome Shigeru.

The morning of 21 December was relatively quiet as by now the recent Japanese convoys had completed their missions and returned to Rabaul. However, a single B-24 found a 2,000-ton cargo vessel in Finschhafen harbour at 0600. Eight 500-pound bombs were dropped, with two landing close to the starboard side. This prompted the despatch of a follow-up trio of 65th BS B-17s to Finschhafen which arrived early that afternoon.

The Fortress crews reported finding two small vessels of 500- and 750-tons, both of which were extensively camouflaged with jungle foliage. The B-17s dropped 24 x 500-pound bombs from 4,500 feet and a hit was claimed on the 500-ton ship which was left burning. A near-miss off the stern of the 750-ton ship was thought to have left it damaged. Both vessels were subsequently thoroughly strafed with 0.50-inch calibre machine guns.

At Port Moresby, four 2nd BS B-26s were also readied with loads of 300-pound bombs to attack these vessels but the mission was cancelled due to heavy cloud over the Owen Stanleys.

The two vessels match the description of the 384-ton *Hakuyo Maru* and the 550-ton *Takasaka Maru*, both of which were cargo vessels cited by various sources as sunk due to air attack on 22 December "near Rabaul". It is also possible that the *Takasaka Maru* was attacked at Arawe on 22 December (see below).

In other missions on 21 December, a B-24 strafed barges at the Mambare River mouth, while five B-25s raided Buna with 43 x 100-pound bombs. However, about half of these overshot the target area and landed in the water.

That evening two No. 751 *Ku* Bettys departed Kavieng to raid Port Moresby, each carrying 11 x 60-kilogram bombs. Although these had difficulty locating the target area, they were spotted from the ground at 0225 after being momentarily silhouetted by the moon. The bombs landed near Seven-Mile but there was no damage or casualties. The anti-aircraft defences were ordered to hold fire as an intrepid 39th FS P-38 launched to intercept the intruders but failed to find them. This was Port Moresby's 96th air-raid, and the last for 1942.

At 2130 that evening No. 11 Squadron Catalina A24-17 was making a nightly patrol of the Lae-Buna area when a destroyer was sighted 31 miles north of Cape Ward Hunt. Four 250-pound bombs were dropped from 4,000 feet, with the closest landing an estimated ten feet from the stern of the destroyer. However, the vessel took evasive action and could not be located again in the darkness after an hour of searching.

Some hours later, at 0330 on 22 December, the same Catalina spotted a 3,000-ton motor vessel 35 miles west of Gasmata. One 250-pound bomb was dropped which landed 25 yards off the bow of the ship.

Daylight on 22 December saw three 65th BS B-17s out hunting for the vessel, and at 0910 they found a small ship anchored off Arawe Island, about 100 miles west of Gasmata. This was attacked with 24 x 500-pound bombs, one of which exploded just five feet from the stern. The Fortresses then strafed it, firing 2,000 x 0.50-inch and 600 x 0.30-inch rounds, after which a fire was started amidships. The vessel is sometimes attributed as being the 550-ton *Takasaka Maru*.

Six B-26s from the 19th and 33rd Bombardment Squadrons were also ordered to the Arawe area to search for this ship, but one of the Marauders returned to base soon after take-off. The others searched the area but couldn't find the vessel.

At 0930 five No. 22 Squadron Bostons bombed and strafed enemy stores dumps west of Gona, while at midday a single B-24 unsuccessfully bombed a transport off the New Britain coast south of Rabaul. That afternoon, five B-25s bombed and strafed suspected enemy positions near the Mambare River.

An awards ceremony for the 89th BS at Kila 'drome in December 1942.

Meanwhile at 1057 a single 403rd BS B-17E on a reconnaissance flight was intercepted southwest of Rabaul by what the crew reported as three "Zekes". The fighters made determined attacks during a half hour period when the Fortress gunners expended most of their ammunition. The B-17E, 41-2666, was riddled with bullet holes in the tailplane and wings but returned safely to Port Moresby.

However, the attackers were not Zeros but a *shotai* of 11th *Sentai* Ki-43-I Oscars which had flown into Rabaul four days earlier as explained in Chapter 9. Photos of the damaged tailplane show a large hole caused by a 12.7mm High Explosive round as used by the Oscars. The JAAF pilots were likely flying a familiarisation patrol when they spotted the B-17, and the interception is noteworthy as the first JAAF combat engagement in the South Pacific. The arrival of these JAAF fighters freed up a contingent of No. 252 *Ku* Zeros to deploy to the newly completed airfield at Munda in the northern Solomons.

At Milne Bay No. 100 Squadron Beaufort A9-29 was carrying out torpedo dropping practice when it crashed at 1150. One crewman never emerged from the aircraft and drowned, while the other three clambered aboard the emergency dinghy and were rescued.

The following day, 23 December, saw a busy morning of activity. At 0820 a single 90th BG B-24 unsuccessfully bombed a ship 55 miles northwest of Lorengau in the Admiralty Islands. Then at 0940 three B-25s raided Cape Gloucester 'drome with 180 x 20-pound fragmentation bombs. This was the first attack on this location and followed the Japanese landing a week earlier. The raid was followed up later by a single B-24 which unloaded four 500-pound bombs on the airfield.

Meanwhile air support missions continued apace in Papua, with three 89th BS A-20As strafing enemy troops near Gona including multiple personnel seen in a native canoe. Then at 1050 six No. 30 Squadron Beaufighters strafed supply dumps and barges in the Buna-Sanananda area with 2,100 x 20mm and 12,000 x 0.303-inch rounds. In stark contrast to many earlier missions in this area there was no anti-aircraft fire.

Also during the morning, a flight of B-25s dropped 19 x 500-pound bombs on a 1,500-ton ship seen off the southwestern coast of New Britain. Two bombs landed close to the stern of the vessel as it was turning. Later a single B-24 dropped 10 x 500-pound bombs on this vessel near Arawe, but the nearest landed 50 feet away and no damage was apparent.

Meanwhile a 64th BS B-17 on a reconnaissance flight was intercepted at 1020 ten miles south of Kavieng by three No. 253 *Ku* Zeros led by FCPO Uwai Makoto. The Zeros persistently chased the bomber for 25 minutes but there was no significant damage inflicted on either side.

The day also saw Nos. 2 and 3 *chutai* of the 11th *Sentai* redeploy from Vunakanau to Malahang field, near Lae (with a stopover at Gasmata where one *chutai* flew some patrols as noted below). Major Tanaguchi Masayoshi, the 11th *Sentai*'s Executive Officer, was in charge of the contingent.

Malahang was an airfield a few miles north of Lae. It had been built in 1935 as the headquarters of the Lutheran Mission aviation service, but to date had not been used by the IJN. However, for the JAAF it offered an autonomous well-located base near Lae. The Allies first saw evidence of activity at Malahang on 7 December when No. 30 Squadron Beaufighters noted two trucks present.

That evening eight No. 751 *Ku* Bettys departed Kavieng to raid targets near Buna, while seven No. 701 *Ku* Nells took off from Vunakanau bound for Port Moresby. Bad weather over the Owen Stanleys meant the Nells also bombed targets near Buna. The Allies logged three different raids near Oro Bay and Gona between 2130 on 23 December and 0030 on 24 December but there was no damage or casualties.

Daylight on 24 December saw a trio of 89th BS A-20As strafe Japanese troops on the coast west of Gona, while several B-24s flying armed reconnaissances were able to attack enemy targets. These included a schooner in the Vitiaz Strait and the runways at Lae, Madang and Gasmata.

Another B-24 bombed a transport anchored at Arawe and scored a direct hit at 0807, following which the ship was seen to sink within two minutes. This was the 623-ton IJN auxiliary *Koa Maru*. Around five hours later, at 1305, the same aircraft bombed Gasmata's runway, but results were unobserved. The Liberator was then intercepted by thirteen 11th *Sentai* Ki-43-I *Hayabusa* that had stopped overnight at Gasmata *en route* from Rabaul to Lae, but there were no losses to either side. The *Hayabusa* had been returning from an attempted fighter sweep over Buna which was abandoned in the face of bad weather.

Following this activity two formations of heavy bombers were ordered to strike Gasmata late that afternoon. The first formation comprised six 65th BS B-17s which unloaded 48 x 500-pound bombs over a ship anchored off Gasmata. Two direct hits were claimed by Captain Cromer, followed by further hits by other crews. The vessel was left listing and settling by the stern, and the Americans believed they had sunk a 5,000-ton ship. However, underlining the problems of accurate ship recognition within the Fifth Air Force, the victim was in fact the 515-ton IJN auxiliary *Tama Maru No.2*. A handful of *Hayabusa* tried to intercept the B-17s, one of which was misidentified as a FW-190 by the Americans, but no substantive combat ensued.

The second formation of bombers sent to Gasmata was five 90th BG B-24s which dropped 50 x

Lieutenant Walter Beane (centre) with #17, his shark tooth decorated 39th FS P-38F 42-12646 at 14-Mile in late 1942.

500-pound bombs over the runway and dispersal area at 1840.

That night saw nine No. 751 *Ku* Bettys depart Kavieng to raid Buna, while seven No. 701 *Ku* Nells took off from Vunakanau to attack Port Moresby. Unusually, among the 60- and 250-kilogram bombs loaded aboard the Nells one bomber also carried a single 800-kilogram bomb. However, bad weather forced the Nells to bomb Buna instead. These missions by 16 bombers were ineffectual with the Allies recording only single aircraft overhead the Buna area for periods between 2200 on 24 December and 0400 on 25 December. All of the bombs dropped landed harmlessly in the jungle.

Christmas Day was relatively quiet. The morning saw a trio of No. 30 Squadron Beaufighters on a coastal sweep strafe grass huts west of Gona. That afternoon a single B-24 bombed the runways at Cape Gloucester and Lae, while a B-17 briefly strafed a submarine south of Rabaul before it crash-dived.

Despite continuing poor weather in Papua, such was the desperate condition of the Japanese troops at Buna that on 26 December Major Tanaguchi launched a morning mission from Malahang. This consisted of fifteen Ki-43-Is led by Captain Miyabayashi Shigenori which flew southeast at 13,000 feet. On arrival over the Buna area at 1100, they spotted four Hudsons of the No. 1 OTU Detachment at Dobodura and descended to 1,000 feet to strafe them.

Two of the Hudsons, A16-2 flown by Squadron Leader Pat Hall and A16-127 flown by Flight Lieutenant Fred Landrey had just taken off and were pursued by several *Hayabusa*. The Hudson crews fought back with their turret and waist guns, using tracer rounds as Landrey explained:

> The shortcomings of tracer to show the true flight of normal bullets I knew … the idea was to let the enemy see that they had not taken on a defenceless cargo aircraft.

Landrey was a No. 1 OTU instructor and a pilot of some experience, having joined the RAAF in 1925 and accumulated 3,600 flying hours. Both Landrey and Hall made evasive manoeuvres at treetop height while heading south knowing it would draw the attackers out of range. Both Hudsons made it back safely to Wards 'drome, although A16-2 sustained a dozen bullet holes and a damaged tailplane, with the latter due to striking trees during the low-level evasive action.

Meanwhile, the pilot of another Hudson, A16-110, elected to land at Dobodura rather than risk combat with the Japanese fighters. The aircraft was subsequently damaged by strafing, while a fourth Hudson was less fortunate. This was A16-3, flown by Flight Lieutenant Neville Hemsworth which had just been loaded with four wounded soldiers as passengers.

On seeing the Japanese fighters overhead Hemsworth considered evacuating the aircraft but believed that would leave the wounded as easy targets, two of whom were stretcher cases. Instead, he elected to take-off in the hope of quickly reaching the cover of low cloud. However, the slow climbing Hudson was quickly attacked by *Hayabusa*, with the turret gunner being wounded and the aircraft catching fire. Hampshire ditched the crippled Hudson in Oro Bay where those onboard were rescued by a USN PT Boat, although the turret gunner subsequently died of his wounds.

With Dobodura under attack, the air controller there urgently called for fighter cover. A dozen 9th FS P-40Es were patrolling nearby at 9,000 feet and quickly intervened. Soon Warhawks and *Hayabusa* were engaged in dogfights, and Darwin veteran First Lieutenant John Landers was forced to bale out of his P-40E *The Rebel* after its engine seized. The American pilots optimistically claimed seven "Zekes" destroyed but the 11th *Sentai* suffered just one loss: Sergeant Major Imamura Ryoichi was shot down and killed.

Then, one of the more famous and unlikely aerial victories in the South Pacific occurred at 1135. A No. 4 Squadron Wirraway on an artillery spotting mission flying at 1,000 feet saw a "Zeke" flying below in the vicinity of the Gona wreck. Being in a favourable position, Pilot Officer John Archer made a front quarter attack firing 50 rounds from each of his forward firing 0.303-inch calibre machine guns. Archer's observer, Sergeant James Coulston, saw the aircraft crash into the ocean in flames.

Two days later Australian soldiers swam out to the site of the crash and retrieved the body of 11th *Sentai* pilot Fuji'i Hiroichi who had died instantly with a bullet wound to the head. It is possible that his *Hayabusa* might have been damaged after earlier combat with the Hudsons, explaining why Fuji'i was heading back to Malahang alone at relatively low altitude.

Elsewhere on the morning of 26 December two 90th BG B-24s bombed Cape Gloucester, Finschhafen and Madang. A third Liberator attacked a merchant ship 25 miles southeast of Rabaul with 10 x 500-pound bombs. Multiple bombs struck the rear quarter of the vessel which was left stationary and burning. The ship was likely the 451-ton *Izumi Maru* which is recorded as lost due to aircraft attack on this date "in the South Seas area".

The afternoon saw a pair of No. 22 Squadron Bostons bomb and strafe enemy positions and barges on the coast west of Gona. Meanwhile a single B-17 on a reconnaissance mission strafed a launch off the New Britain coast south of Rabaul until five Zeros intervened. The Zeros were

Nakajima Model I Ki-43 Hayabusa of the Headquarters chutai, 11th Sentai. This fighter was shot down by a No. 4 Squadron Wirraway on 26 December, with the loss of pilot Fuji'i Hiroichi.

Pilot Officer John Archer and observer Sergeant James Coulston in Wirraway A20-103 after shooting down a Ki-43 on 26 December. The forward fuselage of A20-103 is preserved at the Australian War Memorial.

from No. 582 *Ku*, with the encounter representing one of four attempted interceptions of B-24s and B-17s throughout the day.

The night of 26/27 December saw the Fifth Air Force strike Rabaul for the first time in some weeks as a Christmas Day raid by 11th BG Fortresses from Guadalcanal had reported the harbour full of ships. After flying through heavy cloud three separate 43rd BG B-17 formations struck the harbour between 0101 and 0240 on 27 December. The total force comprised 18 bombers which unloaded 138 x 500-pound bombs into the harbour as well as eight clusters of incendiaries over the town.

The Fortresses made individual runs from 5,000 feet in the face of dozens of searchlight beams and flares fired from ships in an effort to ruin the night vision of the attacking crews. Major Edward Scott claimed to have left a cargo ship burning and other crews observed two smaller vessels to be on fire. The 5,859-ton IJA transport *Italy Maru* carrying a load of aviation fuel was hit during these attacks and later exploded and sank. In addition, the destroyer *Tachikaze* was damaged by a hit on the bow.

Also ordered to raid Rabaul was a force of 90th BG B-24Ds from Iron Range. However, the mission was cancelled after one of the bombers crashed on take-off at about 2200 on 26 December. This was 400th BS B-24D 41-23875 which clipped trees on the side of the runway and was destroyed in a large explosion. The entire crew of ten was killed.

Daylight on 27 December saw eight B-26s of the 2nd and 408th Bombardment Squadrons searching unsuccessfully for a reported destroyer seen off the beachhead area. Instead, the Marauders dropped 38 x 300-pound bombs on the Gona wreck, claiming three direct hits and leaving it listing. During the morning three No. 22 Squadron Bostons led by Squadron Leader Learmonth bombed and strafed enemy positions on the coast west of Gona, while later that evening a B-24 dropped six 500-pound bombs on Finschhafen's runway.

Meanwhile a large-scale air combat unfolded over the Buna area just after midday. With Japanese ground forces in a dire situation, a dozen No. 582 *Ku* Vals departed Rabaul each loaded with one 250-pound and two 60-kilogram bombs. This was a maximum bomb load for the Vals which would have to land at Lae rather than return to Rabaul. The Vals were escorted by a dozen No. 582 *Ku* Zeros, and these formations were scheduled to arrive over Buna at the same time as four more No. 582 *Ku* Vals from Lae escorted by around a dozen 11th *Sentai* Ki-43s.

However, most aircraft departing Lae and Malahang were visible to Australian spotters, and this enabled the Buna area to be cleared of transport aircraft and for fighter cover to be ready and waiting.

Patrolling high above the area at 21,000 feet were a dozen 39th FS P-38s, which jettisoned their drop tanks and dove onto the incoming Japanese formations before the Vals could make their attacks. The American pilots accurately described their opponents as a mix of Zeros, Vals and Oscars and claimed fourteen shot down. While the P-38s had the better of this combat, the actual losses were only a single Oscar flown by Warrant Officer Yoshitake Tadashi and a Val which was badly shot up and written off when landing at Lae.

A mixed formation of 7th and 9th FS P-40s joined the combat but the P-38 pilots mistook some of them for the green-painted Oscars. Amid much confusion and frantic radio calls, several of the P-40s were hit by American 0.50-inch bullets before their pilots broke off the combat and returned to Port Moresby. On landing several of the 49th FG pilots jumped into a jeep and drove to the 39th FS base at 14-Mile, where a heated confrontation took place. Two of the 49th FG squadron commanders wanted charges laid however the matter was eventually dropped.

Among the pilots to make claims from the combat were two from the 49th FG who were getting operational P-38 experience with the 39th FS. One of these pilots was Second Lieutenant Richard Bong who was destined to become the highest scoring American ace of WWII.

During the night of 27/28 December four Nos. 11 and 20 Squadron Catalinas raided Kavieng 'drome with 20-pound fragmentation bombs, 30-pound incendiaries and 250-pound general purpose bombs. The bombs landed in the runway and dispersal areas with several fires started. Intense anti-aircraft fire was encountered aided by multiple searchlights, with two of the flying boats receiving minor damage.

Also that night six 90th BG B-24s set out to raid Rabaul after their mission had been cancelled 24 hours earlier following the crash at Iron Range. Shortly before dawn the Liberators dropped 80 x 500-pound bombs over the harbour and town, claiming a hit on a ship and a possible ammunition dump where a very large flash was observed. Gasmata was also bombed on the return journey, presumably by an aircraft which had bomb release difficulties over Rabaul.

Later that morning three No. 30 Squadron Beaufighters swept the coast between Gona and Salamaua under friendly fighter cover. Little activity was observed, with one possibly serviceable barge and two camouflaged rafts strafed near the Kumusi River. During the day two B-24s made individual bombing attacks on the airfields at Lae and Gasmata.

Another engagement on the morning of 28 December saw a lone Airacobra pilot claim to have shot down an unidentified twin engine aircraft over Goodenough Island. As no IJN twin engine aircraft were active in this area this was likely one of the first Allied encounters with a 76th *Dokuritsu Chutai* Ki-46 Dinah. Unfortunately, limited JAAF records do not confirm the loss.

Bad weather over Papua the following day of 29 December resulted in little air activity. Three 89th BS A-20As strafed canoes and huts on the coast west of Gona, while two 90th BG B-24s individually bombed Lae and Gasmata.

In the early hours of 30 December seven 43rd BG B-17s were in the air for a predawn strike on Rabaul Harbour. The raid commenced at 0520 when four Fortresses swept over the target area at 6,000 feet to catch the attention of anti-aircraft guns and searchlights. This enabled three 63rd BS B-17s to come in at low altitude and make skip-bombing attacks: the pilots involved were Captain McCullar (flying *The Mustang*), Lieutenant James Murphy (*Pluto*) and Lieutenant Berry Rucks Jr (*Panama Hattie*). Lieutenant Murphy barely cleared the mast of his target, and then circled around to see two ships on fire:

> Both ships were filled with fire, and smoke was billowing from the decks. It looked like an early New Year's Eve celebration, with all of the light from the fires.

Direct hits were claimed on 8,000-ton and 10,000-ton transports. Although the American pilots once again overestimated the size of their targets they had hit and sunk the 3,821-ton IJA troop transport *Tomiura Maru*. Five of the Fortresses received minor damage from anti-aircraft fire.

At 0840 three 89th BS A-20As strafed suspected enemy positions near the Mambare River, while a B-24 bombed Madang at 1015 and Lae three and a half hours later. Also during the morning, a 64th BS B-17 on a reconnaissance mission strafed a schooner off the coast of New Britain.

Meanwhile with Nos. 2 and 3 *chutai* of the 11th *Sentai* now established at Malahang field, plans were underway to start moving the remaining No. 1 *chutai* from Rabaul. Four No. 701 *Ku*

Nells were loaded with 11th *Sentai* ground crews and departed Vunakanau at 0835 escorted by nine No. 1 *chutai* Ki-43-I *Hayabusa* led by *chutaicho* Captain Miyabayashi Shigenori. The Nell crews were warned to expect interception by Allied fighters; however, none were encountered. On landing at 1130, Warrant Officer Yamada Takeshi ran his Nell afoul of a bomb crater. It was destroyed killing and wounding an unknown number of those aboard. The remaining three Nells unloaded as fast as possible and were back at Vunakanau by 1450.

At 1515 a B-24 attacked Lae and claimed to have destroyed a medium bomber: doubtless a reference to Yamada's abandoned Nell. Earlier the same B-24 raided Wewak where trucks were left burning.

On the night of 30/31 December a No. 11 Squadron Catalina was over Bougainville dropping supplies to coastwatchers when at 0220 on 31 December four 20-pound bombs were dropped over Buin's runway. Some 90 minutes later two No. 11 Squadron Catalinas raided Buka 'drome. An assortment of 20-, 250- and 500-pound bombs were dropped from 5,000 to 6,000 feet and landed within the target area, but no results were observed.

The morning of 31 December saw another contingent of 11th *Sentai* ground crews transported from Vunakanau to Lae by four No. 701 *Ku* Nells. Escort was once again provided by nine Ki-43s from the No. 1 *chutai* of the 11th *Sentai*, with all of the aircraft returning to Rabaul by midday.

The Japanese were fortunate to avoid several Fifth Air Force squadrons which raided Lae from 1215. The raiding aircraft comprised six 89th BS A-20A strafers, six B-25s from the 71st and 405th BS and six B-26s from the 33rd BS. The Mitchells unloaded 72 x 100-pound bombs while the B-26s dropped 36 x 300-pound bombs. Escort was provided by eleven 39th FS P-38s.

The 11th *Sentai* had six Oscars aloft on a patrol which had just chased a B-24. These quickly caught up with the Allied bombers, all three formations of which reported engaging enemy fighters. One B-26 was damaged, but the B-25s flying at only 2,200 feet caught the heaviest attack. The B-25s correctly reported being intercepted by six fighters, which they misidentified as "Zekes". Fortunately, after the first few passes the Mitchell crews reported that the fighters mostly stayed out of range, likely because of the intervention of the P-38s.

In the subsequent combat the 39th FS described fighting "11-12 Zekes" of which nine were claimed as shot down. This was another example of excessive over-claiming which mirrored what had occurred three days earlier. Just one Ki-43 was shot down, that flown by Captain Shishimoto Hironojo who baled out safely despite being shot at by the P-38s during a parachute descent. After landing in the ocean, he was soon rescued by an IJN launch. Given that the B-25s gunners also made a claim, the Fifth Air Force overclaiming on this occasion was in a ratio of 10:1.

While this activity was occurring over Lae, three 89th BS A-20As strafed targets on the coast between Sanananda Point and the Kumusi River. In other missions on the last day of 1942 a B-24 bombed and strafed Gasmata 'drome, with the crew claiming to have set on fire a twin-engine aircraft. Off Rabaul another B-24 bombed and strafed a submarine but with no visible results.

In a sad note to the end of the year, 13th BS B-25D 41-29733 *Deemie's Demon* departed Port

Moresby bound for Charters Towers. Onboard were three crewmen and eight passengers travelling to a 3rd BG New Year's Eve party. The aircraft disappeared over the Coral Sea in bad weather with all eleven men declared missing in action. The loss was compounded by the crash of 90th BS B-25D 41-29698 *The Early Bird* which flew into a mountain killing all seven onboard after encountering the same weather system on a short flight from Charters Towers to Townsville. The pilot was intending to pick up passengers at Townsville to bring back to Charters Towers for the party which would also celebrate the opening of the newly completed Officers' Club at Charters Towers Airfield.[1]

General Douglas MacArthur had this staged publicity photo taken of him on Christmas Day 1942 titled "somewhere in New Guinea". The location is actually on Port Moresby's Tuaguba Hill, looking towards the harbour side.

---

1   The loss of this second Mitchell is not included in the losses in Appendix 1 as it was a transport flight within Australia.

An abandoned No. 582 Ku D3A2 Val dive-bomber following a forced landing at Salamaua.

CHAPTER 16

CONCLUSION

The period chronicled by this fifth volume of *South Pacific Air War*, 9 September – 31 December 1942, arguably saw the biggest reversal in Japanese fortunes in the South Pacific since the beginning of the war. Early September saw Japanese land forces threatening Port Moresby while American forces in the Solomons were struggling to secure Guadalcanal. From the Allied point of view, it was a time of extreme crisis. However, by the end of the year both of these campaigns were firmly resolved in favour of the Allies evidenced by Japanese plans to evacuate both Guadalcanal and the Papuan beachheads. Such an outcome had been barely perceivable just weeks earlier.

The air war had evolved in a somewhat peculiar manner with IJN airpower at Rabaul being at times completely focused on the Solomons and virtually absent from Papua. While there were regular night-time nuisance raids over Port Moresby, these caused negligible damage and were far removed from the pitched air battles over the Papuan capital of mid-1942.

The IJN suffered horrific attrition over the Solomons. While several fresh *kokutai* were available to reinforce the theatre, the veteran Tainan and No. 4 *Ku* were all but exhausted both qualitatively and quantitively. No. 4 *Ku* had mostly returned to Japan by early October while the remnants of the Tainan *Ku* followed a month later.

Following the IJN restructure of 1 November, continued Betty attrition in the Solomons meant the main force available for offensive operations over Papua were the Kavieng-based Bettys of No. 751 *Ku* which were mainly used for the nocturnal Port Moresby missions noted above. This small force was supplemented by the antiquated Nells of No. 701 *Ku* and the Val dive-bombers of No. 582 *Ku*. The Nells were also used for night-time missions but proved vulnerable when employed during the day, as evidenced by the loss of three Nells to 49th FG P-40s on 7 December.

The Vals had some success against the small supply ships operating along the northern coast of Papua. Losses of several of these ships briefly threatened to upset the Allied assault on Buna, but like many Japanese tactical successes during 1942 they were unable to follow it up. A problem for the Vals was their preferred ordnance of 60-kilogram bombs: these were too small to inflict heavy damage on most targets.

IJN airpower firmly rested on the shoulders of its Zero fighter units. These flew offensive missions over Allied territory as well as providing defensive patrols over supply convoys and key bases. Wherever they were encountered the Zeros remained a deadly threat to Allied aircraft, such that heavy bomber raids against Rabaul and the Shortlands were usually conducted under the cover of darkness.

Unsurprisingly, more Zeros were lost than any other Japanese aircraft type. Appendix 2 shows that 19 Zeros were lost during the period which represents almost half the 41 Japanese aircraft lost (ignoring the loss of ten unknown aircraft on the ground on 12 October).

Given their pivot to the Solomons, it is perhaps surprising that Japanese losses over New Guinea were roughly comparable to each of the earlier periods as shown in Appendix 3 (allowing for the blip in carrier-based aircraft lost during the Battle of the Coral Sea).

When compared to the Allied losses, the Japanese losses were relatively light at least in New Guinea: just 51 aircraft and 72 aircrew. Guadalcanal was another matter. However, these numbers concealed a growing problem in respect to the inexperience of replacement aircrews. After the war, Vice Admiral Sakamaki Munetaka, who had commanded the 26th Air Flotilla, gave his opinion to American intelligence that by the end of December 1942 replacement bomber and fighter crews arriving at Rabaul possessed just one third of the skill of those they were replacing.

Unlike the Japanese, the Fifth Air Force was heavily engaged in direct air support of ground forces. This was aided by the proximity of Port Moresby to the Kokoda Track and Buna beachhead areas. Particularly during the peak of the Papuan crisis in September, the air support effort against enemy forces along the Kokoda Track was considerable. In parallel, many missions were flown against the supply route from Buna to Kokoda including the supposed critical choke point of the Wairopi bridge. Overall, some 2,000 sorties were flown over these areas between August and November.

Many historians give considerable credit to this air campaign, but the hard evidence detracts from this assertion. Dr Peter Williams' *The Kokoda Campaign 1942 Myth and Reality* is the only authoritative study of the campaign to reference detailed IJA records. Williams concludes that actual casualties inflicted as a result of these attacks were almost negligible, while there is little evidence that the attacks on the supply line significantly impeded the delivery of supplies to the frontline troops (most of the supplies were moved during the night).

These conclusions are supported by a 1944 USAAF study of the campaign:

> Little evidence exists to support the glowing claims as to the damage done to the enemy along the Kokoda Track. Over much of it jungle foliage made possible effective concealment ... even the bombing and strafing of villages did not necessarily result in the wholesale destruction of stores since it is doubtful trained soldiers would have conveniently concentrated supplies in such obvious targets; in spite of losses the Japanese Navy was able to reinforce the New Guinea invaders almost at will.

The Allied focus on the Wairopi bridge became almost obsessive as it was one of the few clearly identifiable targets in the Buna-Kokoda area. Yet along that stretch of the Kumusi River the Japanese used at least five other bridge locations which were concealed by jungle foliage, as well as several fordable crossings available when the river was low. Certainly, the attacks prevented the use of the bridge by day, but when it was destroyed the flimsy crossing made from ropes and planks was inevitably quickly repaired. Nevertheless, there can be little doubt that the incessant Allied air attacks contributed to a decline in morale of certain Japanese units, particularly from early November.

During the Battle of Buna-Gona Allied airpower was expected to have a decisive effect as the beachhead areas were supposedly well-defined targets. However, it was soon realised that the Japanese were well dug in and could not be eliminated by airpower alone. The campaign also saw repeated examples of bombs falling amid friendly positions. The answer was direct liaison between air and ground units, and a step in the right direction was the employment of No. 4 Squadron in the army cooperation role with its Wirraways.

More significant was the role played by the Fifth Air Force in deterring Japanese supply and reinforcement convoys during this period. A continuing theme in the theatre was the inability of the B-17 heavy bombers to sink enemy ships. A post-war USAAF survey concluded that, in the Pacific, B-17 bombs hit less than one per cent of shipping targets.

However, during this period there were creeping signs of success, starting with the sinking of the destroyer *Yayoi* on 10 September. This was the first Japanese warship to be sunk by land-based aircraft in the theatre after many attempts. More successes by B-17s followed with the net tender *Kotobuki Maru No. 5* sunk on 25 October, the IJA transport *Yasukawa Maru* sunk on 2 November, the destroyer *Umikaze* heavily damaged on 18 November, the destroyer *Hayashio* sunk on 24 November, the destroyer *Shiratsuyu* damaged on 28 November, the armed merchant cruiser *Gokoku Maru* damaged on 18 December, the IJA transport *Italy Maru* sunk on 27 December and the IJA transport *Tomiura Maru* sunk on 30 December.

These successes were due to the adoption of low altitude bombing tactics and had a significant deterrence effect on the convoys. First, merchant ships were no longer sent to Buna with the IJN preferring the use of destroyers as fast transports. Then some of the destroyer convoys were forced to turn back, while others unloaded their troops far to the west of the beachheads at the Kumusi and Mambare river mouths. By late December only submarines were taking supplies direct to the beachheads.

All in all, this was a significant victory for the Fifth Air Force and directly contributed to the Japanese decision to evacuate the Buna area altogether.

Meanwhile the B-17 crews believed they had inflicted heavy damage during night attacks against shipping at Rabaul and the Shortlands. Actual results fell far short of claims, however, and the need for the cover of darkness during these missions is a testament to the effectiveness of the Japanese defences. Indeed, low-level daylight missions by B-17s without fighter escort against these locations would have been suicidal.

Much of the development of the low-level B-17 tactics was due to the 43rd BG, which boasted a number of exceptional combat pilots such as Kenneth McCullar. It is perhaps ironic that the 43rd BG had begun the period with only one operational squadron. However, after suitable effort had been put into combat training the unit became highly effective.

Arguably Kenney made a mistake by too quickly committing the inexperienced 38th and 90th Bombardment Groups to operations. The 38th BG also initially suffered from poor leadership, and both groups were plagued by difficulties including, for the 90th BG, primitive conditions at Iron Range. However, with proper operational training the 90th BG had begun to show a respectable sortie rate by December. Further, the impressive endurance of the B-24s enabled them to range over northern New Guinea and the Bismarck Sea, greatly expanding the reconnaissance cover previously provided by B-17s.

The period also saw the New Guinea debut of the P-40E-equipped 49th FG. Appendix 1 shows this was at the vanguard of Fifth Air Force fighter operations, with 20 P-40Es[I] lost as compared to only six Airacobras. The Airacobra squadrons of the 8th and 35th Fighter Groups had previously born the brunt of these operations but had enjoyed a relatively quieter period. Among the Airacobra squadrons were two that were based at Milne Bay which saw virtually no combat there.

Looking to the future the 39th FS had discarded its well-worn Airacobras in exchange for brand new P-38F Lightnings. With their excellent range and high-altitude performance, the Lightnings arrived with much promise. However, the technologically advanced fighters proved difficult to maintain and instead spent much of their time on the ground. While they did make their combat debut in the theatre, the full impact of the new P-38 would not be felt until 1943.

One of the most consistent performers in the theatre was the 89th BS, which had the advantage of the 8th BS providing maintenance and training backup in Australia. Certainly, the modifications for low-level use including the fitting of 0.50-calibre machine guns in the nose was a great success. Indeed, a program had begun to make similar modifications to B-25s.

The mixed bag of RAAF squadrons also made key contributions during the period, none more so than the heavy hitting Beaufighters of No. 30 Squadron. The speed and 20mm cannons of these aircraft fitted perfectly with emerging Fifth Air Force attack doctrine, and the squadron was well led by Wing Commander Brian "Blackjack" Walker. Also playing important roles were the Catalina flying boats of Nos. 11 and 20 Squadrons and the Hudsons of No. 6 Squadron.

The Beauforts of No. 100 Squadron suffered from defective torpedoes and had frustratingly failed to strike a blow against the enemy. Similarly, the Bostons of No. 22 Squadron suffered three catastrophic mid-air explosions and struggled with its small fleet of ex-Dutch aircraft, just nine of which were operational by the end of December.

Among the most important contributions by the Fifth Air Force was that made by its transport squadrons, in particular the newly arrived 6th and 33rd TCS. The C-47s of these units were the best and most capable of the transports in the theatre and were augmented by others including Lodestars and Hudsons. During the Battle of Buna-Gona the Allied land campaign was wholly dependent on these transports. From Dobodura an average of 100 sick and wounded soldiers was flown out daily, with a peak of 280 being evacuated on 8 December.

Appendix 1 shows that Allied aircraft losses blew out during the period to 115 accompanied by the horrendous loss of 348 personnel. The increased personnel losses were explained by the Fifth Air Force very much taking the offensive, with losses of American bombers now far exceeding fighter losses:

> Aircraft losses from Appendix 1:
>
> US bombers: 53   (15 B-17s, 9 B-24s, 18 B-25s, 6 A-20s, 5 B-26s)
> US fighters: 28   (20 P-40s, 6 P-39/P-400s, 2 P-38s)

I   Another P-40E lost was an RAAF machine, so there is a total of 21 lost P-40Es given in Appendix 1.

The loss of 24 heavy bombers alone accounted for the loss of 154 crewmen. Appendix 3 shows that the personnel loss during this period was by far the greatest of any of the five periods in question. Likewise, if the carrier-based aircraft losses during the Battle of the Coral Sea are excluded then the aircraft losses for this period were also the greatest.

Hence the end of the year saw the Allies on the brink of victory in Papua and the Fifth Air Force poised for increasingly offensive operations. However, the Japanese were far from spent and had another card to play, largely unforeseen by the Allies.

This was the arrival of the JAAF and the occupation of locations in northern New Guinea at Wewak, Madang and Cape Gloucester. The 11th *Sentai* had quickly deployed to Malahang outside Lae and its *Hayabusa* made their combat debut in the theatre during the last week of December. These nimble and lightweight fighters still have a reputation as being lightly armed, but the fuselage mounted 7.7mm machine guns were easily replaced by much heavier 12.7mm "machine cannon". In addition, the 11th *Sentai* arrived in some numbers and represented as big a threat as the Tainan *Ku* Zeros did at Lae some months earlier.

To some extent the challenge for both sides in early 1943 was to quickly commission new airfields. Could the JAAF turn the likes of Wewak and Madang into strong bastions to rival Rabaul? Likewise, the Allies had been quick to develop fields at Popondetta and Dobodura for the use of transports. Could such airfields north of the Owen Stanleys be used by fighters and bombers? That would markedly extend the range of Allied aircraft and eliminate much of the danger posed by flying over the mountains.

The end of 1942 neatly bookended months of hard fighting in the theatre. The new year of 1943 promised a new adversary in the JAAF and their expansion of the air campaign into northern New Guinea.

APPENDICES

APPENDIX 1 – ALLIED AIRCRAFT LOSSES & FATALITIES
Confirmed Allied Military Aircraft Losses
9 September to 31 December 1942*

* Note as a general rule, accidents in North Queensland not directly involved with operational flying have been excluded from these tables. However, such distinctions are often not clear-cut and have been left to the discretion of the authors.

	DATE	TYPE	SERIAL	UNIT	COMMENTS	FATALITIES*
1	10 Sep 42	A-20A	*Little Ruby*	89th BS	Pilot and gunner baled out over mountains after a raid on Buna. Both hospitalised.	
2	10 Sep 42	A-20A	*The Comet*	89th BS	Ditched short of Port Moresby after a raid on Buna. Two crew rescued.	
3	11 Sep 42	B-17E	41-2663	28th BS	Hit by anti-aircraft fire during low level bombing run over Buna. The pilot Lt Gilbert Erb ditched 20 miles southeast of Buna. Three crewmen drowned and two were captured and killed by the Japanese. Erb led three others to Milne Bay after weeks in the jungle.	5 killed
4	11 Sep 42	B-26	40-1433 *Kansas Comet #2*	19th BS	Crash landed at Iron Range. Pilot Lieutenant Walter Krell and four crew survived; the co-pilot was killed.	1 killed
5	11 Sep 42	P-40E	41-24874	7th FS	Crashed into ocean during flight from Cairns to Horn Island. Lt Robert Hazard MIA.	1 killed
6	14 Sep 42	B-17F	41-24391 *Hoomalimali*	63rd BS	Suffered an engine failure soon after take-off from Mareeba, crashed and destroyed in large explosion. Capt Herschell Henson and ten crew killed.	10 killed
7	15 Sep 42	B-17F	41-24427	30th BS	Aircraft vanished following night raid over Rabaul. Capt Robert Williams and crew MIA.	9 killed
8	16 Sep 42	A-20A	40-3148 *The Comet II*		Wrecked after crash landing at Kila 'drome.	
9	18 Sep 42	B-17E	41-2650	93rd BS	Became lost while trying to find Horn Island. Lt Claude Burcky ordered his crew to bale out. Eight men were rescued by an RAAF Catalina on the coast of the York Peninsula the next day. One man remains MIA and likely baled out over the ocean.	1 killed
10	23 Sep 42	Beaufighter	A19-1	No. 30 Sqn	Shot down by anti-aircraft fire over Buna with the loss of pilot Flt Sgt George Sayer and observer Sgt Archie Mairet.	2 killed
11	24 Sep 42	B-17E	41-9206	435th BS	Lost in bad weather after returning from a reconnaissance flight over Rabaul and the Shortlands. Pilot Lt George F Newton made a forced landing in shallow water in Orangerie Bay on the south coast of Papua where the bomber was abandoned.	
12	25 Sep 42	B-25C	41-12910 *Suicide's Flying Drunks*	405th BS	Wrecked after collision with P-40 during take-off from Horn Island.	
13	25 Sep 42	Beaufighter	A19-39	No. 30 Sqn	Collided with a truck during take-off from Wards 'drome. Sent to an air depot for repairs but never returned to service and eventually used for parts.	
14	28 Sep 42	Beaufort	A9-89	No. 100 Sqn	Crashed during flight between Port Moresby and Milne Bay. Three crew killed, two OK.	3 killed

	DATE	TYPE	SERIAL	UNIT	COMMENTS	FATALITIES*
15	30 Sep 42	B-26	40-1403 *Bunagoon*	22nd BG	Nose badly damaged in landing accident at Iron Range. Rear section later used to rebuild another damaged B-26.	
16	4 Oct 42	Beaufort	A9-60	No. 100 Sqn	Did not return from night raid over the Shortlands. Flt Lt Donald Stumm and three crewmen missing.	4 killed
17	5 Oct 42	B-17E	41-9196	30th BS	Shot down by Zeros over Rabaul. Lt Earl Hageman and eight crewmen are MIA.	9 killed
18	5 Oct 42	B-25D	41-29701 *Battlin' Biffy*	405th BS	Crash landed near Buna after being attacked by Zeros. Pilot Lt Terrence Carey and two crewmen were executed soon afterwards, the remainder died in the crash.	7 killed
19	10 Oct 42	B-25D	41-29703 *Mississippi Rebel*	405th BS	Crashed after take-off from Horn Island following a false air raid alarm. Written off.	
20	13 Oct 42	Beaufighter	A19-68	No. 30 Sqn	Crashed into mountain near Kokoda with the loss of pilot Sgt Thomas Butterfield and the observer Sgt Rupert Wilson.	2 killed
21	16 Oct 42	C-47	41-18585 *Maxine*	6th TCS	Crashed into the jungle near the village of Kagi on the Kokoda Track while airdropping. Three crewmen killed.	3 killed
22	23 Oct 42	B-25C	41-12889 *Yankee Vengeance*	38th BG	Missing during flight between Port Moresby and Townsville.	4 killed
23	27 Oct 42	Beaufighter	A19-49	No. 30 Sqn	Shot down by anti-aircraft fire over Lae with the loss of pilot Flt Lt Edward Jones and observer Flt Sgt Eric Richardson.	2 killed
24	28 Oct 42	Hudson	A16-246	No. 6 Sqn	Disappeared during reconnaissance mission over the Solomon Sea.	4 killed
25	29 Oct 42	B-17E	41-9235 *Clown House*	30th BS	Lost following night raid over the Shortlands and ditched on Great Barrier Reef near Cooktown. Maj Allen Lindberg and his crew were able to reach shore and return to Mareeba.	
26	30 Oct 42	B-25D	41-29731 *L'il De-Icer*	90th BS	Crashed into a mountain near Kokoda with the loss of Lt Robert Miller and his crew.	6 killed
27	1 Nov 42	B-17E	41-2635	30th BS	Crashed near Milne Bay after raid on the Shortlands with the loss of Lt John Hanock and his crew.	8 killed
28	1 Nov 42	P-40E		8th FS	Lt Glenn Wohlford shot down by Zeros near Lae.	1 killed
29	1 Nov 42	B-25D	41-29738 *The Iroquois*	90th BS	Following combat with Zeros crash landed at Kila and exploded, with only one member of the crew surviving.	4 killed
30	1 Nov 42	P-400	AP266	41st FS	Lt Joel Zabel remains MIA after vanishing when returning to Port Moresby after escorting C-47s to Pongani.	1 killed
31	1 Nov 42	P-400	AP367	41st FS	Lt Thomas Ingram remains MIA after vanishing when returning to Port Moresby after escorting C-47s to Pongani.	1 killed
32	2 Nov 42	B-26	40-1503 *Maybe*	33rd BS	Written off in landing accident at 14-Mile.	
33	2 Nov 42	B-26	40-1493 *Ole '93*	33rd BS	Written off in landing accident at 14-Mile.	
34	2 Nov 42	P-40E	41-5313	7th FS	Ditched in Bootless Inlet off Port Moresby, Lt Bryant Wesley was able to swim ashore.	
35	4 Nov 42	P-38F	42-12649	39th FS	Lt Richard Cella ditched during flight from Milne Bay to Port Moresby.	

	DATE	TYPE	SERIAL	UNIT	COMMENTS	FATALITIES*
36	4 Nov 42	P-38F		39th FS	Capt Jim Porter ditched after taking off from Horn Island.	
37	5 Nov 42	C-47	41-38615 The Broadway Limited	6th TCS	Crashed into mountain while dropping supplies with the loss of eight men aboard.	8 Killed
38	6 Nov 42	P-40E	41-25178	8th FS	Lt Nelson Brownell was killed after his engine stopped and the P-40 crashed near Kokoda.	1 killed
39	8 Nov 42	P-40E		8th FS	Following engine problems Robert Howard crash-landed his P-40E into trees at Myola.	1 killed
40	10 Nov 42	Boston	A28-12	No. 22 Sqn	Exploded in mid-air during bombing practice off Port Moresby.	3 killed
41	10 Nov 42	C-47	41-18564 Flying Dutchman	33rd TCS	Crashed into Mount Obree at 9,000 feet. Only six men survived after lengthy ordeals.	17 killed
42	10 Nov 42	Hudson	A16-205	No. 6 Sqn	Crashed in bad weather after departing Milne Bay on a reconnaissance mission.	4 killed
43	15 Nov 42	B-24D	41-23760 Lady Beverley		Ditched near Milne Bay on return from the Shortlands; only two survived.	6 killed
44	15 Nov 42	B-24D	41-11828 The Condor		Experienced fuel transfer problems on approach to Iron Range and was belly landed on a beach and abandoned.	
45	16 Nov 42	B-25C	41-12982 Old Victory		Shot down by anti-aircraft fire over Buna. Lt Richard Yeager and five crew killed.	6 killed
46	16 Nov 42	A-20A	40-155 Abijah Gooch	89th BS	Disappeared on an administrative flight from Cairns to Port Moresby.	4 killed
47	16 Nov 42	B-24D	41-23942 Bombs to Nippon	400th BS	Crashed on take-off from Iron Range and exploded.	11 killed
48	16 Nov 42	B-17F	41-24522	403rd BS	Destroyed on ground at Iron Range in crash of B-24 Bombs to Nippon, above.	
49	17 Nov 42	B-24D	41-11902 Punjab	320th BS	Disappeared during Rabaul raid. Ten MIA including Col Arthur Meehan, the 90th BG CO.	10 killed
50	17 Nov 42	P-40E	41-24821	9th FS	Lt Floyd Finberg ditched off Papuan coast after running out of fuel.	
51	17 Nov 42	P-40E	41-36166	9th FS	Lt William Hanning ditched off Papuan coast after running out of fuel.	
52	21 Nov 42	A-20A	40-101 Old Man Mose	89th BS	Damaged by anti-aircraft fire over Buna and made emergency landing at Pongani. The aircraft never flew again and was stripped for parts.	
53	21 Nov 42	P-40E	41-5607		Lt BA Makowski force-landed at Kokoda.	
54	21 Nov 42	Wirraway	A20-519	No. 4 Sqn	Written off in landing accident near Wairopi, crew OK.	
55	22 Nov 42	Ford Trimotor	A44-1		Crashed and written off while landing at Myola.	
56	22 or 23 Nov 42	O-49A	41-18959		Crashed at Myola and later salvaged for parts.	
57	22 Nov 42	P-400	BW105	41st FS	Lt Herbert Hill baled out over Buna and likely executed by Japanese.	1 killed
58	22 Nov 42	P-40E	41-24811	7th FS	Lt Donald Dittler MIA after battling Zeros over northern Papua.	1 killed

	DATE	TYPE	SERIAL	UNIT	COMMENTS	FATALITIES*
59	22 Nov 42	P-40E	41-5610	49th FG	Lt Donald Sutliff baled out near Wairopi.	
60	22 Nov 42	P-40E		9th FS	Lt Ralph Wire baled out near Myola.	
61	22 Nov 42	P-40E	41-36089		Lt Robert McComsey baled out near Kokoda after experiencing engine trouble.	
62	22 Nov 42	B-17E	41-2536	65th BS	Crashed after being hit by anti-aircraft fire from torpedo boats running supplies to Lae. All ten onboard MIA.	10 killed
63	24 Nov 42	P-40E		7th FS	Capt William Martin hit by anti-aircraft fire over Buna and force landed.	
64	24 Nov 42	Hudson	A16-225	No. 6 Sqn	Crashed and burned after take-off accident at Wards 'drome.	
65	24 Nov 42	B-25C	41-12996	90th BS	Hit by debris from the exploding destroyer *Hayashio* near Lae. After crashing into the ocean two men survived.	2 killed
66	25 Nov 42	Beaufort	A9-82	No. 100 Sqn	Ditched safely near Wanigela after night attack on Japanese destroyers in bad weather.	
67	26 Nov 42	P-40E	41-24866	7th FS	Lt Dean Burnett downed by anti-aircraft fire while strafing Buna.	1 killed
68	26 Nov 42	Boston	A28-22 *Retribution*	No. 22 Sqn	Exploded in mid-air while bombing Buna.	3 killed
69	26 Nov 42	C-47	41-38601 *Swamp Rat*	6th TCS	Shot down by Zeros after taking off from Dobodura.	4 killed
70	26 Nov 42	C-47	41-38631 *Shady Lady*	33rd TCS	Shot down by Zeros after taking off from Dobodura.	4 killed
71	28 Nov 42	F-4 Lightning	41-2123	8th PRS	Following engine trouble Lt Philip Lissner crashed at 12-Mile.	1 killed
72	29 Nov 42	B-25D	41-29699 *White Russian*	405th BS	Crashed into mountains near Lae.	7 killed
73	29 Nov 42	B-25D	41-29724	405th BS	Ditched off Yule Island after a navigation error on a return flight to Port Moresby.	
74	29 Nov 42	Boston	A28-20	No. 22 Sqn	Exploded in mid-air while bombing Buna.	3 killed
75	29 Nov 42	B-17F	41-24546	403rd BS	Missing while shadowing Japanese destroyers near Vitiaz Strait. 11 crewmen MIA.	11 killed
76	30 Nov 42	P-40E		7th FS	Lt John Johnson shot down by Zeros near Buna.	1 killed
77	30 Nov 42	P-40E		7th FS	Lt Irving Voorhees shot down by Zeros near Buna.	1 killed
78	30 Nov 42	P-40E	41-5313	7th FS	Lt Bryant Wesley baled out near Dobodura after combat with Zeros.	
79	30 Nov 42	Lodestar	VHCAH		Destroyed in Buna area due to Japanese air attack.	
80	1 Dec 42	B-17E	41-2645 *Miss Carriage*	64th BS	Missing after shadowing a Japanese convoy, possibly shot down by Zeros.	9 killed
81	1 Dec 42	B-25D	41-29707 *The Sunsetter's Son*	38th BG	Shot down by Zeros after attacking Japanese convoy north of Buna.	7 killed
82	2 Dec 42	B-17E	41-9194	65th BS	Crashed in Port Moresby circuit area in darkness, five of the crew survived.	4 killed

	DATE	TYPE	SERIAL	UNIT	COMMENTS	FATALITIES*
83	2 Dec 42	B-24D	41-23762 *Little Eva*	321st BS	Lost while trying to find Iron Range in darkness. Four killed in crash; remainder of crew baled out of whom three died after a long ordeal in the outback.	7 killed
84	3 Dec 42	C-47	41-18571 *Johnny Reb*	6th TCS	Crashed at Popondetta and burned out.	
85	3 Dec 42	Anson	DJ437	No. 1RCF	Crashed at Vivigani on Goodenough Island.	
86	4 Dec 42	B-17F	41-24429 *Dumbo*	63rd BS	Crashed in bad weather near Finschhafen after searching for a Japanese ship.	9 killed
87	4 Dec 42	Wirraway	A0-551	No. 4 Sqn	Damaged beyond repair when taking off from Popondetta.	
88	5 Dec 42	B-25C	41-12974	90th BS	Hit a tree and destroyed in explosion during pre-dawn take-off from 17-Mile, flown by Lt Charles Richards.	5 killed
89	5 Dec 42	B-25C	41-12907 *The Happy Legend*	405th BS	Flew into mountains near Myola in cloud.	7 killed
90	5 Dec 42	B-25C	41-12911 *Per Diem*	405th BS	Hit by anti-aircraft fire over Buna and written off after landing accident at Seven-Mile.	
91	9 Dec 42	P-39		40th FS	Lt John Hall baled out due to engine trouble.	
92	10 Dec 42	Beaufort	A9-161	No. 7 Sqn	Force landed in the sea near the Palm Islands north of Townsville.	
93	10 Dec 42	Beaufort	A9-119	No. 7 Sqn	Ditched soon after take-off from Horn Island.	
94	11 Dec 42	Wirraway	A20-51	No. 4 Sqn	Crew baled out due to cloud while flying in the mountains. Only the pilot, Flying Officer Arthur Dineen, survived.	1 killed
95	11 Dec 42	Wirraway	A20-51	No. 4 Sqn	Missing, likely crashed into Owen Stanleys in cloud.	2 killed
96	14 Dec 42	A-20A	40-090 *Pride of the Yankees*	89th BS	After attacking enemy positions at the Mambare River, was damaged by its own bomb blasts and written off after emergency landing at Soputa.	
97	14 Dec 42	B-17F	41-24550 *The Stingaree No. 2*	403rd BS	Ditched in Bootless Inlet following engine failure after take-off from Seven-Mile.	
98	15 Dec 42	B-25D	41-13091 *Stinky Pinky*	90th BS	Crashed in mountains northwest of Townsville during flight to Charters Towers from Port Moresby.	11 killed
99	15 Dec 42	Hudson	A16-36	1OTU Det	Hit by ground fire and crashed near Soputa during airdropping mission. Sqn Ldr William Pedrina and two crewmen killed.	3 killed
100	16 Dec 42	P-39K	42-4362	41st FS	Lt Robert Tucker missing after baling out in cloud over the Owen Stanleys.	1 killed
101	16 Dec 42	P-39K	42-4346	41st FS	Lt Alexander Currie baled out in cloud over Owen Stanleys and walked to safety.	
102	17 Dec 42	B-26	40-1529 *Fury*	2nd BS	Missing in cloudy conditions over Kokoda. Lt Franklin Anderson and six crewmen MIA.	7 killed
103	18 Dec 42	P-40E		8th FS	Lt Richard Dennis missing over Kokoda area.	1 killed
104	18 Dec 42	B-24D	41-23835	320th BS	Crashed in cloud near Bulldog in the Owen Stanleys. Lt Harold Adams and eight crewmen killed.	9 killed
105	19 Dec 42	B-24D	41-23709	319th BS	Shot down by Zeros over the Bismarck Sea. Lt Elmo Patterson and 10 crewmen killed.	11 killed

	DATE	TYPE	SERIAL	UNIT	COMMENTS	FATALITIES*
106	19 Dec 42	P-40E	A29-137		Aircraft had been under repair at Milne Bay since Sept when it ditched soon after take-off.	
107	20 Dec 42	B-24D	41-23766	400th BS	Crashed into mountains southwest of Lae while returning from Wewak area. Lt John Rafferty and nine crewmen were declared MIA, the wreckage was not found until 1984.	10 killed
108	20 Dec 42	B-25D	41-29706 *Lola*	90th BS	Crashed into ocean north of Cairns *en route* for Port Moresby. Lt Donald Emerson and 10 passengers and crew were killed.	11 killed
109	20 Dec 42	B-25D	41-29709 *Eight Ball Esquire*	13th BS	Ditched in ocean soon after leaving Cooktown for Port Moresby. Lt William Hellriegel and 11 others were rescued three days later.	
110	20 Dec 42	P-40E			Lt King Pipes MIA during delivery flight from Townsville to Port Moresby.	1 killed
111	22 Dec 42	Beaufort	A9-29	No. 100 Sqn	Crashed during torpedo dropping practice in Milne Bay. One crewman drowned.	1 killed
112	26 Dec 42	Hudson	A16-3	1OTU Det	Ditched in Oro Bay after combat with Oscars; the turret gunner died of wounds.	1 killed
113	26 Dec 42	P-40E	41-25164 *The Rebel*	9th FS	Lt John Landers baled out after combat with Oscars near Dobodura.	
114	26 Dec 42	B-24D	41-23875	400th BS	Crashed while taking off from Iron Range and destroyed in explosion.	10 killed
115	31 Dec 42	B-25D	41-29733 *Deemie's Demon*	13th BS	Disappeared over the Coral Sea while flying from Port Moresby to Charters Towers. 11 onboard MIA.	11 killed
					* Total Fatalities (note other fatalities occurred in aircraft not classed as lost; does not include fatalities on the ground due to air crashes)	348

Breakdown of aircraft lost:

P-40E Warhawk	21
B-25 Mitchell	18
B-17 Flying Fortress	15
B-24 Liberator	9
P-39 / P-400 Airacobra	6
Beaufort	6
C-47	6
A-20A	6
B-26 Marauder	5
Hudson	5
Beaufighter	4
CAC Wirraway	4
Boston	3
P-38 Lightning	2
Other	5 (O-49A, Ford Trimotor, F4 Lightning, Lodestar, Anson)
	115

APPENDIX 2 – JAPANESE AIRCRAFT LOSSES & FATALITIES
Confirmed Japanese Military Aircraft Losses
9 September to 31 December 1942*

* from 7 August onwards all losses in the Solomons are excluded excluded unless there is Fifth Air Force involvement.

	DATE	TYPE	SERIAL / UNIT	COMMENTS	*FATALITIES
1	17 Sep 42	Betty	Misawa *Ku*	*Shotaicho* pilot FPO1c Sasaki Hideo and crew missing in bad weather after Port Moresby raid.	8 killed
2	17 Sep 42	Betty	Misawa *Ku*	Observer FPO1c Sato Yoshio and crew missing in bad weather after Port Moresby raid.	7 killed
3	17 Sep 42	Betty	Misawa *Ku*	Pilot FPO2c Nishigai Mitsuo and crew missing in bad weather after Port Moresby raid.	7 killed
4-5	11 Oct 42	Rufe	No. 14 *Ku*	Two destroyed on deck of *Kiyokawa Maru* following attack by No. 6 Squadron Hudson.	
6-15	12 Oct 42	Unknown	Unknown	10 unidentified aircraft destroyed during air raid on unidentified location, possibly Buka.	
16	23 Oct 42	Model 21 Zero	No. 3 *Ku*	FPO3c Koji Ikeda missing in bad weather after mission over Goodenough Island.	1 killed
17	28 Oct 42	Model 21 Zero	No. 751 *Ku*	FPO3c Echi Yuki disappeared while trying to intercept a B-17E near Kavieng.	1 killed
18	1 Nov 42	Model 32 Zero	No. 251 *Ku*	FPO1c Kaneko Toshio shot down by P-40Es near Lae.	1 killed
19	2 Nov 42	Model 32 Zero	No. 251 *Ku*	FPO1c Yasui Kozaburo force landed after combat with B-17s but was returned to Japanese forces.	
20	17 Nov 42	Val	No. 582 *Ku*	Ditched on return to Rabaul after attacking ships off Buna. The crew were rescued.	
21	18 Nov 42	Zero	No. 582 *Ku*	FPO1c Ohara Yoshikazu shot down during combat with B-17s near Lae.	1 killed
22	20 Nov 42	Zero	No. 252 *Ku*	FPO2c Gono Iwao shot down during combat with USAAF bomber over Buna.	1 killed
23	20 Nov 42	Zero	No. 252 *Ku*	Leading Seaman Kanoya Yasutaka shot down after combat with USAAF bomber over Buna.	1 killed
24	22 Nov 42	Zero	No. 252 *Ku*	Leading Seaman Maeda Tomio shot down by Airacobras over Buna.	1 killed
25	22 Nov 42	Zero	No. 252 *Ku*	FPO3c Oda Toru shot down by P-40s over northern Papua.	1 killed
26	24 Nov 42	Val	No. 582 *Ku*	Force landed 20 miles from Lae after attacking Dobodura	
27	24 Nov 42	Val	No. 582 *Ku*	Force landed after attacking Dobodura	
28	26 Nov 42	Zero	No. 582 *Ku*	Flyer1c Yoshio Nobuto shot down by P-40s over Buna.	1 killed
29	30 Nov 42	Zero	No. 582 *Ku*	Lieutenant Sakai Tomoyasu shot down by P-40s over Buna.	1 killed
30	30 Nov 42	Zero	No. 582 *Ku*	FPO1c Yokoyama Takashi shot down by P-40s over Buna.	1 killed
31	1 Dec 42	Zero	No. 582 *Ku*	FPO2c Sekiya Kiyoshi baled out after combat with B-17s, later rescued by an IJN destroyer.	
32	1 Dec 42	Zero	No. 582 *Ku*	Damaged during combat with B-17s and written off during landing at Gasmata.	
33	3 Dec 42	Zero	No. 252 *Ku*	Damaged during combat with B-17; FCPO Yoshihashi Shigeru later died from injuries in landing accident.	1 killed
34	7 Dec 42	Zero	No. 582 *Ku*	FPO2c Uematsu Nau shot down by P-39s near Buna.	1 killed
35	7 Dec 42	Val	No. 582 *Ku*	Shot down by P-39s near Buna.	2 killed
36	7 Dec 42	Val	No. 582 *Ku*	Shot down by P-39s near Buna.	2 killed

	DATE	TYPE	SERIAL / UNIT	COMMENTS	*FATALITIES
37	7 Dec 42	Val	No. 582 *Ku*	Written off during emergency landing at Salamaua following combat with P-39s.	
38	7 Dec 42	G3M2 Nell	No. 701 *Ku*	Shot down by P-40s near Buna. Ensign Shirai Senjo and crew killed.	7 killed
39	7 Dec 42	G3M2 Nell	No. 701 *Ku*	Shot down by P-40s near Buna. FCPO Agui Yoshihito and crew killed.	7 killed
40	7 Dec 42	G3M2 Nell	No. 701 *Ku*	Shot down by P-40s near Buna. FCPO Sakamoto Yoshikane and crew killed.	7 killed
41	8 Dec 42	Zero	No. 252 *Ku*	Leading Airman Echi Horoshi shot down during combat with a B-17 near Rabaul.	1 killed
42	13 Dec 42	Betty	No. 751 *Ku*	Ditched off New Britain after combat with B-24. The crew came ashore and were rescued.	
43	14 Dec 42	Betty	No. 751 *Ku*	FCPO Shibada Yago and crew missing after night raid against Port Moresby.	7 killed
44	14 Dec 42	Zero	No. 582 *Ku*	Leading Airman Sato Toshimi shot down by B-24 defensive fire while flying convoy protection mission.	1 killed
45	19 Dec 42	Zero	No. 582 *Ku*	FPO2c Morioka Tatsuo baled out after combat with B-24s near Madang, he was rescued by a destroyer.	
46	26 Dec 42	Ki-43–I Oscar	11th *Sentai*	Sergeant Major Imamura Ryoichi shot down by P-40s near Dobodura.	1 killed
47	26 Dec 42	Ki-43–I Oscar	11th *Sentai*	Shot down by Wirraway near Gona, pilot (unknown rank) Fuji'i Hiroichi killed.	1 killed
48	27 Dec 42	Ki-43–I Oscar	11th Sentai	Warrant Officer Yoshitake Tadashi shot down by P-38Fs over Buna area.	1 killed
49	27 Dec 42	Val	No. 582 *Ku*	Damaged during combat with P-38Fs over Buna and written off on landing at Lae.	
50	30 Dec 42	G3M2 Nell	No. 701 *Ku*	Written off in landing accident at Lae with unknown number of injuries and fatalities.	?
51	31Dec 42	Ki-43–I Oscar	11th *Sentai*	Captain Shishimoto Hironojo baled out safely after combat with P-38s near Lae, rescued by launch.	
				* Total Fatalities (note other fatalities occurred in aircraft not classed as lost)	72

Breakdown of aircraft lost:

Zero	19
Val	7
Betty	5
Nell	4
Oscar	4
Rufe	2
Unknown type	10
	51

APPENDIX 3 – CUMULATIVE AIRCRAFT LOSSES & FATALITIES
8 December 1941 to 31 December 1942

Allied Losses

	Volume 1 8 Dec 41 – 9 Mar 42	Volume 2 10 Mar – 30 Apr 42	Volume 3 1 May – 18 Jun 42	Volume 4 19 June – 8 Sept 42	Volume 5 9 Sept – 31 Dec 42	Totals
Airacobra	1	1	59	21	6	88
P-40E Kittyhawk / Warhawk		19	2	11	21	53
B-25 Mitchell		4	15	4	18	41
B-17 Flying Fortress	2	1	3	19	15	40
SBD Dauntless		1	37			38
B-26 Marauder		8	12	9	5	34
F4F Wildcat	2	2	26			30
Hudson	9	2	4	5	5	25
A-24 Banshee		7	10	5		22
Wirraway	10	2		2	4	18
TBD-1 Devastator			15			15
PBY Catalina	8	1	4			13
Beaufort				4	6	10
B-24 Liberator					9	9
C-47					6	6
A-20					6	6
Beaufighter				1	4	5
Lodestar				3	1	4
Boston					3	3
F4 Lightning		1	1		1	3
Other*	2	1		5	5	13
Totals	**34**	**50**	**188**	**89**	**115**	**476**
Fatalities	**63**	**53**	**172**	**191**	**348**	**827**

* Walrus, SOC Seagull (2), Ford Trimotor (2), P-38 Lightning (2), Empire flying boat, DC-2. DC-5, LB-30, Anson, O-49A

Japanese Losses

	Volume 1 8 Dec 41 – 9 Mar 42	Volume 2 10 Mar – 30 Apr 42	Volume 3 1 May – 18 Jun 42	Volume 4 19 June – 8 Sept 42	Volume 5 9 Sep – 31 Dec 42	Totals
A6M2 Zero	2	26	41	21	19	109
B5N Kate	2		35			37
G4M1 Betty	15	4	7	5	5	36
D3A1 Val	3		21	5	7	36
H6K4 Mavis	5		4			9
A5M4 Claude			6			6
G3M2 Nell		1		1	4	6
E13A1 Jake	4		1			5
F1M2 Pete			5			5
A6M2-N Rufe				3	2	5
Oscar					4	4
E8N2 Dave		3				3
Unknown type			10		10	20
Other *		1	2	2		5
Totals	**31**	**35**	**132**	**37**	**51**	**286**
Fatalities	**139**	**49**	**187**	**46**	**72**	**493**

* H8K1 Emily, E7K Alf, E9W Slim, J1N1-C Irving, Babs

SOURCES & ACKNOWLEDGMENTS

Research for this volume focuses on primary sources. As with all previous four volumes of *South Pacific Air War*, the private collections of authors Michael Claringbould and Peter Ingman including private letters, diaries, microfilms, photos and captured documents, contain considerable information for which it is not practicable to further credit, other than select sources listed below. Special acknowledgements again go to Pacific War Air Historical Associates (PAWHA) members Ed DeKiep, Osamu Tagaya and Jim Lansdale (deceased) for their advice on Japanese aircraft markings; also to PAWHA member Luca Ruffato (deceased) for research on the Tainan *Ku* and translation of the relevant *Sentoshoho*. Thanks also to Justin Taylan and his website www.pacificwrecks.com; Thanks to Russell Harada in Papua New Guinea for *kanji* translation work. Thanks also to websites www.combinedfleet.com and www.adf-serials.com.au.

Books and Documents

Bullard, Steven (translator). *Japanese Army Operations in the South Pacific Area; New Britain and Papua Campaigns, 1942-43*. Australian War Memorial, Canberra, 2007.

Claringbould, Michael and Ruffato, Luca. *Eagles of the Southern Sky*, Tainan Books, 2013.

Ferguson, SW & Pascalis, William K. *Protect & Avenge – The 49th Fighter Group in World War II*. Schiffer, USA, 1996.

Finch, Frank and Lunney, Bill. *Forgotten Fleet: a history of the part played by Australian men and ships in the US Army Small Ships Section in New Guinea*, Forfleet Publishing, 1995.

Hickey, Larry et al. *Revenge of the Red Raiders, The Illustrated History of the 22nd Bombardment Group during World War II*. International Research and Publishing Organisation, USA, 2006.

Hickey, Lawrence J et al. *Ken's Men Against the Empire, The Illustrated History of the 43rd Bombardment Group during World war II, Volume 1: Prewar to October 1943 the B-17 Era*. International Historical Research Associates, USA, 2016.

Gill, G. Hermon. *Royal Australian Navy 1942-1945, Australia in the War of 1939-1945, Series Two Navy, Volume II*. Canberra, Australian War Memorial, 1968.

Gillison, Douglas. *Royal Australian Air Force 1939-1942, Australia in the War of 1939-1945, Series Three Air, Volume I*. Canberra: Australian War Memorial, 1962.

Kenney, George C. *General Kenney Reports – A Personal History of the Pacific War*. Reprint (originally published 1949), Air Force History & Museums Program, 1997.

King, Colin M. *Song of the Beauforts - No 100 Squadron RAAF and Beaufort Bomber Operations*, Air Power Development Centre, Canberra, 2008.

McCarthy, Dudley. *South-West Pacific Area First Year Kokoda to Wau*, Series One Army, Volume V. Canberra, Australian War Memorial, 1959.

Musumeci, Michael D. *Iron Range Airbase Carved in the Cape York Jungle 1942-1945*. M Musumeci, Mareeba, 2008.

Page, Charles. *Wings of Destiny - Wing Commander Charles Learmonth, DFC and Bar and the air war in New Guinea*, Rosenberg Publishing, NSW, 2008.

Salecker, Gene Eric. *Fortress Against the Sun The B-17 Flying Fortress in the Pacific*. USA: Da Capo Press, 2001.

Vincent, David. *The RAAF Hudson Story Book One*. D Vincent, Highbury, South Australia, 1999.

Vincent, David. *The RAAF Hudson Story Book Two*. Vincent Aviation Publications, Highbury, South Australia, 2010.

Walker, Alan S. *The Island Campaigns, Australia in the War of 1939-1945, Series Five, Medical, Volume III*. Canberra, Australian War Memorial, 1957.

Watson, Richard L. *The Papuan Campaign, Chapter 4, The Crisis in the South and Southwest Pacific, Army Air Forces in World War II Vol. IV The Pacific: Guadalcanal to Saipan August 1942 to July 1944*, Office of Air Force History, 1950.

Williams, Peter. *The Kokoda Campaign 1942 Myth and Reality*, Cambridge University Press, Port Melbourne, Victoria, 2012.

Other Sources

RAAF 4, 6, 7, 11, 20, 30, 33, 75, 76 & 100 Squadron operations logs September to December 1942.

Australian Infantry Brigade and Anti-Aircraft unit War Diaries, numerous.

Allied Air intelligence logs

Microfilm histories/ documents pertaining to 5th Air Force establishment, 8th Fighter Group, 35th Fighter Group, 435th Reconnaissance Squadron, 22nd Bombardment Group, 3rd BG; including 2nd BS, 19th BS, 28th BS, 30th BS, 63rd BS, 64th BS, 89th BS, 90th BS, 13th BS, 8th BS, 8th FS and 9th FS.

Japanese POW sources & Diaries

Allied interrogations of Japanese POWs make curious reading but should not be treated as definitive. They include JAAF POWs interviewed from the 1st Air Route, 1st Mobile Air detachment, 5th Signals Section, 12th Air Sector detachment, 13th, 20th, 22nd, 25th, 38th, 41st and 51st Airfield Construction Battalions, 39th Anti-aircraft Battalion and the 11th *Sentai*.

Japanese Language Sources

Diaries/ memoirs of pilots (various units) Tanaguchi Masayoshi, Shishimoto Hironojo, Harumi Takemori, Shiromoto Nauharu, Yoshida Masa'aki, Muraoka Shinichi, Shimizu Kazuo, Katsuaki Kira, Kimura Toshio, Hasegawa Tomoari, diary of 6 *Ku* pilot FPO1c Murakami Keijizo, memoirs of No. 2 *Ku* Zero pilot WO Tsunoda Kazuo.

Senshi Sosho Tobu Nyu-Ginia Homen Rikugun Koku Sakusen (JAAF Operations, Eastern New Guinea) Tokyo, Asagumo Shinbunsha, 1967

Senshi Sosho Rikugun Koku no Gunbi to Unyo Daitoa Senso Shusen (Equipment and Operation of Army Air Forces, (Asagumo Shinbunsha, 1976)

Radio Tokyo transcripts 1942

Maboroshi, privately published in Tokyo in 1986 by the Rabaul-New Guinea Army Air Units Association

Haraguchi Kichigoro, Soretsu Bakuso Hayabusa Sentai (The Intrepid Exploits of a *Hayabusa* Unit), Maru Special 2, No.1 (1958)

Otaka Nakajima, The Pacific War as Viewed from Combined Fleet Operations Room

Hata Ikuhiko (editor), The Imperial Army and Navy Comprehensive Encyclopaedia, University of Tokyo Press

Tokuki Matsuda, *Kakuta Kakuji*: The Warrior who Pushes Through the Enemy, PHP Bunko 2009

Meiji Centennial Series (Volume 74) History of the Naval Academy Hara Shobo

Admiral Kusaka Junichi, private diary hand-written in kanji

Memoirs of Commander Okumiya, staff officer to Rear Admiral Kakuta Kakuji

Diary of Vice-Admiral Ugaki Matome, Chief of Staff of the Combined Fleet

Diary of Rear Admiral Sanwa Yoshiwa, Chief of Staff (aviation), Southeast Area Fleet

Organization of the Naval Air Groups: Wartime Organization, 15 November 1940, Secret Order No.824. Revised 1941, No.366, No.618, No.994, No.1171, No.1497.

Senshi Sosho Volume 49

Japanese Naval Units and Air Bases - ATIS captured document dated 26 Nov 42 (via Jim Lansdale)

Organization & history of 25 Air Flotilla, ATIS captured document dated 16 Oct 42 (via Lansdale)

Manual of Military Secret Orders ATIS captured document dated 20 Jul 43 (via Lansdale)

Japanese Naval Air Service Intelligence memorandum No 28, ATIS captured document dated 7 Jul 43 (via Lansdale)

Japanese Air Terms in *kanji*, Squadron Leader A. R Boyce, Far Eastern Bureau, Calcutta 1944

Historical Monograph Series - summary of aerial operations in New Guinea in late 1942 by Japanese high Command - Southeast Naval Operations part 2 (translated by US General Headquarters Far East Command, Military Intelligence Section 1952)

Japanese Naval Air Organization CINCPAC Bulletin Nos. 18-45

The Achilles Tendon of the IJN by Yoshida Toshio (CDR, 59th class, Secretary to ADMs Yonai, Shimada, and Nagano).

Translation of Japanese Navy Messages, Japanese Naval Forces, Sep-Dec 1942

Tabulated Records of Movement (TROMs) for relevant Japanese ships cited in text.

Japanese Newspapers

Japan Times and Advertiser, newspaper, articles September to December 1942

Asahi Shimbun, newspaper, articles September to December 1942

Imperial Navy Magazine – numerous articles late 1942 including by reporter Takeda Michitaro

Unit Operations Logs (*Kodochosho*)

No 2 *Kokutai*, No. 3 *Kokutai*, No. 6 *Kokutai*, No. 252 *Kokutai*, No. 253 Kokutai, No. 251 *Kokutai*, No. 582 *Kokutai*, No. 202 *Kokutai*, No. 204 *Kokutai*, No. 751 *Kokutai*, No. 801 *Kokutai*, No. 802 *Kokutai*, No. 851 *Kokutai*, Kisarazu *Kokutai*, Yokohama *Kokutai*, No. 14 *Kokutai*, Tainan *Kokutai*, Misawa *Kokutai*, Chitose *Kokutai*, No. 204 *Ku* unofficial History (post-war, compiled by veterans)

Ship Operations Logs (*Sentochosho*)

Kiyokawa Maru, Kamikawa Maru, Sanuki Maru, Sentoshoho, No. 6 *Sentai Sentoshoho* (various cruisers and ships)

INDEX OF NAMES, MILITARY UNITS AND SHIPS